DUST JACKET ILLUSTRATION shows the ultra-modern 747-400, designed specifically for Northwest's Pacific routes, which will set a new standard of efficiency and passenger comfort to and from Far East markets. Note distinctive red winglets, which improve aerodynamic efficiency.

FLIGHT TO THE TOP

Flight to the Top

*How a home town airline made history
. . . and keeps on making it*

By Kenneth D. Ruble

The absorbing 60-year story of Northwest Airlines

Printed in the United States of America at the Viking Press

A "People Story"

An airline is far more than planes and routes and glamorous destinations . . . an airline is people.

This is the story of a tiny independent carrier born into a shaky new profession 60 years ago, and of the people — 30,000 of them today and tens of thousands more over the years — whose commitment to the traveling public helped transform that pioneer puddle-jumper between the Twin Cities and Chicago into an industry leader spanning two oceans and serving three continents.

How did a "home town airline" in the middle west — headquartered far from the sophisticated money centers that are supposed to have a corner on financial genius — manage to build the strongest balance sheet in the business and set a standard of excellence that has baffled competitors, some of them already awash in red ink even before the Airline Deregulation Act of 1978 triggered cutthroat competition from upstart nonunion carriers?

This history provides a behind-the-scenes look at a number of answers to that question, while it traces the exciting and often bumpy path Northwest Airways — as Northwest Airlines was known originally — has traveled through six decades on its hard-earned way to the top.

Only 23 years after the Wright brothers launched the air age, and nearly eight months before Minnesota's Charles Lindbergh gave aviation a spectacular shot in the arm by soloing the Atlantic, Northwest began carrying mail with two rented open cockpit biplanes and a pocketful of dreams on October 1, 1926.

Today Northwest serves Europe, North America and the Orient with the most up-to-date custom-built fleet anywhere, featuring an industry high in the percentage of wide-bodied jets. The story behind this amazing growth involves the history of many states, 16 foreign lands and innumerable men and women who devoted an important part of their lives to Northwest's exciting career. Among them were several remarkable leaders whom fate supplied just when they were needed most.

The first of these men was Col. Lewis H. Brittin, whose missionary zeal got Northwest off the ground. Next, Croil Hunter brought to the airline's presidency a restless ambition to expand on Brittin's dream. Then Donald W. Nyrop provided the know-how and selfless dedication that made dreams into reality by turning an ailing Northwest into a phenomenon of American business, with the nation's top operating efficiency and the soundest financial strength of all U.S. carriers.

He was followed by NWA's first "home grown" President and Board Chairman — M. Joseph Lapensky — whose stewardship during the chaotic aftershocks of airline deregulation helped bring Northwest through as the only major carrier with sustained profitability and the lowest debt-to-equity ratio.

This kind of strength has been good for air travelers and shippers because Northwest is financially able to update its fleet continuously with better planes, better schedules, better service. And it has been good for employees, who have carried home full paychecks throughout deregulation. They have watched many other airlines — heavily in debt — slash wages, lay off workers wholesale, "wash out" pension plans, demand one concession after another, go through bankruptcy (such as Continental and Braniff, with Continental returning as a nonunion carrier) or sell out to a holding company that controls two nonunion airlines, as Eastern did.

The 60 years chronicled in this book are spiced with anecdotes, dozens of photos and personal recollections gathered from scores of men and women who participated in many of the absorbing, and sometimes desperate, events that highlighted Northwest's past.

A dramatic push west during the Great Depression of the Thirties preceded NWA's monumental World War II performance for the U.S. military, after which postwar expansion led to Hawaii, Alaska and the Orient before a major crisis threatened the airline's very existence. This set the stage for a long, resolute uphill battle to earn the leadership position Northwest enjoys today.

Now, with a "youth movement" bringing comparatively young but seasoned executives to the fore, the airline has geared up for the kind of teamwork needed to build on its historic past for an equally lustrous future.

Dramatic evidence of this forward-looking kind of leadership was provided early in this sixtieth anniversary year when Northwest negotiated an $884 million purchase of Republic Airlines to create the third largest U.S. carrier.

K.D.R.

Contents

vii

Part IV Reaching Out (1945-1950)

Part V Rough Air (1950-1954)

Part VI Uphill Struggle (1954-1976)

Part VII Europe, Deregulation and the First Merger Ever (1977-1986)

Appendix

Illustrations

PART I

The Fledgeling
(1926-1930)

Ticket Number One

THE MAYOR OF ST. PAUL chickened out at the last minute, so the urgent question of the day on that hot, sultry July noon was: who in the assembled band of well-wishers would replace the missing mayor as the first ticketed passenger of Northwest Airways on its nine-month-old air mail run to Chicago?

The date was July 5, 1927 — only 23½ years since the Wright brothers first achieved man's age-old dream to fly, and just a few weeks after Lindbergh had electrified the world by soloing the Atlantic. The place was Speedway (later Wold Chamberlain) Field, an old automobile raceway-turned-airport off the southern outskirts of Minneapolis and St. Paul.

Perspiration stood out on the forehead of Colonel Lewis H. Brittin, "father" of the infant air service that is known today as Northwest Airlines.

His tall, scholarly appearance — heightened by a pair of rimless granny glasses and a gray Homburg perched squarely atop his head — concealed a restless inner dynamo that had driven him to surmount one obstacle after another in order to put Minnesota's Twin Cities on the slowly growing U.S. air map.

Suddenly Col. Brittin spotted Byron G. Webster, a dapper young St. Paul businessman, in the small crowd that had gathered to cheer the beginning of Northwest's passenger service.

"Come on, Byron," urged the Colonel in his well-modulated voice, "let me write you the number one ticket on Northwest Airways."

Webster didn't wait to be asked twice. He

INITIAL LOGO. Airmail was the only pay load for the first nine months of operation.

marched forward and eagerly shook hands with the man whose spirited leadership he had followed just a few months earlier in an all-out drive that pushed through a $295,000 bond issue to build an airport near downtown St. Paul.

In a matter of minutes, Brittin wrote the ticket and lanky Charles Holman, at 28 a living legend known to an adoring public as "Speed" (but to his closest friends as Charlie) boosted Webster into a black-bodied biplane known as the Stinson Detroiter. Northwest thus became the first airline to operate a closed cockpit plane for passenger service. Holman hoisted his own 6-foot 5½-inch frame in after Webster and settled into the pilot's seat of the tiny three-passenger aircraft.

Andy Hufford, chief engine mechanic and widely regarded as a genius of the tool bench,

COLONEL LEWIS H. BRITTIN, the dynamo who got Northwest off the ground October 1, 1926 in Minneapolis-St. Paul.

slouched forward out of the crowd and gave the propeller a preliminary spin.

Then Holman turned the switch on, yelled "Contact!" and Andy twisted her tail again.

The roaring engine drowned out encouraging yells of the small audience as Holman taxied to the sod runway, revved up and vaulted into the steamy Minnesota atmosphere at 2 p.m. on the dot.

Closed cabin or not, Holman wore the same helmet and goggles that were his trademark whether he was flying the mail, winning major races in an open cockpit plane against the nation's leading aviators, or drawing "ohs" and "ahs" with his famous stunt flying exhibitions. He first won national prominence as a 24-year-old when he defeated the country's best in a stunt flying contest at the Pulitzer races in St. Louis.

These aerial gymnastics both thrilled and chilled Colonel Brittin. He appreciated the publicity Speed's exploits gave his fledgeling airline, but worried like a fond parent about his number one pilot, who also doubled in brass as operations manager — all for a munificent $75 a week.

As they gained altitude, Holman tapped Webster on the shoulder and pointed down at the Mississippi River, snaking its way through the Twin Cities. Webster nodded, since the Detroiter's clattering pistons made conversation all but impossible.

"We followed down the Mississippi," Webster recalled later, "and at its junction with the St. Croix River near the Wisconsin state line, the engine suddenly went deader than a smelt."

Unruffled as always, the square-jawed Holman calmly looked over the countryside with his keen blue eyes, then expertly floated the silent plane into a small field for a perfect three-point landing.

"He gave me that sleepy grin of his," Webster recalled later, "hauled out a tool kit and started working on the engine. Pretty soon he was satisfied he had found the problem, but the field was too small to get out of unless the load could be lightened."

2

Holman walked to a nearby farm house, telephoned Colonel Brittin, and the two men waited patiently for a Northwest truck to reach them from St. Paul, about 35 miles away. While Webster and the mail sacks were being trucked back to the Twin Cities, Holman bounced the plane skyward and flew back to Speedway Field. He was waiting when Webster alighted from the truck, and grinned: "Shall we try 'er again?"

"Sure," came Webster's ready answer.

Once again mail sacks were put aboard, and they took off — this time with no audience except a few Northwest employees.

First stop: La Crosse, Wis., about 120 miles down river from the Twin Cities. A welcoming committee had been standing by for three hours, through a thunderstorm that drenched the crowd and turned the airfield into a sea of mud and goo.

Holman gentled the Detroiter onto the field, and the soggy welcomers conducted a brief ceremony to mark the occasion, then fled for cover as the rain picked up again.

Next stop: Madison. It was dark by now, and Wisconsin's capital city delegation, pelted by a heavy downpour from the same weather front that had soaked La Crosse, was long gone. Holman loaded on another mail sack, phoned ahead from the airport office to check the weather in Milwaukee, then announced casually: "Gotta sit here for a while until things clear up a little. I'll go get some coffee and sandwiches to take along with us."

Soon after the takeoff for Milwaukee, another thunderstorm shook the little plane as if it had been a naughty child.

Holman's impromptu lunch tumbled to the floor in a mess as the Detroiter bucked and pitched along, far below its normal 85-mile cruising speed. The pleasant aroma of coffee and the sharp odor of gasoline mingled in their nostrils. Webster didn't feel much like eating, anyway, and Charlie Holman was too busy fighting the controls to worry about food.

At the stroke of midnight, Speed settled the Detroiter smoothly down on the Milwaukee

BYRON WEBSTER, St. Paul businessman, holds the ticket that made him Northwest's first official passenger. Storms made his flight to Chicago a 12½-hour adventure.

airport in almost total darkness. ("He must've had cat eyes," reported Webster.) In those days, "lights out" time was seldom later than 9 p.m. because night flights were a rarity.

The mayor and his welcomers had retired to dreamland long before, but a rain-soaked reporter — Robert H. Wills of the Milwaukee Journal — was on hand to record the arrival of Northwest's first official passenger. By then, Holman and Webster had developed a comradeship that required few words. They scared up a cup of coffee with the Journal reporter's help, and Holman asked:

"You game to try Chicago?"

"Why not?" laughed Webster. "I don't think we could get a date at this hour of the night, anyway."

In clearing skies, the two soared out of Milwaukee, and the first commercial passenger flight between the Twin Cities and Chicago became history at 2:30 a.m., July 6, 1927. The 370 zig-zag miles had taken 12½ hours, plus a lot of faith, courage and skill.

Today, the Chicago-Twin Cities flight is a relaxed trip of just over an hour in one of

3

CHARLIE "SPEED" HOLMAN, first operations manager. His major race triumphs and aerobatic exhibitions made him a legend in his twenties, but he was all business when on the job.

NORTHWEST BECAME THE FIRST AIRLINE to introduce a closed cabin plane for passenger service. This 1926 Stinson Detroiter wore skis in the wintertime.

NORTHWEST AIRWAYS, INC.
U. S. AIR MAIL C. A. M. 9
CHICAGO, MILWAUKEE, LA CROSSE, ST. PAUL-MINNEAPOLIS

N⁰ ... 1

Amount Paid $ ....

Date _July 5_ 192_7_

From _Saint Paul_   To _Chicago_

CONDITIONS OF PASSAGE

It is understood that Northwest Airways, Inc., is incorporated as, and is, a private carrier only, and has not held itself out as, and is not, a common carrier of passengers. In consideration of said Northwest Airways, Inc.'s issuance to me of a ticket for transportation in one of its planes it is agreed by me as follows:

1. That said ticket represents merely a revocable license, and that said Northwest Airways, Inc., may with or without cause and in its sole discretion decline to carry me, and that in that event its sole responsibility shall be to refund the price paid by me for said ticket.

2. That after the commencement of the flight I may be landed and discharged in such manner and in such place as the pilot, with or without cause and in his sole discretion, shall see fit, and that in that event the sole responsibility of Northwest Airways, Inc., shall be to refund to me such proportion of the price paid by me for said ticket as the distance between the place of land-

ing and destination bears to the whole length of the flight for which said ticket has been issued.

3. That the maximum amount for which said Northwest Airways, Inc., its servants and employes, shall in any event be liable to me or my representatives on account of my personal injury or death, caused in any manner whatsoever during or arising out of the said transportation, shall be the sum of $20,000.00, and I hereby, for myself and my representatives, release and forever surrender all claims or causes of action for amounts in excess of the said sum.

NORTHWEST AIRWAYS, INC.
L. H. Brittin, V. P. and Gen. Mgr.

L. H. Brittin.
Signature of Agent.

Grace Webster
Signature of Passenger.

660 Summit Ave.
Address of Passenger.

PASSENGER TICKET NO. 1, issued July 5, 1927, for flight to Chicago.

Northwest's comfortable, wide-bodied jets, and millions of passengers have followed Byron Webster during the intervening years.

Nevertheless, that trail-blazing 12½-hour odyssey helped set the stage for six decades of battling against odds, culminating in what some observers have called a "miracle of modern business."

But to place a measuring stick on the present, we must examine the past, so — logically enough — our story begins at the beginning.

ORIGINAL NORTHWEST HANGAR at Speedway Field, now "grown up" into Minneapolis-St. Paul International Airport — known for many years as Wold-Chamberlain Field.

2

How it All Started

AIR MAIL was the name of the game in the early years of United States commercial aviation. Passenger service, by itself, did not pay its own way.

World War I speeded up the development of both planes and pilots, so shortly before the Roaring Twenties, the Post Office Department answered a growing demand for faster mail service by launching an experimental air route between Washington and New York. By September 8, 1920, the project had inched along until Post Office planes were flying one coast-to-coast route, connecting New York, Chicago and San Francisco.

But not without a price. Crashes, deaths and miraculous escapes were commonplace.

One young Air Corps reservist — Charles A. Lindbergh — parachuted to safety four times while flying the mail. Many others were not so lucky. (Interestingly, Lindbergh didn't even wear a chute on his history-making Atlantic solo crossing May 20 and 21, 1927. He took along five sandwiches and a quart of water, but eliminated both his parachute and radio so the "Spirit of St. Louis" could carry more gasoline.)

Among the Post Office feeder lines attempted with left-over World War I planes in 1920 was one between Minneapolis-St. Paul and Chicago,

with no beacons, no radio and lots of weather. In nine months, four pilots were killed and eight planes wiped out, so the line was discontinued.

Even the feeder from New York to the nation's capital was dropped. While the Post Office continued flying its lone transcontinental route, the speed-minded public of that era complained that progress was woefully slow.

In Congress, there was a growing sentiment to "take government out of business." The Contract Air Mail Act of 1925 was a major step, providing a plan of competitive bidding to establish air mail service in the hands of private operators instead of the Post Office. And the Air Commerce Act of 1926 — signed by President "Silent Cal" Coolidge on May 20 (exactly one year before Lindbergh's famous flight) — put teeth in the 1925 law by directing the Secretary of Commerce (then Herbert Hoover) to establish airways, organize air navigation, conduct research, to license pilots and aircraft, and to promote safety by investigating causes of accidents.

Only days after Coolidge signed the Air Commerce Act, a well-to-do Chicago seed dealer and aviation enthusiast named Charles "Pop" Dickinson — who had a Santa Claus beard and a friendly disposition to match —

7

filed a bid at $2.75 a pound to resume the Twin Cities-Chicago air mail route that had been abandoned by the Post Office six years earlier. The news was hailed ecstatically by the press. Business and civic officials got behind a move to collect several thousand letters for the initial flight.

Dickinson was awarded the contract — C.A.M. (Contract Air Mail) No. 9 — effective June 7, 1926. Fifteen minutes after Elmer Lee Partridge took off with a load of mail on that date, the plane was demolished and Partridge was killed in the midst of a violent summer storm.

Tough luck stalked Pop Dickinson from that day forward. The enthusiastic press coverage of June had turned sour by July. Even the Minneapolis postmaster charged that the public

CHARLES "POP" DICKINSON, like the U.S. Postal Service before him, failed in his attempt to establish a Twin Cities-Chicago air mail service. Northwest then made a go of it.

was "paying 10¢ for two-cent service," because so many sacks of air mail wound up traveling by rail when flights were forced down or canceled.

One by one Dickinson's pilots resigned in disgust, until toothbrush-mustached Eddie Ballough — the man who taught Speed Holman to fly — was the only one left.

Dickinson had a foreboding when his phone rang one day in early August, 1926.

"Pop?" asked the caller.

"Yeah, Eddie," he replied. "What've you got to tell me?"

"I've just been forced down again," said Ballough. "This is the end, Pop. I quit."

"For God's sake, don't leave me now," pleaded Dickinson. "We'll get things squared away any day now."

"Sorry, Pop. You're a great guy. That's why I hung on as long as I did. No hard feelings, but I'm quitting just as soon as you can get out of your contract, and that's final."

Dickinson's contract with the government had a 45-day escape clause, so he reluctantly filed notice that he was going out of business October 1, 1926.

One of the first persons he told was his good friend, Colonel Brittin, because he knew the colonel — as director of industrial development for the St. Paul Association (predecessor of the Chamber of Commerce) was vitally interested in aviation as a key to future growth of the Twin Cities.

Everybody called Brittin "Colonel" — a rank he had earned — but while many assumed he had been an army flyer, he had no aviation background at all. He was a volunteer artilleryman in the Spanish-American war, and a Lt. Colonel in the Quartermaster Corps in World War I.

Orphaned as a child in his native Connecticut, Brittin spent his boyhood in a boarding school, and eventually passed entrance examinations for both Yale and Harvard. He chose Lawrence Scientific School at Harvard, went broke before completing his second year, then found a menial job with a construction firm while continuing his engineering studies at night. Eventually Brittin became an industrial engineer, spent five years building factories in Mexico, then returned to the United States to help General Electric Company plan new installations, warehouses and other facilities.

One of his G.E. projects brought him to Minneapolis, and Brittin — a go-getter and mixer despite his professorial appearance — soon knew many Twin Cities businessmen on a first name basis.

When a number of these leaders decided to back the development of a multi-million dollar industrial district offering the combined facilities of all railroads serving the Twin Cities, they put Brittin in charge as general manager of what became a highly successful operation known as the Northwest Terminal.

Brittin laid out and superintended the total development, yet still found time to attend night school at the University of Minnesota, taking courses in traffic management and commercial law.

Impressed by his Northwest Terminal success, directors of the St. Paul Association decided to harness Colonel Brittin's dynamic energy by putting him in charge of their own business development activities.

He quickly justified their faith in his ability. Auto pioneer Henry Ford — one of the early promoters of aviation — sponsored a number of Ford Reliability Tours, in which a dozen or more airplanes flew from city to city to demonstrate the practicality of flying. The Colonel induced Ford (whose famous Model T "tin lizzie" was the fastest-selling automobile of that day) to send one of these tours to the Twin Cities. Brittin cultivated the friendship of several key Ford associates and Detroit industrialists who participated in the aerial visitation.

No one realized it then, but history's die had been cast.

In his role as business developer, the colonel — aided by his G.E. background — had a much more ambitious project in mind than the mere hosting of a Reliability tour. He had his eye on

SPEEDWAY FIELD, forerunner of today's Twin Cities International Airport, in 1926. This view is to the northeast, with Thirty-fourth Avenue S. running left to right tangent to the oval raceway on which cars and motorcycles once competed. Far right, crossing Thirty-fourth Avenue, is Sixty-sixth Street.

an unused government power dam spanning the Mississippi between St. Paul and Minneapolis, and with the help of the men whose acquaintance he had made so recently, went directly to Henry Ford with his idea.

Ford agreed with Brittin that the unused dam was a waste of water power. He also agreed to build an automobile assembly plant — his largest outside the Detroit area — across from the dam on the banks of the Mississippi.

Meanwhile, back to Pop Dickinson. When he sadly told Brittin that once again, the Twin Cities would be without air mail service, the colonel galvanized into action.

He headed east that same day and called on Robertson Aircraft Corporation (one of Eastern's "ancestors"), urging them to bid for Dickinson's expiring contract. They laughed at him. He tried National Air Transport and Stout Air Service (two of United's many forerunners) with the same result. They knew all about Pop's problems, and saw no future in serving Minneapolis-St. Paul.

The 1920s — sometimes called an "era of wonderful nonsense" — saw the United States fling off its memories of World War I in wild abandon.

Shieks in balloon trousers and flappers featuring the stringbean look danced the Charleston, competed in goldfish swallowing contests and sang ditties like "Baby Face," "Crazy Over Horses" and "I Found A Million Dollar Baby". In 1926, sportswriter Grantland Rice christened Notre Dame's dazzling backfield "The Four Horsemen," Jack Dempsey lost his heavyweight boxing title to ex-Marine Gene Tunney, Babe Ruth belted 47 home runs as a warmup for his record 60 the following year, and rum-running escapades frequently grabbed big headlines as the United States entered its seventh year of national prohibition.

A much smaller headline that September reported: "Air Mail Service Ends October 1." But Lewis Brittin had not yet begun to fight.

"If nobody else will keep this thing alive, then I'll do it myself," he told his friend Bill Kidder, a

Curtiss airplane dealer who also had served as Pop Dickinson's Twin Cities manager.

"Why not?" encouraged Kidder. "I'll give you all the help I can."

By then, the colonel had burned up nearly two weeks in the futile hunt for a going airline to assume Dickinson's route, so with just 31 days left he was playing a desperate game against time.

He had no money, no planes, no pilots, no tools, no air mail contract and no personnel except Lewis H. Brittin, a man with a mission.

Once again, Brittin telephoned his friends at Ford, and quickly won their agreement to set up a Detroit meeting of well-heeled individuals to listen to his proposition. He took Kidder along to help answer any technical questions that might come up, and in one monumental session persuaded 29 Detroiters to establish Northwest Airways, Inc., as a Michigan corporation with stock having a par value of $300,000.

The new firm was incorporated September 1, 1926, and Brittin was dispatched to Washington to file a $2.75-per-pound bid for C.A.M. No. 9. Eight days later, Harold H. Emmons, Detroit attorney and financier, was elected a director and president; Frank W. Blair, president of the Union Trust Co. in Detroit, director and treasurer; William B. Stout (then working on his design for what became the famous Ford Tri-motor airplane, affectionately known as the "Tin Goose") director and secretary; and Brittin, director, vice president and general manager.

With no other offers, the new airline's bid was accepted by the Post Office Department. The starting date of October 1 meant Col. Brittin had little more than three weeks to turn his penciled notes into a going organization with aircraft, personnel and a base of operations.

Anticipating success with their air mail bid, the backers approved placing an order for three Stinson Detroiters, but these ships couldn't be completed until a month or more after service had to begin. To fill the gap, Brittin rented a pair of two-seater open cockpit biplanes — an OX-5 Curtiss Oriole and an OX-5 Thomas Morse —

HAROLD H. EMMONS of Detroit, an original investor, was Northwest's first president when the airline was incorporated in 1926.

from Bill Kidder at a cost of $4,312.50, pending expected arrival of the Detroiters on November 2.

Pilots Speed Holman, Dave Behncke (later co-organizer and first president of the Air Line Pilots Association) and Chester Jacobson began Northwest's flights right on schedule October 1, 1926, and never again — except during a short-lived presidential proclamation in 1934, of which more later — have Minneapolis and St. Paul been without air mail service.

Following in the wake of two previous failures (by the Post Office and by Pop Dickinson) Northwest's new air mail flights captured scant news space at first, in a year that saw newspapers acclaim Gertrude Ederle as the first woman to swim the English Channel, Bobby Jones as winner of the U.S. Open golf championship, Admiral Byrd as first to fly over the North Pole

and "Scarface Al" Capone as top dog of Chicago's gangland.

The Northwest Airways "family" in those opening months totaled 11 hard-working persons, (versus 30,000 today) including Colonel Brittin, who worked full time with no pay. He didn't starve because the St. Paul Association, in the conviction that Northwest would be a major factor in developing future Twin Cities business, kept him on its own payroll for months until the fledgeling airline could afford to put him on salary.

That's how Northwest acquired "Rosie," too.

Her real first name was Camille, but nobody knew or cared. Rosie Stein was loved by everyone, including the newspaper reporters who nicknamed her. No matter how tough things were going — and on plenty of days they were going very tough, indeed — she always answered their query: "How are things?" by insisting: "Everything's rosy."

CAMILLE "ROSIE" STEIN, Colonel Brittin's "right hand man" and later a company officer, director and first stewardess supervisor.

11

She had been Colonel Brittin's secretary — he called her "my right hand man" — at the St. Paul Association, and she moved right along with him to the tiny little operations office in which the budding young airline set up business at Speedway Field, near a barny 80-by-100-foot hangar.

Rosie did anything and everything that needed doing, with a smile and without being asked. She tended a coal fire in the pot-bellied little stove that kept the operations shack warm on chilly days, she answered the phone, sold tickets, took deposits (when there were any) to the bank, bought engine parts, chased an occasional stray cow off the landing field and —if a passenger got "weathered in" — she'd whip up a lunch over the coal stove, clean off the colonel's desk and invite the passenger to sit down.

Later, Rosie was hailed as the first woman airline officer in the United States when she was elected assistant secretary and director of the company. She eventually became director of passenger service and (in 1939) was named the first superintendent of stewardesses (long before the designation "cabin attendant" was coined) when cabin service went formal. To her, flight attendants were always "my girls." And for someone who never had any children of her own, Rosie probably has more namesakes across the length and breadth of this country than anyone you could think of — but we're getting ahead of our story.

Julius Perlt, hired as a $125-a-month clerk in the fall of 1926 (he later had a long career as a Chamber of Commerce official in the Twin Cities) says Rosie's office stove served still another useful purpose on bitter winter days.

"When the engine oil was too stiff to pour," he recalls, "we'd stoke up the fire and put the oil cans right on the stove."

Perlt's voice, by the way, is known to generations of midwest football fans because for several decades he has manned the public address system at all University of Minnesota home football games, and continues this hobby today, even though semi-retired.

One of many times that Rosie had difficulty mustering her perennial smile came on the day Chester Jacobson cracked up in the Thomas Morse, reducing the infant Northwest "fleet" to one rented Curtiss Oriole two weeks before the Stinsons were due.

Jacobson was so embarrassed by the whole thing that he resigned, and was replaced by Robert Radoll — a former barnstormer — while the colonel scrounged around and managed to borrow a Travelair monoplane to fill the gap.

As things turned out, even the anxiously-awaited Stinson Detroiters didn't go into service without a struggle.

3

Getting Off the Ground

COLONEL BRITTIN was less than enchanted with the fact that financial control of his new baby was centered so far from home base, but a Detroit-backed airline was better than no airline at all, and he was deeply pleased when the board approved his proposal to carry out a stock subscription campaign among Twin Cities businessmen.

To develop publicity for the stock drive, Brittin persuaded the other officers — Emmons, Stout and Blair — as well as Carl Kellar, a Michigan investor, to join him as passengers aboard the three new Stinson planes when they were ferried from Detroit to the Twin Cities.

Everybody cooperated except the weather man. A blinding snowstorm forced Speed Holman and Eddie Stinson, builder of the planes, to land in Milwaukee. The only Detroiter to get through on schedule was flown by Dave Behncke, with Stout and Kellar aboard.

Despite the storm delay, all three of the black-bodied aircraft were present in time to go "on line" as advertised, November 2, 1926.

Behncke, incidentally, is better remembered for his flying ability than for his spelling of the word "taxi." Here, featuring nostalgic meal prices that today's generation might find hard to believe, is the expense account he submitted for the week of October 7, 1926:

Oct. 2	Taxie at La Crosse	$1.50
	Dinner	.85
Oct. 5	Long distance call to Milwaukee	.50
Oct. 7	Taxie at St. Paul	1.00
	Dinner	.75
	various wires	2.00
	total	6.60

Behncke, the first pilot hired by Speed Holman in the latter's role as operations manager, reminisced years later: "We flew part of the route to Chicago almost completely after dark during the winter months. There were no emergency fields and no radio — no aids of any kind except one revolving beacon atop the Milwaukee airport hangar.

"When bad weather trapped me at night, I circled a farm house and the farmer would come out with the family car, light up a field with his headlights and down I'd come.

"I used my father's farm near Cambria, Wis., which is on the route, and quite a number of times my brother wheeled out his car to help me make a landing during a bad snowstorm.

"One time I made an unscheduled stop with the mail on my dad's farm and had chicken dinner with the family, after which I again took off for the Twin Cities. Somehow the information leaked out that I was going to do this, and the Milwaukee Journal had a photographer at the field to meet me. The Sunday edition devoted a full page to the story, including a picture of my mother waving goodbye to her son, taking off from the old hayfield."

The information, of course, was leaked by none other than Colonel Brittin, who demonstrated a flair for publicity on many occasions. During the first year's operation, he spent a mere $367.58 for advertising, and $1,106.71 on publicity.

The books also show an expenditure of $169.70 that first year for air mail postage. As Damon Runyon used to say, "a story goes with it."

Every budding airline in those days — Northwest included — assigned someone to air mail one envelope daily (usually it contained a blotter) to each destination on that airline's route. This cost only 10¢ per half-ounce letter, and it positively insured the fact that at least one mail sack would go to every city every day. The economics of all this were quite simple. A mail sack plus padlock weighed two pounds. At the $2.75-per-pound rate from the Post Office, this added up to $5.50, even if the sack contained only one half-ounce letter.

Bert Ritchie, now a retired captain, remembers one of his first assignments as a relief pilot was to handle the blotter-mailing chore in his spare time. "At least, it was legitimate mail," he smiles, "which is more than some sneaky devils at certain other airlines could say when they tossed old engine parts into mail sacks to build up the weight."

In the early days of air mail, postage rates varied by destination — the half-ounce cost to Chicago from Minneapolis-St. Paul (or closer) was 10¢, to New York 15¢, to San Francisco, 20¢, to Boston, 25¢ and to Los Angeles, 30¢. But on Feb. 1, 1927, this was simplified to 10¢

DAVID L. BEHNCKE, first pilot hired by Charlie Holman, later became co-founder of the Air Line Pilots Association (ALPA.)

regardless of the destination, in a move by the postal service to subsidize both carriers and the public while promoting wider use of air mail.

Even at $2.75 a pound, Northwest's income per flight between Chicago and the Twin Cities averaged only $96.25 each way (on 35 pounds of mail) during the first few months of operation. By the following summer this mail pay had improved to $171.87 for each flight, on an average 62½-pound load of air mail.

In contrast, even if a passenger weighed 200 pounds, he paid only $40 for a one way trip between the Twin Cities and Chicago, so it's easy to understand why mail was the operation's bread and butter. In fact, it was to be 15 years before passenger revenues finally outdistanced mail income.

During their first three months of operation, Northwest planes completed 88.9% of a scheduled 52,000 miles between Chicago and the Twin Cities, despite an unusual number of storms and foggy days. Severe weather was encountered on 47 of the 122 total trips. The Detroiters averaged four hours 40 minutes for the eastbound trips, and five hours 5 minutes on the westbound flights from Chicago.

Eastbound mail added up to 2,521 pounds, westbound another 1,759, for a grand total of 4,280 pounds, which figured out to 40 pounds headed for Chicago each trip and 30 pounds for the Twin Cities. Total mail revenue for the three months was $11,770, amounting to 27.65¢ per mile flown. Uncle Sam was not exactly hurting from the $2.75-per-pound mail pay, because with a 10¢ postage rate per half ounce, the 4,280 pounds of mail meant sales of $13,696 in air mail stamps.

(In its 1976 jets, Northwest hauled 4,750-pound containers of mail between the Twin Cities and Chicago for 4¢ a pound, and bulk mail for 8¢ a pound!)

Northwest's payroll for the first three months totaled $6,191.60, or 13.4¢ per mile, while gas and oil for the same time period amounted to $3,694.74 — 7.9¢ a mile.

Other operating expenses for the first three months were not kept separate from the full year's figures, but minutes of the Board show a net loss of $897 for October, November and

PILOTS LOADED the air mail sacks in the early days. Here's Deke DeLong at work.

December — a far better showing than the Board had expected, during the rigors of an early winter. The minutes add: "By unanimous consent, congratulations were extended to Col. Brittin and the operating staff for the splendid results achieved during these exceptionally difficult months."

A prized possession of retired Northwest Captain Vince Doyle, who has collected much memorabilia of the airline's past, is the log of the original Milwaukee airport. Here are several entries that illustrate flight problems of those days:

Jan. 15, 1927, 1:30 p.m. NWA telegram: Ask if field can be rolled. Snow 14 inches deep. (NOTE: there were no snowplows at the field, but rollers sometimes were effective in packing the snow down.)

Jan. 21, 1927, 10:10 a.m. Flying impossible here. Radoll in Maywood (Chicago airport) awaiting instructions.
11:32 a.m. Telegram from Col. Brittin: Advise Radoll if mail cannot be brought thru today, stay there until tomorrow. Prepare plane for zero weather tonight. Holman leaves here on time.

Feb. 16, 1927, 6:10 p.m. Holman, Perlt passenger, depart for Maywood with mail. Beacon on.
7:10 p.m. Holman returns. Ground fog. Called P.O. truck, mail trained from Milwaukee.

Feb. 17, 1927, 9 a.m. Holman takes off to test ceiling. Find ceiling 300 feet and visibility ½ mile.
11:10 a.m. Holman and Perlt, passenger, depart for La Crosse with mail.

Early in 1927 — the year Al Jolson gave talkies a sensational introduction in "The Jazz Singer," Hirohito became emperor of Japan, Stalin assumed power in Russia and Mussolini was fascinating the Italians on his way up the ladder to eventual dictatorship — Brittin had sold $23,000 worth of stock, mostly to well known St. Paul business men.

The largest individual purchaser, however, was none other than Charlie Holman. Most of the buyers pledged $1,000 each, a few invested $500, but Speed was so confident about Northwest's future that he ponied up $2,000 in cash — almost half his annual salary.

Based on the showing of tangible though modest home town interest, the Board shortly agreed to add three St. Paulites — J.M. Hannaford, Jr., Roger B. Shepard and C.E. Johnson as directors, along with three more Detroiters — E.S. Evans, E.W. Lewis and William B. Mayo, Henry Ford's chief engineer.

It was also in 1927 that Northwest first flirted with the idea of expanding its service, when the Daniel Guggenheim Fund for the Promotion of Aeronautics showed some interest in helping extend the line to Detroit, Cleveland and Buffalo. Nothing came of these negotiations, so the Board voted to turn the matter of future expansion over to Brittin.

Some of the bookkeeping perpetrated half a century ago is enough to make any self-respecting accountant tear his hair out, so the records on Northwest's first full year of operation leave several items to the imagination.

It's a cinch that outgo exceeded income, even though hangar space and airfield usage were gladly provided free by the communities served —not to mention the fact Colonel Brittin was working for zero salary.

The old books show no profit and loss figures — in fact, they don't even show the expense of buying the three Detroiters — but $74,678.52 is listed as "operating expenses." Largest single item of "overhead" was $5,379.05 for insurance and bonding; "equipment maintenance" took another $8,276.61, and the three largest items under "transportation expense" of $32,470.27 included pilot salaries ($13,758.96), gasoline ($7,901.04) and rental of the two open cockpit planes used until the Stinsons arrived ($4,312.50).

Charlie Holman's personal fortunes improved in the fall of 1927 when he was granted time off to enter the National Air Derby, a grueling cross-country race from New York City to Spokane.

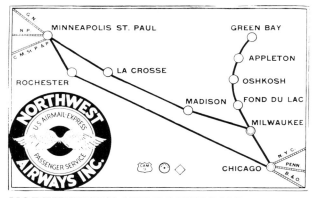

NORTHWEST'S 1929 ROUTE MAP

By the time the nation's top pilots (including such luminaries as Jimmy Doolittle) had reached the Twin Cities, Holman was running a poor second, but he had cut his deficit to 16 minutes when he reached Butte, Mont. Always a fierce competitor, Speed quickly decided to shoot for the $10,000 first prize by leaving the best known route through the Rockies to take his chances on finding a shortcut that would pick up those precious 16 minutes. He roared into Spokane, a victor by 19 seconds over his one-time teacher and good friend, Eddie Ballough.

A few days later, Ballough ate Holman's prop wash again when Speed beat him out by 29 seconds in a race from Spokane to Portland.

Speed returned to the Twin Cities and a thunderous hero's welcome. Editorials in the newspapers proclaimed "Welcome to Speed Holman," and when St. Paul and Minneapolis each demanded the right to stage a gigantic parade in his honor, Colonel Brittin took a leaf from Solomon's book.

"Why don't you *both* stage a parade?" he suggested to the city fathers.

They did, and everybody was delighted. Everybody but unassuming Speed Holman, who didn't fly because he was interested in fame — he flew because he loved it.

Despite the storm-tossed experience of Holman and Byron Webster which had opened Northwest's passenger service on July 5 that same year, 106 brave souls flew the Twin Cities-Chicago route before the young airline suspended passenger travel for the winter. Those 106 persons wouldn't make a full load for just one of Northwest's "small" jets of today — the 727-200 — nor half a load for the wide-bodied DC-10s, nor a third of a load for the big 747s.

Even a mere 106 passengers brought in about $4,000 income, and before the first 12 months had been completed, Brittin was hard at work on several new ideas to improve the financial picture. One of these ideas created a "first" in U.S. air history, just a year before the United States was engulfed in the most devastating world-wide depression of all time.

4

The (tin) Goose Hangs High

ONE OF THE REMARKABLE FACTS about Colonel Lewis Brittin is that despite his lack of aviation background — or maybe *because* of it — he grasped many of the key principles necessary to transform flying from a gay adventure into a successful business enterprise.

Writing in the University of Minnesota's "Gopher Business News" for February, 1928, Brittin pointed out that "aviation is essentially a young man's industry . . . it has the romance, the adventure, the associations that have great appeal. Its future, however, lies in something entirely different.

"However inspiring its beginnings, the cold facts of economic need will govern its ultimate development. The transition from one to the other will be worth studying, and young men will find this study very much worth while. Commercial flying must develop its own business techniques. Aviation accounting and aviation *organizational methods* will constitute a special field of modern business.

"Obsoleteness is more to be considered than depreciation from wear and tear. The cost to lift and carry a pound of pay load is the secret of the future. In this industry, rigid economy in operating costs is absolutely essential."

To demonstrate how closely he was watching costs, Brittin summarized his records on 1927 operations: "On a basis of 50½¢ per ship mile as an operating cost, Northwest Airways has found that it requires 15¢ per ship mile for payroll, 7½¢ for gasoline, oil and grease, 5¢ for insurance, 10¢ for depreciation and 13¢ for general expense including maintenance and repairs.

"The interesting thing about the Northwest Airways air mail line," he continued, "is that it was organized just like any other business, and from its inception has been operated on a strictly business basis . . . it has the distinction of ranking second in operating efficiency (among the 20 contract air mail lines in the United States.)

"No group of men could operate an air mail line between the Twin Cities and Chicago, summer and winter, flying under all conditions of good and bad weather without learning a great deal and changing their preconceived notions on aviation at least several times. This is commonly called 'experience.' It is the foundation of every successful pioneering industry and as it develops, becomes invaluable.

"The Northwest Airways has had just this experience and now is trying to use it in a way that will help aviation generally in this section of the country.

"Northwest is the only operating commercial

FORD TRI-MOTOR, alias the "tin goose," shown outside Northwest's second home base, now St. Paul's Holman Field, in 1930. Northwest operated five Tri-motors in the Thirties.

air line today in the states of Wisconsin and Minnesota, and this territory with North and South Dakota, which is the field for logical extension of this line, can never be served adequately by a flying organization that operates only between Chicago, Milwaukee, Madison, La Crosse, Minneapolis and Saint Paul.

"Distances in the Northwest are so great that to realize the real benefit from commercial aviation it is necessary to develop a network of lines throughout the Northwest.

"The extension of this commercial air service depends very largely on the development of adequate landing fields in the principal cities throughout the territory. Like the railroads, adequate terminals are indispensable to aviation.

"In order to stimulate the development of flying fields, Northwest Airways has decided to offer its services gratis to any city or town in Minnesota that wishes to consult its personnel on the subject of landing fields, hangars and flying equipment. This service is being offered as

a practical contribution to stimulate commercial aviation."

The promise was no empty gesture. More than a score of interested communities were aided by Northwest in laying out air fields and hangar facilities, and many cities in nearby states took advantage of the offer in the years that followed.

When representatives of the famed Mayo Clinic joined civic officials of Rochester, Minn., to request that their city be added to Northwest's schedule, Holman was dispatched immediately to help the city fathers select an airport site. It wasn't long until a Rochester stop (known internally as the "Mayo Clinic Special") was included on Chicago-Twin Cities flights.

Nearly 400 miles west, at Bismarck, N.D., city officials named their first airport "Brittin Field" in thanks for the help provided by Northwest.

Aero Digest reported in April, 1928, these Minnesota cities already had taken advantage of Brittin's offer of personnel and equipment to make surveys and lay out airports: Little Falls

CO-ORDINATED AIR-TRAIN mail, express and passenger service was launched by Northwest September 1, 1928, with six railroads participating. Planes carried the load by day, trains at night, before beacons made night flying practical. Aircraft in this picture is the Hamilton Metalplane.

(Lindbergh's home town), Faribault, LeSueur, Marshall, Cass Lake, Austin, Mankato, Virginia, Duluth, Eveleth, Albert Lea, Rochester, Winona, Hastings, Red Wing, Crookston, Fairmont, Owatonna, Redwood Falls, Morgan and — across the western tip of Lake Superior from Duluth — Superior, Wis.

Brittin's determination to put Northwest in the black led him to establish a flight school and "hop" service (sightseeing trips over the Twin Cities), both manned by off-duty pilots, as well as a dealership in Waco airplanes and a coordinated air-rail operation that set the industry buzzing when it was launched September 1, 1928.

Brittin had his work cut out for him when he approached the Great Northern, Northern Pacific, Milwaukee and Pennsylvania Railroads with his ambitious plan designed to cut eight hours from a journey between the midwest and New York.

Railroad officials reacted at first — and with some reason — as if they were being asked to put a mouse in charge of their cheese barrel.

But Brittin sold them, one by one, pointing out that the plan would stimulate business for both methods of transportation, and that the air portion of these trips would be by daylight only — since beacons were not yet widely available — so the railroads would benefit handsomely. (He carefully neglected to mention that once enough beacons and emergency fields dotted the airways, very few passengers or express or mail bags would transfer from plane to train.)

In the summer of 1928, Brittin finalized his plan for a closely coordinated schedule with the four railroads (later, six, when the B. & O. and New York Central signed up) and Northwest's Board unanimously approved this "first" in aviation. They also decided Brittin should enter the sole employ of the company at $1,000 a month, approved Speed Holman's request to compete in the National Air Races, and sold 22½% of Northwest's stock to Transcontinental Air Transport (TAT) for $65,000 to finance the purchase of a 14-passenger Ford Tri-motor needed for the increased passenger travel expected from the new air-rail project.

CHARLES A. LINDBERGH served as a Northwest consultant while the air-train project was being developed. With him are Charlie Holman, left, and Col. Lewis H. Brittin, center.

The all-metal "tin-goose" — in reality it was covered with a corrugated aluminum alloy — was the wonder of its day. In addition to space for 14 passengers, the Tri-motor had ample room for a pilot and — for the first time — a co-pilot, toilet facilities and a smoking area. What's more, it cruised at 125 miles an hour —40 miles faster than the Detroiters.

With his nose for news working overtime, Brittin hired Charles Lindbergh to come to the Twin Cities to give "technical advice" on the plane-train project. His own people needed very little help, but Lindy's arrival generated reams of publicity, and that's what the colonel was seeking.

To dramatize the opening of his new service September 1, 1928, Brittin arranged for Mayor J.H. Dahl of Fargo to participate by taking a train to Minneapolis, then flying to Chicago in the Ford Tri-motor, and proceeding by train on to New York, where he gave interviews as a midwest ambassador of goodwill.

Speed Holman was at the controls of the "behemoth" Tri-motor, as some newspapers called it, and the return flight from Chicago was flown by Chadwick B. Smith, whom Holman had hired as chief pilot in order to give himself more time for his operational duties and for occasional participation in major U.S. air races.

Holman continued on from Chicago to New York to participate in the National Air Derby between New York and Los Angeles. As the saying has it, "you can't win 'em all," and while Speed won more than his share, here's a wire report of September 8, 1928, from Washington, Pa.:

"Charles W. (Speed) Holman of St. Paul, winner of last year's National Air Derby, and his mechanic, Ralph Geror, narrowly escaped death this morning when their 170-mile-an-hour Laird crashed in a forced landing on the side of a mountain near here.

"Forced from the race, and his ship (entered by Northwest Airways, Inc.) badly damaged,

Holman saved his life and that of his mechanic by what fellow pilots today termed an almost miraculous landing in a dense black fog which forced eight other pilots down at various places. Flying blind after not having seen the ground for hours, Holman's limited supply of fuel ran out. Sweeping down through the fog over the side of a mountain, Holman glimpsed a small clearing, and slipped his ship into it to make what seemed like an impossible dead stick landing."

Geror went on to become one of the top airline maintenance men in the business, during a long career with Northwest.

The Ford Tri-motor used to open the air-rail tieup was the first of five eventually bought by Northwest. Almost simultaneously with its arrival, two 6-passenger Hamilton Metalplanes also were purchased at $27,000 apiece. Seven more of these 125-mile-an-hour monoplanes were to follow in the next five years, because the 3-passenger Stinsons were too small to handle the increasing Chicago-Twin Cities traffic.

More planes meant more pilots, and the first of the new crop hired — on September 1, 1927 — was Speed Holman's idol, Walter Bullock, who had fired Speed's ambition to fly by giving him his first airplane ride.

Though a year younger than Holman, Bullock was one of the nation's pioneer aviators. He was acclaimed as "the youngest licensed pilot" when he soloed at 17 and received Certificate No. 630 issued November 29, 1916, by the Aero Club of America. An early day barnstormer, Walter was giving flying exhibitions off the ice of Lake Calhoun in Minneapolis when Speed sought him out and performed odd jobs in return for an occasional ride and some informal flight instruction.

With more than 10 years of flying already under his belt (seat belt, that is) when he came to Northwest, Bullock achieved one of the nation's most distinguished commercial flying careers, eventually being elected to the OX-5 Aviation Hall of Fame. In 1954 he became the first pilot to log 25,000 hours flying for Northwest, on top of

WALTER BULLOCK followed Charlie Holman and Chad Smith as operations manager.

another 4,000 hours accumulated on his own. Walter could fly anything that had wings — with the possible exception of an ostrich — and proved it time and again, even after he reached the mandatory retirement age of 60.

At 76 he still had the same tall, slim build, sharp eyesight and "feel" for a plane that he had in his twenties, which he demonstrated by taking a solo joyride in a small plane he had never set foot in before.

Early in 1928, Northwest attempted to bring weekly service to Fargo and Winnipeg, but a three-month trial produced very little business and very much static from the Canadian government, which decided it didn't want an

American carrier to cross its borders. Wisconsin received the next extension of service that fall, north of Milwaukee to Green Bay, via Fond Du Lac, Oshkosh and Appleton through the Fox River Valley. Stinson Detroiters were assigned to open this run on December 15.

The Kellogg-Briand World Peace Pact was signed by 162 nations in 1928, Hoover was elected President, Eddie Cantor was singing "Makin' Whoopee," another big song hit of the day was "You're the Cream in My Coffee" and Speed Holman added new laurels to his fame by winning the Los Angeles-Cincinnati Air Derby ($2,500 first prize.)

Holman then returned home and set a world's record by looping-the-loop 1,433 times in a five-hour flight over the St. Paul airport that now bears his name. He did it on less than one hour's sleep after being guest of honor at an all-night party celebrating his Air Derby victory.

With mail business growing, a second daily flight between the Twin Cities and Chicago was added, and 428 persons had been carried in one full year of passenger service.

The first regularly scheduled Air Express to reach the Twin Cities was flown in by Charlie Holman April 2, an event which was particularly exciting to department store executives. The Leader's advertising trumpeted: "Leaves New York today, on sale at The Leader tomorrow. The Leader is only one day away from Broadway!"

Twin Cities newspapers did their bit to help boost mail service by listing the locations of all red, white and blue air mail boxes every day — which didn't take a lot of space to begin with, because Minneapolis had only 11 in 1928.

Three more events of note helped close out that year. On September 1, Northwest — with more seats to fill than ever before in its new and larger aircraft — cut the Twin Cities-Chicago fare to $30 one way, and $50 round trip, thus competing head-to-head with first class rail travel for the first time.

In addition, Brittin obtained an agreement from the Post Office to expand the five-day mail service to seven days a week.

Another event was not publicized, but it had far-reaching consequences in the history of Northwest. Richard C. Lilly, president of Merchants National Bank in St. Paul (later re-named First National) attended the October 5 Board of Directors meeting in Detroit as a representative of Roger Shepard, who could not attend, and explained that he was forming a pool of proposed stockholders in Minneapolis and St. Paul.

The Board listened politely. Also a bit skeptically, remembering the somewhat anemic $23,000 stock subscription in the Twin Cities of a few months earlier. What they didn't know is that when Dick Lilly charged into action, he could make a buzz saw appear to be standing still.

5

Home Sweet Home

THE TWENTIES WERE still roaring like a lion, even though they went out like the proverbial lamb.

Business was rocketing along, banks were making loans at a merry pace and investors were buying huge chunks of stock on margin. Only a few students of deteriorating world-wide conditions recognized in 1929 that the U.S. economy was thundering toward disaster, but nobody listened to this kind of alarmist talk.

It was the year of the St. Valentine's Day massacre, when six members of Bugs Moran's gang were lined up in a Chicago garage and machine-gunned to death — presumably by the mobsters of Al Capone, who several months later was given a slap on the wrist in the form of a one-year sentence for carrying concealed weapons. It also was the year Herbert Hoover became president and Ernest Hemingway published "A Farewell to Arms." Speed Holman won the first Gardner Trophy race from St. Louis to Indianapolis that summer and also the closed course competition for 800-cubic-inch engines at the National Air Races in Cleveland.

That historic year also saw Northwest begin night air mail flights — which for the first time enabled next-morning delivery of mail between New York and the Twin Cities, with pinpoint connections in Chicago — and Speed Holman

created a sensation at the National Air Races by stunting the big Ford Tri-motor, putting it through loops, rolls and most of the maneuvers commonly made with small aerobatic planes.

Contrary to one persistent legend, Charlie Holman did *not* perform the dangerous outside loop with a Tri-motor, although he did it many times with single engine aircraft. His old buddy, Walt Bullock, often said: "I don't believe *anyone* ever did an outside loop with the Ford Tri-motor."

The most significant event of the entire year for Northwest came when Dick Lilly brought control of the airline "home."

He personally button-holed the elite of Twin City business leaders, calmly told each man how many dollars he expected him to put up, then astounded the Detroit board members by plunking down $160,000 in cash with an offer to buy all 400 Michigan-held shares for $400 each. (This did not involve the shares owned by T.A.T., nor another 22½% sold to Universal Airlines to finance purchase of the first two Hamilton Metalplanes.)

After an all-night debate, the offer was approved unanimously by the Board, with a recommendation that Michigan shareholders accept the offer.

24

Most of them did, and the new slate of officers and directors was a "Who's Who" of the Minneapolis and St. Paul business community, with only one Detroiter — William B. Mayo of The Ford Motor Company — still remaining on the Board.

Dick Lilly was elected president, with Arthur R. Rogers — president of the Rogers Lumber Company and former head of the Minneapolis Civic and Commerce Association (now Chamber of Commerce) — Chairman of the Board.

The rest of the lineup included Brittin, vicepresident and general manager; Harry C. Piper of Lane, Piper and Jaffray, Minneapolis, vicepresident; Julian Baird, vicepresident of the Merchants Trust Co., secretary and treasurer;

RICHARD C. LILLY of St. Paul brought control of Northwest from Detroit to the Twin Cities in 1929. His fellow Minneapolis-St. Paul investors elected him president.

C.A. Gunderson of the Merchants Trust, assistant secretary and treasurer, and these directors:

From St. Paul, Frank B. Kellogg, attorney, former U.S. Secretary of State and winner of the Nobel Peace Prize; Roger B. Shepard, president of Finch, Van Slyke & McConville; J.M. Hannaford, Jr., vicepresident of Gordon & Ferguson, Inc.; L.J. Shields, president of National Battery Co.; Paul J. Kalman, president of Kalman Steel Co.; George K. Gann, vicepresident of Tri-State Telephone & Telegraph Co.; C.E. Johnson, vicepresident, Empire National Bank; from Minneapolis, Frank T. Heffelfinger, president of F.H. Peavey & Co.; H.R. Weesner, president, Wabash Screen Door Co.; Rufus R. Rand, capitalist; G. Nelson Dayton, treasurer of The Dayton Co.; and from Chicago, Col. Paul Henderson, vicepresident of National Air Transport Co., and Earle H. Reynolds, president of Peoples Trust & Savings Bank.

By this time, the Northwest staff included James B. "Big Jim" LaMont as chief ship mechanic, which was a real coup for the young airline. Bull-voiced Jim LaMont was a crusty individual with a heart of gold and a touch with tools that was sheer poetry.

Jim learned to fly just a few years after Samuel P. Langley built a plane in 1903 that cracked up shortly before the Wright Brothers made the first successful powered flight. LaMont became a mechanic for Glenn Curtiss, who persuaded him to quit flying and turn his talents to airplane maintenance, which was a break for Curtiss and — eventually — for Northwest.

In 1914, the original Langley plane was removed from its pedestal at the Smithsonian Institution, giving Curtiss a chance to prove, or disprove, his contention that — with LaMont's help — Langley could have beaten the Wrights off the ground.

Working with Curtiss, Jim made minor changes in the wings, tail and launching apparatus, took the plane to Lake Keuka in New York — and it flew.

One of LaMont's Northwest crew — Lou Koerner — who arrived in 1928 and went on to become superintendent of overhaul some years later, told this story at the time Big Jim retired in 1945:

"I remember when we had a ship forced down in the hills of British Columbia. The passengers were lavish in their praise of the manner in which the pilot (Frank Judd) handled the ship into a miraculous landing which halted only a few feet from a stone hedge in a lonely mountain road. Bad weather had forced a belly landing at night so the ship, naturally, was badly damaged although no one was hurt.

"The event turned out to be a field day for the natives in those parts. Even the school closed so the kids could watch Jim LaMont and his boys tote the ship down off the hills to a small clearing, where timbers were thrown up to support the fuselage and undercarriage while repairs were being made. After many days and much cussing and sweating, the timbers were

BIG JIM LAMONT, chief ship mechanic in the early days, could fly planes as well as fix 'em.

removed and the ship was ready to be ferried back to the St. Paul shops for final repairs.

"The crucial moment was at hand. There could be no test flight. The ship must fly out of there and keep going. Frank Judd had put it in there and requested he be the one to take it out. Alone. But there was one thing Frank didn't reckon on — Old Jim.

"As Frank was revving up his engines, and with the minimum gas load permissible — to lighten the ship — Old Jim climbed into the cockpit beside him.

" 'Jim, you know it will be tough enough getting this crate out of here without you,' exploded Frank.

" 'Now listen, Frank, if this klunk is going to get off, it won't make any difference whether I'm here or not,' retorted Jim. 'And besides, I told all those school kids I was going out with it. You're not going to make a liar out of me are you?'

"Well, you guessed it, they both came out of there together. That was old Jim. He wasn't handy with a slide rule, but he managed by using his mechanical instinct. He was somewhat akin to the early day pilots who flew by the seat of their pants."

An interesting parallel involving Frank Judd and LaMont is that Judd, too, eventually left the pilot ranks for an illustrious ground-based career. After holding several key administrative posts both before and during World War II, he was promoted to vice president in charge of maintenance and engineering, and served long and loyally in this demanding position through many of the airline's most turbulent years — including the hectic transition from piston aircraft to jets.

With beacons finally installed by the Department of Commerce every 10 miles between the Twin Cities and Chicago, Northwest became a customer of its own Waco dealership by buying the first three (of nine) speedy Waco biplanes to launch night airmail flights August 1, 1929. The open cockpit Wacos were used strictly for mail service, so no space was needed for passengers.

In a steady drizzle, Leon S. "Deke" DeLong flew the opening eastbound flight of the "Nighthawk run," as it was billed, with R.L. "Lee" Smith piloting the first westbound segment. Handsome Mal Freeburg alternated with DeLong and Smith thereafter. All three — along with Smith's identical twin brother Les, who joined the ranks in 1930 — enjoyed long and, on occasion, spectacular careers.

Freeburg, who sometimes stripped down to his BVD's to keep cool on hot summer nights while flying the mail, was following the Burlington tracks on his way to Chicago one night in 1930, when he spotted a flaming railroad trestle over the Chippewa River near Trevina, Wis.

Mal knew the railroad schedules by heart. In a matter of minutes, the crack Burlington Blackhawk was due to cross that trestle.

He shoved the throttle forward and raced toward the oncoming train, banked off to one side when he saw its headlight, and dived repeatedly at the engine cab, with his landing lights blinking wildly. The engineer decided this was just another hot pilot showing off, and made no move to slow down until Freeburg desperately dropped several of the emergency landing flares with which his Waco was equipped.

That did the trick. The train squealed to a halt two blocks short of the burning trestle. One of the passengers saved by Freeburg's quick

FIRST NIGHT AIR MAIL from the Twin Cities to Chicago was flown by Leon S. "Deke" DeLong August 1, 1929. Congratulating him is George Drake, then Minneapolis assistant postmaster. C.L. "Les" Smith flew the Chicago-Minneapolis leg that same night.

thinking was Bobby Jones, on his way to win the U.S. Open golf championship at Interlachen in Minneapolis as part of the only "grand slam" in the history of golf.

Less than two years later, Mal became the first U.S. pilot to win the Air Mail Flyer's Medal of Honor from the Post Office Department for another quick-thinking episode while flying the Ford Tri-motor to Chicago.

With eight passengers aboard and 21-year-old co-pilot Joe Kimm at the controls as they were passing over Wabasha, Minn., on April 12, 1932, a fearful jolt shook the plane.

Freeburg quickly reached over, pulled back the throttle, and gave Kimm a look that — translated — meant: "What the hell did you do now?"

A piece of the propellor of the left wing motor had splintered off, and the unevenly-weighted prop set up such a violent shimmy that the 500-pound motor jerked loose from its mounting and hung precariously from the stricken plane, threatening to plunge down like a bomb on the city below.

"Mal took over the controls," Kimm remembers, "and when I looked out where he was pointing, I damn near died.

"First of all, the engine was endangering the people of Wabasha. On top of that, everybody knew a Tri-motor would fly on two engines, but nobody had any idea how badly the ship would be unbalanced with one outboard motor removed altogether."

With the utmost delicacy and precision, Freeburg gently turned his stricken plane toward the nearby Mississippi river, holding his breath until he was well out over the water. Then he banked left, whipped his controls back and forth, and shook the motor loose. It dropped harmlessly into the Father of Waters.

"The left wheel had been jammed by the falling engine," says Kimm. "In fact, a piece of the tire was chopped off, but Mal carefully put her down right wheel first on a nearby emergency field, for one of the nicest landings you could imagine."

A spontaneous cheer from the passengers saluted Freeburg's expert airmanship. The plane had barely rolled to a halt when one of those aboard — a reporter from the St. Paul Dispatch — raced for the nearest house to telephone in his scoop. The story hit newspaper front pages from coast-to-coast.

Almost unnoticed in all the publicity was the fact that — with the aid of recently installed two-way radio communication — Kimm was able to call home base instantly for a replacement aircraft.

"Operator Bill Edwards took the call," adds Kimm, "and the only casualty of the entire operation was Hank Aune of maintenance, who tripped and twisted his ankle while rushing downstairs from the radio room in his haste to get another Tri-motor ready. The replacement plane reached Wabasha so fast that we delivered our passengers to the Chicago airport barely an hour behind schedule."

Freeburg's written report upon landing was the understatement of the year: "Delayed on

MAL FREEBURG'S HEROICS won a medal from the President of the United States.

28

account of motor trouble. Changed ships at Wabasha." Mal, incidentally, was a civic-minded man as well as a brainy pilot. He onced served as mayor of suburban Richfield on the southern edge of Minneapolis.

Joe Kimm, his co-pilot on that news-making flight, is one of many who started an aviation career as a teen-age model plane builder. Walter Bullock was the adviser of Joe's model airplane club, and shortly after Kimm won the Minneapolis Journal's model airplane tournament of 1928, Bullock casually told him one day:

"If you can sell your folks on the idea, (Kimm was not quite 18) and if you can get a few clothes together in a hurry, Northwest could use you as a steward on our Tri-motor flights to Chicago."

Joe could, and did.

As he said later: "Stewards used to gas the plane, board the passengers, sell tickets, pick up tickets, validate them, serve box lunches, get chocolate bars from a machine on the back wall, load the baggage, sign for registered mail, load it, clean the floor afterward and put in 130 hours each month — all for 78 bucks.

"I realized I had the wrong job, so I figured I'd better learn to fly."

Kimm graduated from the flight school operated by Northwest, was hired as a pilot at age 19, and when he retired in 1971, took with him a record that never will be broken. In addition to many honors and key assignments — including that of system chief pilot during one of the most trying times in Northwest's history — Kimm had been a Northwest pilot for 41 years.

Good news and bad news traveled hand in hand in 1929. Shortly after the young airline had proudly issued a pretentious brochure titled "A Million Miles Without An Accident," pilot Eddie Middagh was killed in the crash of a Tri-motor just after taking off from the St. Paul airport for Wold Chamberlain. Six passengers and the steward — 18-year-old Robert Johnston — escaped.

By mid-year, Northwest's assets of $351,984 included $222,762 worth of aircraft. The first mention of "net profit" to be found in the books is a plus of $18,604 for the month of July, generated by that month's mail revenue of $55,341, passenger revenue totaling $12,044, "hop service" income of $3,148, another $281 from air express and student instruction income of $577.

October's net proft was $16,800, and November's another $21,300, but December showed a loss of $719.66. The pattern of wintertime losses was to hang on for years.

Colonel Brittin, whose many talents included considerable artistic ability, was one of the country's first airline executives to uniform his flight crews, and personally designed a gold pilot's insignia comprising two wings that extended from a replica of the globe, on which the words "U.S. Air Mail" appeared in raised letters.

The Post Office Department was so taken with Brittin's design that the government asked for — and obtained — his permission to adopt the insignia as the official emblem to be worn by air mail pilots of all U.S. airlines. The same design also was placed on huge banners, which flew at airports throughout the nation to mark the point where air mail was dispatched and delivered.

Part of the airline's student instruction income in 1929 came from a 20-year-old named Tom Hillis, who learned to fly in what the students kiddingly referred to as "the A.P. Nelson School of Air Navigation," because Brittin had assigned Nelson to coordinate this flight school with other activities of the airline.

As a bonus for soloing (under the teaching of Chad Smith) Hillis was awarded a free trip to Chicago in the Ford Tri-motor, and the wide-eyed young man gulped in excitement at being allowed to occupy the co-pilot's seat alongside Walter Bullock.

"When Walter decided I was to be trusted," recalls Tom, "he took a nap. I had to wake him up to find out where Maywood air field was."

There were no pilot openings at the time, so Hillis — like several others through the years —

ORIGINATED BY NORTHWEST, this air mail emblem was adopted by the U.S. Postal Service for all carriers flying air mail. Colonel Brittin personally created the design, NWA's oldest tradition.

joined Northwest as a mechanic, later became a foreman and chief mechanic, and finally signed on as a pilot.

To celebrate Northwest's return to home town control — not to mention a record 4,167 passengers carried in fiscal 1929 — the Board that fall authorized construction of a $100,000 hangar, machine shop and administration building at the St. Paul airport. The company's planes were used as auxiliary moving vans when the spanking new quarters were occupied a few months later, just about the time Amelia Earhart set a world speed record for women pilots, and the Post Office again "borrowed" Brittin's air mail emblem for its new 5¢ stamp.

The new company headquarters was a showplace, compared to the dingy old hangar and small operations building that had filled the bill up to that time.

And what became of the old Wold Chamberlain operations office?

"I made a deal with Speed Holman to buy it for $50," recalls Tom Hillis. "We jacked it up, skidded it across Sixty-sixth street and set it down at 7308 Portland Avenue, where I put in some partitions and turned it into my home. So far as I know, it's still there."

Once the new St. Paul headquarters building was in use (Northwest continued to serve Wold Chamberlain field) Brittin insisted that everything be kept meticulously clean and neat.

"The colonel would walk down the middle of the hangar, with Speed Holman walking down one side and Chad Smith down the other," remembers Hillis, "to make sure every tool was in its numbered cabinet, everybody was wearing clean coveralls, and anything not in use was put away properly.

"Colonel Brittin seemed to be around at all hours of the day or night — even on weekends. (A habit that was revived when Donald Nyrop arrived on the scene.)

Flight crews still found it necessary to get weather information — most of it out-dated — by telephone and by telegraph, but the beginnings of a radio network were laid by Northwest in 1930. The first purchase was a $160.99 ground radio installation at the new St. Paul headquarters, and many thousands more were to be expended shortly, bad times or not.

Although the stock market crash of October, 1929, was the most violent evidence that the "great depression" had begun, the full effects of the nation's slowly strangling economy were not yet evident in 1930. Unemployment grew by the month — to 12 million in 1932 — and as conditions worsened, 5,000 banks collapsed, carrying their depositors with them into a despair that gnawed at the country's vitals.

"Retrenchment" became a byword of the times, as business generally pulled in its horns and hoped to ride out the storm. But at Northwest Airways, Colonel Brittin and the new Board of Directors geared up to plunge boldly ahead with an ambitious plan to fight depression with expansion.

PART II

"Go West, Young Airline, Go West"
(1930-1941)

6

A Beginning — and an End

DURING THE THREADBARE THIRTIES, with unemployment eventually reaching 33% in Northwest's home county, U.S. movie theaters staged "dish nights" and "bank nights" to lure patrons out of their homes, but a majority of Americans settled for the cheaper entertainment of family radio.

They chuckled along with "Amos and Andy," agonized over the problems of "One Man's Family" (weakling Clifford, reliable Paul, beautiful Claudia and the mischievous twins — remember?) and raptly followed the backstage drama "Myrt and Marge."

Charlie Holman added his own bit of drama to the beginning of the Thirties when he and his wife went to Chicago with the Walter Bullocks to watch the famous Thompson Trophy race. Charlie wasn't entered, but on the morning of the race he decided to visit his old friend Mattie Laird — builder of the black biplane Speed had flown to victory in several competitions.

He found Mattie desperately making final mechanical adjustments on a new plane named "Solution." Laird's pilot suggested Holman's experience might help win the race.

Mattie didn't say a word — he just gave Holman a questioning look.

"You've got a pilot," Speed told him. "Any-thing you can build, I can fly."

Charlie quickly put on helmet, goggles and flying suit and gave "Solution" a short test hop. Then in record time for the 100-mile triangular course, Holman — the man who wasn't entered — solved the $10,000 question by winning first prize. He averaged 201.9 miles an hour.

In the nation's capital, Congress greeted the start of the Thirties by changing the rules of the game for all U.S. air mail operators.

The McNary-Watres Act turned the Postmaster General of the United States into a virtual dictator, and — in keeping with the national trend toward retrenchment — established lower mail pay rates that reduced the income of most carriers, including Northwest Airways.

Walter Folger Brown, Hoover's Postmaster General, had an important hand in drawing up the bill. Brown was convinced that topnotch air mail service could be provided only by large corporations with strong financial resources, so he wrote into the Watres Act — as it became known for short — a provision giving the Postmaster General power to extend or consolidate routes whenever "in his judgment the public interest will be promoted thereby."

The old method of paying for mail by weight

was abandoned in favor of paying for available aircraft space, with a new maximum rate of $1.25 per mile. One of Brown's objectives in cutting mail pay was to do away with the practice under which some carriers earned so much from Post Office revenue that they made only a token effort to provide passenger service. (Conversely, Northwest eagerly began some of its passenger routes *before* being awarded a mail contract — nearly a year before, in the case of Rochester, Minn.)

Brown's detractors (he eventually was cleared of wrongdoing, after a congressional investigation) claimed the broad powers granted him — and his successors — by the new law gave the Postmaster General an opportunity to "play God."

By forcing consolidations involving many different airlines, and by awarding air mail contracts strictly as he felt the public interest demanded, Brown became "the architect of the major U.S. airline route networks which survive today," according to R.E.G. Davies, veteran aviation writer.

Specifically, Davies singles out Brown as the creator of the so-called domestic "Big Four" — United, American, TWA and Eastern Airlines — and with helping Pan American establish a total monopoly on overseas mail service from the United States, by awarding Pam Am every foreign route for which bids were invited during Brown's regime.

In his own defense, Brown later pointed out that Pan Am's Juan Trippe — a shrewdie if there ever was one — had neatly sewed up foreign landing rights, so most bids lower than Trippe's were meaningless. He also told congressional investigators that on occasions when low bidders failed to receive contracts, it was because his department was "not buying peanuts and pig iron; we were buying a service that was highly specialized and exceedingly hazardous. There was no sense in taking the government's money and dishing it out to every little fellow that was flying around the map and was not going to do anything."

Immediately after the McNary-Watres bill was enacted, Postmaster General Brown invited officers of the nation's largest airlines to a series of Washington meetings which became known as the "spoils conferences."

As one of the "little fellows," Northwest was *not* included in Brown's invitation.

Those attending the "spoils conferences" were Aviation Corporation (forerunner of American), United Aircraft, Western Air Express, T.A.T. (predecessor of TWA), Eastern Air Transport and the Stout line — then part of United. These airlines received all but two of the 22 air mail contracts issued by Brown at that time under the new Watres Act.

In retrospect, it appears Northwest Airways escaped the shotgun weddings engineered by Brown for two reasons: Northwest was small, and it operated in thinly populated areas where there was not enough business to split up among competing carriers — although competition reared its head in earnest as the young airline's ambitions grew.

On occasion, the Postmaster General exercised his dictatorial powers by telling a carrier: "I want you to fly from this point to that point, whether you think it's a good idea or not." In 1930, for example, Northwest was ordered to fly once a week from the Twin Cities to Omaha, connecting with the Central Continental. Like the earlier weekly service to Winnipeg, this anemic schedule produced little business, so Brown finally authorized a halt to the money-losing route.

In his zeal to spread the gospel of air travel, Colonel Brittin was guilty on occasion of a money-losing error that plagued many early day aviation executives. With little or no coercion on the part of the Postmaster General, Brittin happily added seven new short-haul stops at small cities in Wisconsin and Illinois which cost more to operate than could be recouped in revenues.

In 1931 he even bought two Sikorsky amphibian planes to serve Duluth by landing in that city's Lake Superior harbor, when its

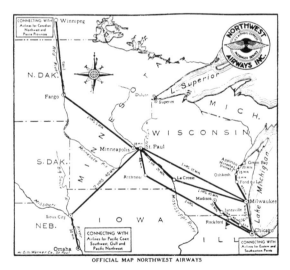

FULL PAGE NEWSPAPER AD shows the route system in 1930.

airport was many months away from completion.

The first Sikorsky — nicknamed the "Duck" — really quacked, because Northwest mechanics rigged up a horn featuring a high-pitched baritone that never failed to attract an audience while a rowboat gondolier plucked passengers from the floating amphibian.

The Duck was reasonably well patronized in good weather, but profits went down the drain before long, because as native Duluthians proudly relate, the air-conditioned city is blessed with "nine months of winter and three months of damn poor sleighing."

As 1931 arrived, coming events were casting their shadows before them.

In the Orient, Japan invaded Manchuria, but the rest of the world paid meager attention to this start on a decade of conquest that was to culminate at Pearl Harbor. Wiley Post and Harold Gatty flew around the world in 8½ days in the "Winnie Mae," federal agents finally put Al Capone away when he drew an 11-year Alcatraz sentence — for income tax evasion — and Colonel Lewis Brittin went to work on his dream of a Northern Transcontinental.

The Colonel's No. 1 problem — at least, to begin with — was that Walter Folger Brown did not share the same dream. Neither did many congressmen, as several hearings were to demonstrate shortly.

Brown, after studying the map and its major population centers, had decided this country should have two transcontinental air routes — one through the central part of the U.S., and another across the south. It was this strategy that led him to whack more than two dozen air carriers into a variety of mergers so his own dream could be accomplished.

Fortunately for Northwest, Brown took a tolerant view of Brittin's westward-ho ambitions across the colder and lesser-populated northern tier of states, largely because Brittin — a highly persuasive man — spent more and more of his time in Washington, where he could argue the merits of his case in person.

Colonel Brittin was a quick study, as they say in show business, and after watching some of the big boys operate in our nation's capital, soon realized it doesn't pay to barge in with an important route request — however deserved — without some backing from the people who go to the polls. Directors of Northwest, headed by Arthur R. Rogers — who had succeeded Dick Lilly as president — became a hard working board, as they pitched in to help Brittin develop grass roots support for his first objectives —

TWO SIKORSKY AMPHIBIANS were added to the fleet in 1931 because Duluth had no airport. These planes operated in and out of the Duluth harbor, carrying a maximum of eight passengers.

Fargo and Winnipeg. In the long range plan were Bismarck, Billings, Helena, Spokane and — hopefully — Seattle-Tacoma on Puget Sound, but Fargo was the key first step.

Delegations of civic leaders and businessmen from the Twin Cities, Fargo, Grand Forks and Pembina (on North Dakota's Canadian border), plus a similar group in Winnipeg, vociferously endorsed the proposed new daily service. Canadian postal officials got on the bandwagon, too.

Then some eagle-eye discovered a route to Winnipeg slightly more than doubled Northwest's main line mileage (Chicago-Twin Cities) of 370 miles. The U.S. comptroller general ruled this was prohibited by the Watres Act. As a compromise, it was agreed Western Canada Airways would meet Northwest flights at the border and carry all traffic over the 67 miles between Winnipeg and Pembina.

Both governments warmly approved the plan as a hands-across-the-border project that materially improved the mail service of each country.

Groundhog Day — February 2, 1931 — was chosen for the start of this new international route. The groundhog didn't see his shadow on that day, mainly because a dense fog also made it impossible for pilots to see the ground. Joe Ohrbeck got as far north as Osakis, Minn. — about 125 miles — with a Northwest Hamilton Metalplane, before being forced down, but his Canadian counterpart was unable to leave Winnipeg. The 18,000 letters which had started from Wold Chamberlain did not reach their destination until February 3.

With the Fargo stop now a reality, the next objective was Bismarck, North Dakota's capital city. Speed Holman and Brittin personally scouted locations for emergency landing fields, helped lay out the Bismarck airport — which was named Brittin Field in the colonel's honor — and enlisted the active support of Governor George Schafer.

The governor called on Postmaster General Brown and presented resolutions adopted by a score of North Dakota communities supporting Northwest's proposed new east-west route and applauding the airline's start on a quarter-million-dollar radio-telephone and telegraph system, with new stations in Fargo and Pembina connected to the parent station in St. Paul.

In early May, 1931, the Post Office announced Northwest had been certified to serve Bismarck, starting June 2, when two-way radio contact with Northwest's 18 planes would become a reality — thus adding another 160 air miles to the west.

The more races Charlie Holman won, the more he was in demand at aviation events around the nation, so with a Bismarck extension now secured, he took a few days off because civic sponsors of the Omaha Air Show had begged him to take part in their two-day event, May 16 and 17.

Holman won a special 25-mile race staged on the opening day, and stayed overnight to chat with Jimmy Doolittle and several other friendly enemies of the race circuit.

On the second day, during an unplanned delay in the program, the spectators began clapping their hands and yelling for action. Holman walked up to the committee in charge of the show and suggested: "Why don't I keep them occupied by going up and doing a few tricks?"

The delighted committee quickly agreed, and the public address system announced sonorously:

"Ladeez and Gentlemen, presenting Charles "Speed" Holman, one of the greatest American pilots, in a daredevil exhibition of stunt flying."

The Minneapolis Tribune carried this eye-witness account of what followed:

Up, up he goes 2,000 feet in the air. Lightly the biplane turns on its side, drifts down. Then as the motor thunders again, it gains speed on its downward dive toward the center of the field.

The spectators gasp as the plane dives steeply toward the center of the earth. Then a hundred feet from the ground the ship "levels off" and Holman skims across the field — a black flash

PRESIDENT FRANKLIN D. ROOSEVELT presented the Air Mail Flyers' Medal of Honor to Northwest Captain Mal Freeburg in 1933. Others, left to right: David Behncke of NWA; W.W. Howes, assistant U.S. Postmaster General; J.M. Donaldson, Howes' deputy; Congressman Clyde Kelly; S.A. Cisler, Superintendent of Air Mail. (Captains wore only two stripes in those days.)

moving 300 miles an hour. Fifty feet from the ground it straightens out, not more than a hundred yards from the stands.

Across the field, Holman begins another of those unbelievable climbs. It seems as if the plane is rushing upward at 200 miles an hour, pulled by the force of the propeller alone. The people in the stands can hear the wire rigging scream in the wind.

At 2,000 feet the ship stalls, slides over on its side. Another wingover. A barrel loop. Then Holman turns again toward the field, turns the nose of the plane down.

Down comes the plane . . . . . down . . . . . down . . . . . down . . . . .

About 300 feet in the air the black plane spins, flops over on its back.

The motor roars on. The wires scream. The plane stays on its back, still headed toward the earth. Three hundred miles an hour.

At 75 feet the plane begins to level off — still on its back. The spectators sit agonized. Still the plane slides down. The speed is blinding, but to the watchers it seems an age.

Then at 50 feet the plane levels off, starts to skim across the field, the landing gear pointing skyward. The wings wabble, quiver. The motor thunders on.

Then as Holman starts to climb with the plane upside down, it happens.

There is a jerk. The plane points downward again. The ship hits the ground, Holman beneath it.

There is a tearing crash. The plane folds up as if

38

it were cardboard. Dust fills the air while pieces of wreckage are still flying.

A sheet of metal goes bouncing to one side as the wreckage settles down. A thin stream of smoke rises from the motor where it lies apart from the other wreckage.

There are screams from the stands. Women faint. Fat policemen, reporters, photographers, officials, a doctor, a priest run toward the heap of fabric, wires, broken metal.

"Get him out. Get him out," someone screams.

But there is no need. Holman's body lies entangled in the wreckage, bound by wires and torn canvas to a heap that two minutes ago was a darting, graceful thing.

The sorrow of Colonel Brittin and the small but closely-knit band of Northwest employees was shared by the entire state of Minnesota and by countless thousands across the nation. The only certainty about the accident that took Holman's life is that the bracket of his seat belt was corroded and broken. Some spectators said they saw Holman grasp the side of the cockpit when — in their estimation — the seat belt fastening snapped. Official records of the investigation do not exist, but Holman's buddies agreed that a mechanical failure of some kind had to be the cause, because Charlie had performed his famous power dives and upside-down flying routines too many times to have made a mistake in handling his black Laird.

Holman's funeral was the largest ever seen in the state of Minnesota. More than 100,000 people lined the route to the highest knoll in Acacia cemetery near Mendota, overlooking the Mississippi river. Governor Floyd B. Olson attended, representing the citizens of Minnesota, and was the first on a long list of honorary pall bearers. (Ironically, the only other funeral in Minnesota history that rivaled Holman's in size was that of Governor Olson, who was being boomed as presidential timber when he was cut down by cancer in 1936.) Active pall bearers were all fellow pilots of Holman — Chad Smith, Walt Bullock, Homer Cole, John Malone, R. Lee Smith and Joe Ohrbeck.

At Northwest headquarters, Holman's fellow employees went about their daily tasks like robots, depressed in spirit and unwilling to touch his office, which was decorated with trophies and pictures, the desk still covered with letters and business documents.

Among a dozen photographs on the wall was one of Charlie Holman's prized possessions — a framed print of Captain Eddie Rickenbacker's famous "Hat in the Ring" squadron insignia from World War I. It was autographed by Rickenbacker:

"To my dear friend, Charles 'Speed' Holman. May all his landings be three pointed."

7

Proof of the Pudding

NOT EVEN THE LOSS of Charlie Holman could halt Northwest's drive westward, although there were inevitable delays as the airline re-grouped its forces — not once, but twice. And there was opposition to be surmounted in Washington, too.

The last official business transacted by Holman in his capacity as "Operating manager" (the term then used) was to finalize preparations for amphibian flights to Duluth and to get ready for the new Bismarck service. Charlie's next project had been to help Mandan, Bismarck's sister city, plan an airport of its own — a task that fell to his successor, Chad Smith.

Tragedy struck again when Smith — one of Northwest's mainstays from almost the very beginning — did not survive an emergency appendectomy. Thus, Walter Bullock became the third man to head Northwest operations in a period of just four months.

Shortly after the new Bismarck flights were launched without a hitch, figures for the year ending June 30, 1931, showed a new high of 7,268 passengers had been carried, plus a quarter million pounds of mail, and — wonder of wonders — this had generated a net profit of $174,072, the first sizeable black figures yet achieved. The airline's planes flew 1,298,000 miles that year, powered by 406,687 gallons of gasoline — considerably less fuel than Northwest jets now require in *one day* over their domestic and international routes while piling up more than 22 *billion* passenger miles a year (before the Republic merger.)

Walt Bullock took over his new duties on Northwest's fifth birthday, just as the young airline retired its No. 1 Stinson Detroiter and donated it to the Minnesota Historical Society. In a trifle less than five years, the little plane had carried 14,720 passengers, 178,429 pounds of mail, and covered 435,721 miles — equivalent to about 17½ times around the world.

The larger 6-passenger Hamilton monoplanes handled traffic to all five North Dakota destinations, and one of them helped contribute to the local folklore near Cleveland, a small town west of Jamestown, N.D.

When a winter blizzard forced Carl Leuthi down on a snow-covered field, he trudged to the nearest farm, leaving his load of mail locked in the plane. A real live pilot, of course, was something of a rarity in your average North Dakota farmhouse, and Carl was treated royally as if he had just dropped in from Mars on a flying saucer.

Leuthi did his part by entertaining the family

40

with yarns about fellow pilots, including a report about the time Mel Fried spotted a midnight resort hotel fire near Pewaukee, Wis. Mel repeatedly zoomed the town until lights began flashing on, and awakened residents carried the hotel's sleeping caretaker to safety — another of many similar lifesaving errands sparked by Northwest flight personnel in the early days.

In 24 hours the snow finally quit, so his benefactors wished Leuthi Godspeed and trooped out to watch his Hamilton take off.

Several days later when Carl flew over the same farm, he couldn't believe his eyes. Down on the snowy landscape, in giant 25-foot dark-hued letters against the white background, was his name: L E U T H I.

Wanting to do something special for his new-found friend, the farmer had come up with an inspiration — he spelled out Carl's last name in the snow with his manure spreader.

(For several weeks, whenever Carl flew over the farm with a load of passengers, he'd point down at his barnyard-inspired monogram and chuckle: "Friends of mine." Then came the sequel. As spring snows melted, the winter-applied fertilizer seeped into the soil, and a vibrantly green L E U T H I continued to salute every passing aircraft all summer long.)

Northwest's passenger traffic for the full year of 1931 — a majority of it rung up through the good weather months of late spring, summer and fall — reached 14,222 — a record that was not to be broken for three eventful years. With 15 million jobless across the nation in 1932, marchers demonstrating for a soldier's bonus rioted in Washington, John Dillinger was on his way to becoming Public Enemy No. 1 and kidnappings became a cancer on the body of America. The most poignant case of all, widely known as the "crime of the century," marred the early spring of that year.

A stealthy intruder climbed his home-made ladder to a second story window near Hopewell, N.J., and snatched the first-born son of Charles A. Lindbergh. In a series of bizarre midnight negotiations with go-betweens, the kidnapper collected $50,000 ransom provided by the tortured parents, who did not know the baby already lay buried in a shallow grave not far from the national hero's home.

After a sensational trial in which the kidnap ladder's origin was traced to the home of Bruno Richard Hauptmann (ransom money was found there, too) Hauptmann paid with his life in the electric chair.

Less than three months after the Lindbergh kidnapping, Amelia Earhart Putnam became the first woman to solo the Atlantic — five years to the day after Lindy's historic crossing.

One of Amelia's friends, whom she had met while he was attending Yale University, was a personable young Fargo man named Croil

CARL LEUTHI received the keys to the city of Los Angeles from actress Loretta Young several years after his North Dakota experiences related in this chapter. On this occasion he had made a demonstration flight to several West Coast cities with one of Northwest's first Stratocruisers.

Hunter. Their paths were to cross again, but it was another of Hunter's friends — Yale classmate Julian Baird of St. Paul — who introduced him to Dick Lilly as "the kind of young go-getter we ought to put on the payroll."

Lilly first put Hunter on his own payroll, by sending him east as New York manager of the First Bancredit Corporation. He liked the way the young man operated. With Colonel Brittin fighting the "battle of Washington" almost full time, Lilly decided Croil would be a valuable addition to the management group at Northwest Airways, so after a four-year stint in New York, Hunter was appointed traffic manager on March 15, 1932. E.I. Whyatt came aboard at the same time as assistant treasurer and chief accountant — eventually becoming executive vicepresident of the airline.

Seven weeks later the Board of Directors voted Colonel Brittin a $1,000 bonus for "meritorious service" because he had "spent his entire time in Washington over a period of many months." While no external announcement was made, the Board also voted that "on account of the importance to the corporation of its air mail contracts, Colonel Brittin has been relieved of responsibilities in respect to the *operation* of the corporation so he could devote all his time and efforts to contracts with the Post Office Department, members of congress and to public relations in the territory we serve."

All the evidence indicates Brittin relished his role in the "battle of Washington," which was heating up to a point where some of the major airlines kept entire teams of lobbyists at the nation's capital. Brittin performed superbly, considering the lack of clout he had as the lone representative of a small independent line.

Through an ironic twist of fate, the job he loved and performed so well was to be his undoing.

The first problem faced by Northwest in 1932 is that one school of thought believed north-south lines radiating from the existing Central Continental air route — like rib bones extending from the spine of a fish — would provide adequate service to key cities north of that line.

At a hearing of the House Committee on Post Office and Post Roads, several witnesses pointed out Seattle and Spokane already had north-south lines (United) connecting them to the Central Continental, and three Montana points (Great Falls, Helena and Butte) were connected to Salt Lake City by a small north-south route known as National Parks Airways.

"Our proposed Northern Transcontinental is much more practical because it is far shorter," testified Colonel Brittin. "The natural flow of traffic is east-west across the northern states."

One congressman interrupted him: "Your northern route will provide too many flying hazards. You could not maintain a decent flying schedule on a Northern Transcontinental with all those mountains, not to mention the weather problems."

Brittin answered this objection with actions rather than words.

While Billings — Montana's largest metropolis — was the next Northwest objective, Brittin set out that fall on a demonstration flight to the capital city of Helena, considerably farther west, with Walter Bullock at the controls of a Hamilton Metalplane.

They made the Helena-Twin Cities flight — 1,025 air miles — in the amazing time (for then) of 9 hours 15 minutes, on September 14, 1932.

Their itinerary included Fargo, Valley City, Jamestown and Bismarck, N.D., as well as Glendive, Miles City and Billings in Montana. Brittin spent several days enlisting the support of local civic leaders for Northwest's bid to extend west from Bismarck. The Montanans were so enthusiastic that, before Northwest's Hamilton took off on its return trip, the Livestock Breeders Association presented Col. Brittin with a fuzzy white lamb.

This was some years before Congress passed a law permitting "certain animals" to be transported by air (excluding skunks), but the lamb became a non-revenue passenger on the return flight nevertheless, wearing a gunny sack diaper provided by the livestock men.

TWO HORSEPOWER "TRACTOR" tows a Northwest Hamilton Metalplane at the Pembina, N.D., airport in 1932. At the reins is Charlie "Snakes" Bouvette, station manager. Joe Kimm took this shot from the cockpit of another Hamilton he had just flown in from the Twin Cities.

On their arrival home, Brittin — in his typically thoughtful way — gave these chops-on-the-hoof to Bullock's nine-year-old daughter, Marilyn. Marilyn had a little lamb for several months, after which it turned into a full grown sheep and was presented to a farmer who had better housing facilities for animals of that size.

Upon landing back in the Twin Cities, Brittin told news reporters: "We have proved the flying hazards on this route (to western Montana) are no greater than those on other Northwest lines, and that there will be no difficulty in maintaining a flying schedule. We crossed the Bad Lands and two mountain ranges with no trouble whatever."

Scoffers in Washington asked: "But what could you do in the dead of winter?"

The next proof served up by Northwest put that question to rest permanently, with Croil Hunter now beginning to participate actively in the struggle to reach Puget Sound. Hunter took to the airline business like a kitten takes to catnip, and in a few months felt completely at home in his new job as traffic manager.

"Croil was easy to know, easy to like, had a sense of humor that could rescue a lost cause, yet he could take the hide off a rhinoceros when riled," in the words of Frank Judd. Hunter had served overseas in World War I, returning as a captain, and before going to work for Dick Lilly, was called home from Yale to take charge of the family mercantile business in Fargo following the death of his father.

Standing almost a head shorter than Colonel Brittin's six feet three, Croil made up in energy what he lacked in height, and enthusiastically joined in plans to fly a Ford Tri-motor west and show the Washington doubters that mountains and winter held no terrors for Northwest Airways.

Hunter enjoyed the limelight, and assured

43

plenty of publicity for the flight by inviting his friend, Amelia Earhart, to ride along, since she was headed for some speaking engagements on the west coast anyway.

On January 28, 1933, with snow falling briskly, Northwest launched its historic "proof of the pudding" flight on behalf of the Northern Transcontinental. On board were Colonel Brittin, Hunter, Mrs. Hunter (who de-planed in Bismarck), Miss Earhart, Medal of Honor winner Mal Freeburg — then system chief pilot — mechanic Heinie Wahlstrom, Captain Hugh Rueschenberg and co-pilot Joe Kimm.

After leaving Minnesota's lake country behind, they crossed the "bread basket of the world," spending a night in Bismarck before pushing on to Billings, trading kingpin of the Midland Empire. The weather was bitter cold. Each night the Tri-Motor had to be staked down as protection from strong winds, because its wingspread was too great for the hangars available.

By then, Northwest owned eight radio stations over which pilots received weather advice every 15 minutes on routes from Chicago to Bismarck. But the Tri-motor soon was far beyond reach of the airline's western-most station, adding to the problems of the flight crew as they went deeper and deeper into unfamiliar terrain.

A Montana sheep rancher who claimed to know "every pass, every stream, every salt lick and every tree blaze," volunteered to go along from Helena and guide the plane across the Continental Divide and on toward Spokane.

The first doubt of his infallibility came when the grizzled old-timer pointed to a cut between two peaks and announced: "Thar she be. You fly through that canyon, and there's open country just beyond."

Kimm, who was at the controls at the time, suddenly found himself pocketed on all sides, and managed a heart-stopping turn that got the Ford back to safety. The second time it happened, Hugh Rueschenberg — always a perfect gentleman — gently informed the self-

AMELIA EARHART rode along as an observer on Northwest's 1933 "proof of the pudding" flight to convince Washington officials that a route to Seattle via the northern tier of states was feasible in the wintertime. At left, co-pilot Joe Kimm and Captain Hugh Rueschenberg.

appointed Dan'l Boone: "We've appreciated your help, but I believe we can make it through the Rockies from here."

Their route took them over Missoula, up the Clark Fork River, across Idaho's Lake Pend Oreille and finally — through a blinding snowstorm that dropped the ceiling to 300 feet — into Spokane, center of the farm, lumber and mine-rich Inland Empire.

The snow continued for two days, which didn't bother Brittin and Hunter at all, because they had "missionary work" to do with local business and civic leaders, to develop backing for Northwest's proposed northern route to the coast. Amelia Earhart received interviewers in a $75-a-day suite, and Northwest sponsored a local dinner party at the Davenport Hotel the night before the traveling group capped its performance by flying through the dangerous but breathtakingly beautiful Cascade mountains to Seattle, queen city of the Pacific Northwest.

As the Northwest survey party got ready for its flight back to the Twin Cities (it took just two days) a representative of well-entrenched United — which already operated the Central Continental route with spur lines up to Spokane and Seattle — airily told Brittin: "If you Swedes from Minnesota don't keep out of these mountains, you're gonna break your goddam necks."

He was wrong about the necks, but there was bumpy air ahead for the "Minnesota Swedes."

8

Battle for Seattle

THE MOST CRUCIAL PERIOD in Northwest's early history followed the successful demonstration flight to Seattle. It was a critical time for the entire nation, as well.

With unemployment still climbing and "Apple Annies" reduced to selling fruit, pencils and trinkets on city street corners to keep body and soul together, U.S. voters had swept Franklin D. Roosevelt into office with the fond hope that his campaign theme song, "Happy Days Are Here Again," would become a reality.

Public confidence in the economy was so shaken that as one bank after another failed, panic-stricken depositors queued up in long lines to withdraw their money from institutions still open, leading Roosevelt to launch his presidency by closing all the nation's banks temporarily in order to prevent total financial chaos.

Two days before Roosevelt took office on March 4, 1933, the outgoing administration — which had been holding out against Northwest's fight to serve Montana — suddenly approved the 392-mile extension from Bismarck to Billings.

This move amounted to a "consolation prize" from Postmaster General Brown, and here's how it developed. Whenever Brown felt the public would be served by allowing a large airline to absorb another one, he always insisted that the seller must receive a generous price. Brown had proposed that John B. Kohler sell his short route from Milwaukee to Grand Rapids, across Lake Michigan, to a subsidiary of American Airlines, but E.L. Cord, American's president, offered Kohler a niggardly price.

Brown angrily retaliated by "asking" Northwest to take over the Kohler mail contract and then sub-lease it back to Kohler. Under duress, the Board of Directors agreed. Brown sugar-coated the pill by allowing Northwest to discontinue some of its unprofitable short-haul stops in Wisconsin and Illinois, so the 392 miles to Billings would be offset by roughly an equivalent distance in canceled routes. This, in effect, allowed westward expansion but with little or no increase in air mail payments.

On the same day the Billings extension was approved (with stops at Glendive and Miles City), Northwest directors promoted Croil Hunter to general manager, and designated Col. Brittin as executive vicepresident — a move which led to an occasional spark between the two. Each respected the other, but neither man qualified as a shrinking violet, so it was natural that Hunter felt a manager should manage, and

46

Brittin felt an executive vicepresident should "exec."

With Montana now on line, Northwest directors took a deep breath and committed half a million dollars for a fleet of bigger, faster, more comfortable planes (the Lockheed 10-A "Electra"), in order to be up to date for long-haul traffic when and if the battle for Seattle proved successful. These all-new-design ships were to be twin-motored metal monoplanes capable of 215 miles an hour and a guaranteed cruising speed of 180, carrying 10 passengers and two pilots.

Shortly after this aircraft order was placed, even the newly acquired extension to Billings was threatened with cancellation as soon as Roosevelt's campaign manager, James A. Farley, was appointed Postmaster General.

Farley's first move after taking office was to cut more than $5 million from the $20 million previously allotted for U.S. air mail pay, with a corresponding slash in rates paid to the airlines. Next he decreed a virtual freeze on further extensions of air mail routes.

W.W. Howes, genial, double-chinned assistant under Farley, told reporters flatly that while "there may have been nothing wrong" with the Billings award to Northwest, the route was a definite candidate for oblivion. Colonel Brittin

rushed west from Washington and joined Hunter in an all-out campaign for support in Montana and its neighbor states. They developed a lot of it.

Several members of Congress demanded that the Bismarck-Billings extension be rescinded, but more than a dozen Montana civic groups bombarded their own senators and congressmen with telegrams urging retention of the service, *plus* its extension to Seattle.

Elroy H. Westbrook, president of the Midland National Bank in Billings, assembled a committee of prominent Montanans and traveled to St. Paul to argue the case personally with Postmaster General Farley, who was making an inspection trip of the U.S. postal service. More committees in Spokane, Seattle and Tacoma joined in, and Governor William Langer of North Dakota — after a meeting with Croil Hunter — telegraphed Farley that a Northern Transcontinental "would be of tremendous military value, as it is the shortest route to the Pacific Coast, the Orient, Alaska and western Canada." (Hunter helped write this prophetic telegram.)

In a subsequent letter, Hunter reported: "The Montana delegation made a favorable impression at the conference with Mr. Farley. It

ONE "NOSE HANGAR" was the only shelter this Hamilton had when Northwest first began serving Fargo, N.D., with continuing flights on to Winnipeg, thus becoming an international airline.

was decided the entire proposition should also be put up to Mr. Howes. The delegation, accompanied by Colonel Brittin, has proceeded to Washington, where . . . a conference has been arranged for them with Howes by Mr. Farley."

Brittin's written follow-up to Dick Lilly said North Dakota's senators Nye and Frazier joined the Montanans in calling on Howes, who "criticized the extension and advocated its cancellation from the beginning to the end of the conference. The three delegations, however, (senators, congressmen and civic groups) remained steadfast . . . and impressed on Mr. Howes that the service could not be discontinued without open and militant opposition."

Colonel Brittin, meanwhile, was told by a mutual acquaintance that Alfred Frank, operator of National Parks Airways (connecting Salt Lake City with three Montana communities) was willing to sell his 509-mile line. This was exciting news to the colonel, because with more route extensions nearly impossible to come by, his idea was to buy up those 509 north-south miles and then apply them on further expansion to the west. Brittin asked Fred B. Sheriff of Helena to look into the possibility of acquiring National Parks.

When Croil Hunter learned this, he promptly hit the roof.

His page-and-a-half memo to Brittin of May 20, 1933, started by bawling out the colonel for his expense account ("far in excess of what it should have been"), and went on: "This matter of working for our Billings extension, and all other policies of the Northwest Airways, is not a one-man show . . . I have repeatedly requested that you keep me fully informed as to what you are doing and to discuss with me any activities you contemplated, so we could all be working to the same end with the best advice that all of us may have.

"When Mr. Lilly left for Europe, he wrote instructing you to do this, which you entirely disregarded, and proceeded to make this deal through Fred Sheriff . . . having National Parks approached on the matter of our buying them

out . . . There is a possibility that the steps you have taken may result most unfavorably for our interests and before going ahead should have been discussed with Mr. (Julian) Baird and myself . . . You have repeatedly given me the run-around . . .

"I do not like to write you in this manner but we might just as well understand each other now as later . . . As General Manager, I am going to be held responsible for the success or failure (so) I want it distinctly understood that from now on all matters pertaining to the company are to be taken up with me."

Without question, Brittin was having trouble adjusting to the fact that he no longer sat alone in the left seat. But if he felt annoyance, none showed in his answering letter, which began with the colonel's invariable form of salutation: "My Dear Hunter."

His opening line was a masterpiece of turning the other cheek: "In reference to your recent inquiry."

He went on to say "the mere fact that Alfred Frank opposed our westward expansion with one hand, and offered to sell out to us with the other, would in itself show pretty conclusively which company was trying best to serve Montana."

The letter continued: "I explained the situation to Mr. Lilly in New York, and he authorized me to open negotiations with Mr. Frank . . . As Senator (Burton K.) Wheeler and others in the Montana delegation felt such a move very desirable, I authorized Mr. Sheriff to enter preliminary negotiations with Mr. Frank . . . A few days ago I called on Mr. Howes and advised him what had been done so there could be no misunderstanding in the matter . . .

"Should Mr. Frank indicate a willingness to sell and Mr. Lilly approved of such a plan, I could lay the matter before Mr. Howes and ask the Post Office Department to fix a valuation on the equipment and contract of the National Parks Airways, with the understanding that it would later be transferred to an east-west line between Seattle and Billings or Spokane and

Billings.

"In this way, we would not purchase this line unless it was done with the consent and help of the Post Office Department and with assurances that the mileage could be used to complete a Northern Transcontinental.

"I have not received further advice from Mr. Sheriff, but when I do I will be very glad to keep you informed."

Hunter and Brittin buried the hatchet after this exchange of letters, and both men continued working shoulder-to-shoulder in the struggle to reach Puget Sound, once Farley and Howes finally decided to keep hands off the Billings extension.

The battle shaping up was described briefly but accurately by the Chicago Tribune: "Creation of a new northern route to the Pacific Coast by Northwest Airways is expected to result in a battle between that system and United Airlines for the passenger, mail and express traffic between the Pacific Northwest and Chicago gateway. United operates west from Chicago to Salt Lake City, then northwest to Spokane, Portland and Seattle."

As part of Northwest's campaign literature, Brittin and Hunter issued a map and small accompanying handbill pointing out that "if efforts of the northern states are defeated, Montana and the adjacent regions in all probability will be served by a series of north-south feeder lines. This would give Montana a purely local air mail system, at right angles to the natural flow of traffic."

When the extension to Billings was granted, Department of Commerce regulations required emergency landing fields at 50-mile intervals, and here Brittin's earlier assistance to a number of cities in establishing local airports paid off handsomely. It cost Northwest only $5,000 to arrange for necessary intermediate airport facilities, plus several thousand dollars more for added radio equipment.

Next objective: Spokane, with both eyes peeled for the jackpot — Seattle-Tacoma. Hunter and Brittin themed their campaign to hammer on three basic points:

1. Northwest's proposed Northern Transcontinental would bring Chicago and Seattle 250 miles closer — and thus faster — than the

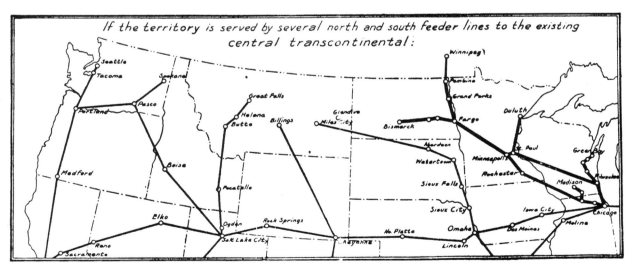

"AMMUNITION" IN COLONEL BRITTIN'S BATTLE for a direct route to Seattle was this map showing how government concept of north-south feeder lines would deprive northern cities of timesaving east-west air service. The map helped Northwest enlist many allies.

existing Central Continental which reached the Pacific Northwest only through a spur line from the south.

2. The natural flow of traffic is east-west.

3. Contrary to general belief, the northern route permitted a lower crossing of the Rockies (6900 feet) than the central route, and had 315 miles less mountain flying.

Support snowballed. D.M. Merrin of the Spokane Chamber of Commerce wrote Croil Hunter: "It is mighty good news that the Billings extension will evidently stay put. We have advised our congressional delegation of our attitude toward your line and have urged them to support any plans for an extension to Puget Sound."

J.C. Crichton, manager of the county municipal airport in Tacoma, reported the Pierce County Commission and the Tacoma Chamber of Commerce were solidly behind Northwest's extension to Puget Sound, and Amelia Earhart — who had just toured the Lockheed plant to observe work on Northwest's newly ordered Electras — wrote Hunter: "I am still keen about the plan which originated this order." She enclosed a Washington Post clipping which said airlines in the west were staging "a battle for business comparable to that of the railroads several decades ago."

In August, Brittin reported both good news and bad news to Lilly. First, Stephen A. Cisler, superintendent of air mail for the Post Office, was about to recommend a 5% cut in air mail rates (on top of the earlier 25% reduction). That was bad. But Cisler had decided to encourage departmental approval of a plan under which Northwest might buy out National Parks. That was good. Cisler also "would not authorize air mail service between Billings and Seattle unless a lighted airway were provided" over the entire route from the Twin Cities to Puget Sound. That was iffy, to say the least.

Early in the Roosevelt administration, during what has been nick-named the "alphabet soup" era, a rash of programs came into being to create jobs or otherwise prime the pump of the economy — the WPA, PWA, NRA, AAA, CCC, NIRA, and several others.

With various "made work" programs gearing up for action, Northwest and its backers went all out to promote this idea among congressmen: as long as jobs were to be created, why not devote some of the effort to giving a Northern Transcontinental route the same facilities the government already had provided for airlines serving the more southerly routes — beacons, a teletype system and radio weather service?

Without any question, in the airline business the "haves" were in a lot better shape than the "have nots."

Figures presented to Congress revealed there were 21,000 miles of U.S. government-illuminated airways, of which less than 1,000 miles were provided for independent lines such as Northwest.

Post Office Department statistics in July, 1933, showed the three major airline groups then operating in the United States — American, United, and the so-called General Motors Group (TWA, Eastern and Western Air Express) were receiving 90.35% of all domestic air mail pay.

At that time, American was flying 9,402 route miles, serving population centers such as Boston, New York, Chicago, Memphis, Fort Worth, Dallas, Galveston, Atlanta, New Orleans, Cincinnati, Houston, and Los Angeles. Western Air Express had 1,762 miles of routes, with Chicago, Atlanta, Salt Lake City, San Diego, Albuquerque and El Paso as principal destinations.

United then had 6,518 route miles, and its main terminals were New York, Chicago, Dallas, Salt Lake City, Seattle, San Diego, San Francisco, Omaha and Kansas City. TWA had a 4,000-mile cross-country system, with the key terminals of New York, Kansas City and Los Angeles. Eastern covered 2,412 miles, with New York and Miami as its leading revenue producers. At that time, a good third of Northwest's 2,014 miles represented branches from the main line.

The battle for Spokane and Seattle-Tacoma, of course, was far more important than the mere 677 miles involved — it was a fight to keep from being bottled up short of the Pacific coast.

Under the Postal Department's reduced $15 million air mail budget, $9 million was provided by postage sales and the remaining $6 million by government subsidy — a pipsqueak figure by today's standards, but not in the Thirties. In July, 1933, mail pay issued that month stacked up like this: $415,000 to United, $359,340 to American; $216,500 to TWA, $118,100 to Eastern, $59,030 to Western Air Express and $58,145 to Northwest.

"This indicates the monopolistic hold the three big groups have on the nation's domestic air mail service," wrote Brittin to the Board of Directors. He pointed out that of the remaining 5 lines in the country, Pennsylvania Airlines was under the control of TWA, National Parks Airlines was under the control of United and United States Airways was a sub-contract of American, so "this leaves Northwest Airways and its sub-contract — Kohler Airlines (which operated between Grand Rapids and Chicago) the only remaining independent air mail lines in the United States."

The airline industry in the early Thirties had formed an organization known as the Aeronautical Chamber of Commerce, but Brittin recommended to his Board of Directors that Northwest stay out because "as an independent, we will always be a factor, but as a member we will merely be a small minority, bound by the policies of the majority."

The Board agreed with him.

Representatives of National Parks Airlines and United launched a vigorous "stop Northwest" campaign, button-holing congressmen and civic leaders alike in a last ditch effort to kill off any further expansion west of Billings.

But the thorough spadework of Brittin and Hunter was tough to combat. The Spokane and Tacoma Chambers of Commerce, as well as the Northern Transcontinental Airway Association — of which Spokane banker R.L. Rutter was president — telegraphed Jim Farley and W.W. Howes, urging approval of the Northern Transcontinental and requesting them to "use your influence to induce consummation of purchase of National Parks Airlines so that present north and south mileage can be turned around by Northwest Airways to fill in the gap between the present Montana terminus at Billings and Spokane."

Farley's reply said his department "finds it impracticable at this time to consider any extension involving service to any territory at present without service, nor can it properly take any action with a view to urging one carrier to enter into negotiations for purchase of another."

That seemed to end the matter, but an earlier ploy of Brittin's provided a breakthrough. By discontinuing mail flights to Duluth, Green Bay, and Madison — plus the west-bound stop at Rochester — Northwest more than offset the postal mileage (447) between Billings and Spokane. Farley and Howes threw in the towel, and granted the Spokane extension via Helena and Missoula, effective October 23, 1933.

This was great news, but there was no time for celebration. On November 29, the Department of Commerce was granted a federal Public Works Administration appropriation of $655,445 to develop a fully lighted airway between the Twin Cities, Spokane and Seattle, via Fargo, Bismarck, Glendive, Billings, Helena and Missoula.

This fueled up the already white-hot battle over who was to control the last leg in Northwest's dream of reaching Puget Sound — the 230 miles over the Cascades from Spokane to Seattle — and like many a football team that has stomped 98 yards down the field, Northwest ran smack into a goal line stand that threatened to stop them short of a touchdown.

The battle culminated in a dramatic series of events that began in Washington, D.C., on Saturday, December 2, when Colonel Brittin —true to his habit of working weekends — decided to poke around at the Department of Commerce.

Due to divided authority in Washington, Commerce was in charge of the airways, while the Post Office handled air mail decisions. Brittin suspected his competitors might try to circumvent the ban on new mail contracts and ace out Northwest by going direct to the Commerce Department for approval on a *passenger* route between Spokane and Seattle. He was so right. Here, in Brittin's written report, is what followed.

"Saturday noon (today) one of my friends in the Department of Commerce advised me that James Murray, one of the Washington representatives of United Airlines, had filed with the Department this morning a brief request for permission to initiate air transport (passenger) service between Spokane and Seattle on Monday morning, December 4, 1933.

"My informant stated Mr. Murray had been holding the request in United's Washington office for nearly a week under instructions to file it with the Department of Commerce if the Northern Transcontinental airway project (beacons, weather service and teletype system) was authorized for construction.

"Mr. Murray made the interesting statement that 'if the National Parks Company cannot stop Northwest Airways, United will.'

"United evidently has become reconciled to our operations as far west as Billings, but they are bitterly opposed to any extension of our line west of this point. They make it very plain to certain officials of the Commerce Department that they are acting jointly with National Parks Airlines in this opposition.

"My informant agreed with my contention that Northwest Airways already has earned at least a *moral priority* on the northern route to Seattle, and that our recent fight to get the northern transcontinental airways built was altogether too tangible to be ignored. He agreed United had no right to grab off — at the last minute — the western end of this airway three days after it had been authorized, when for three years prior to this authorization they had never made the slightest effort to aid in bringing it to

reality.

"My informant felt that United's latest move to beat us to it was indefensible and that it would be judged by both the Commerce Department and the Post Office Department as a 'dog in the manger' act prompted purely by selfish motives.

"We therefore agreed Northwest Airways could not afford to permit United to acquire a tangible priority between Spokane and Seattle uncontested, and in order to protect our own interests, that Northwest Airways should promptly file a request and if possible turn the tables by beating *them* to it, if only by a margin of 24 hours.

"I therefore immediately served notice on the Aeronautics Branch of the Department of Commerce that I would file on behalf of Northwest Airways late Saturday afternoon a brief request to initiate air transport service between Seattle and Spokane via Wenatchee . . .

"I immediately contacted Stephen A. Cisler, superintendent of air mail service, and informed

DRAMATIC CONCLUSION to the "battle for Seattle" came when Nick Mamer brought Northwest's first flight to the shores of Puget Sound on December 3, 1933.

him fully . . . stating that United's move in suddenly filing a request to initiate service between Spokane and Seattle forced Northwest Airways to do the same. I pointed out United was the aggressor in this instance, just as National Parks Airlines was the aggressor in forcing us to suddenly establish service between Billings and Spokane. Mr. Cisler was very much surprised at United's action . . .

"He obviously resented the fact that in filing their application . . . United had ignored the recent instructions he issued to all air mail lines to the effect that no air mail operator should establish passenger line extensions without consulting the Post Office department first.

"I took pains to point out in our interview that National Parks had established their Billings-Butte extension and their Great Falls-Havre extension without notice of any kind to the Post Office department, in contrast to the fact that I secured his consent to our Billings-Spokane extension nearly a week before it was inaugurated.

"Mr. Cisler finally agreed with me that United's sudden move gave us no other alternative, if we wish to protect the western end of our transcontinental route, and thereupon informed me that he would make no objection to the extension of our passenger service from Spokane to Seattle.

"I then talked to Mr. Hunter over long distance telephone at St. Paul," Brittin continued, "and secured some technical data for my formal request from Mr. (Fred) Whittemore (operations manager) and talked to Mr. (Nick) Mamer over long distance telephone in Spokane.

"I then prepared a brief form of request to initiate air transport service between Spokane and Seattle on Sunday morning December 3, 1933, and submitted a schedule for one round trip per day, which was agreed to by Mr. Hunter.

"I handed this application personally to an informal conference in the inspection division of the Aeronautics Branch of the Department of Commerce shortly before 4:30 p.m. Saturday afternoon." (Attending the meeting were Luke Harris, assistant director of aeronautics; Major Cone, director of air regulations; George E. Gardner, head of the inspection division, and J.H. Geisse, special assistant to the director of aeronautics.)

"I was assured that the request of Northwest Airways was entirely acceptable and that permission to initiate service on Sunday morning, December 3, was authorized.

"I wired this authorization to Mr. Hunter in St. Paul. On Saturday afternoon I received a Postal Telegraph wire from Mr. Hunter stating the service would be started Sunday morning (December 3.) I immediately telephoned Mr. Gardner that service would be initiated as requested."

The "Mr. Mamer" referred to by Brittin was an old friend and — for a time — a would-be competitor. Nick Mamer, an experienced pilot who knew the western mountains better than any man alive, had launched Mamer Air Transport at the start of the Thirties, attempting to connect the Twin Cities with Spokane and —later — Seattle, without benefit of an air mail contract. Northwest, in fact, served as his Twin Cities ticket agent in 1930. But pickings were too slim on three weekly passenger flights, so Nick finally returned to operating an air charter business.

When Brittin telephoned Mamer, offering him an opportunity to become a Northwest captain and nail down the airline's claim to the key Spokane-Seattle segment, Nick jumped at the chance to help make history.

Using Fred Whittemore's open-cockpit taper wing Waco (Northwest aircraft No. 7, at that time) Mamer — carrying no passengers or mail — left Spokane at 7:45 a.m. Sunday, Dec. 3, 1933, soared past majestic Mount Rainier and landed in Seattle at 10:10 a.m. He was back in Spokane at 1:05 p.m. the same day.

True to Croil Hunter's promise while seeking west-end support for the expansion to Puget Sound, Mamer re-traced his route on December 4 and went on to the nearby Tacoma airport, as well.

J.R. Wiggins, writing in the St. Paul Pioneer Press, reported that during a few tense and busy hours December 2, Northwest "settled plans for commencement of service that ordinarily would occupy months of planning and negotiation."

"When a plane of Northwest Airways roared over the route from Spokane to Seattle last Sunday morning," Wiggins wrote, "its throbbing motor heralded the finish of one of the most dramatic fights for an air route in the history of commercial aviation. It marked the end of a contest, reminiscent of the early days of the railroad when competing lines fought tooth and nail for first entry into regions unreached by the iron horse.

"The flight from Spokane to Seattle brought to a spectacular close a stirring battle within the walls of the new Department of Commerce building.

"It marked the final phase of a contest unexceeded for thrills and dramatic interest by any episode in the long fight between the several great airways for control of the traffic of the Pacific Northwest. Even the achievement of the northern transcontinental route, in many ways, could not surpass for thrills and action the several hours over the past weekend that determined which airway should dominate in traffic over the new route."

One of the big winners, of course, was metropolitan Minneapolis-St. Paul. As Minnesota Senator Henrik Shipstead had declared during hearings before the 72nd Congress: "This new air route facility will give the Twin Cities a key position. It is as important as was the original building of railroad connections. The tendency hitherto has been to direct commercial aviation by way of the south and southwest. With this new line built, the Twin Cities will come into their own."

But for Colonel Brittin, the hour of triumph preceded a time of despair.

9

Cloak and Dagger

A NEW KIND OF DRAMA was about to unfold in the nation's capital, while Northwest tackled the twin jobs of training pilots to fly mountain routes and organizing the necessary aircraft to serve its hard-won new extensions to Spokane and Seattle-Tacoma.

Speedier equipment was a must, to serve a main line that suddenly had grown to 1,944 miles — from Chicago to Puget Sound.

The "big" 10-A Electras, on which the Board had risked half a million dollars before the Battle for Seattle was won, were behind schedule at the factory — a common problem with most totally new aircraft. Three 200-mile-an-hour Lockheed Orions — each with a capacity of five passengers plus mail and express — were ordered on a hurry-up basis to fill the gap. These small but fast wooden frame monoplanes were a standard production model, and thus could be delivered in 90 days or less.

In the meantime, Pilots F.E. Kelch and A.W. Olson flew the Billings-Spokane segment with taper wing Wacos, carrying mail only, until six-passenger Hamiltons were brought in to carry both passengers and mail. By agreement with Uncle Sam, no passengers were to be carried over the Cascades to Seattle until beacons and radio weather transmission stations were completed by the Department of Commerce.

The year 1933 had been an eventful one both at home and overseas. In Germany, Adolf Hitler rode a wave of depression and discontent to become chancellor of the Third Reich. Wiley Post set a new solo round-the-world flight record of $7\frac{1}{2}$ days, President Roosevelt launched his famous radio "fireside chats" to reassure a depression-jittery American populace, and prohibition was repealed December 5.

Colonel Brittin — encouraged by the Board of Directors — had been pressuring T.A.T. (an affiliate of North American Aviation) to sell back their $22\frac{1}{2}\%$ interest in Northwest Airways for many months, and finally won their agreement to do so late in 1933. They sold back 2,250 shares at $60 each. (The $135,000 price brought them double their original investment.)

When Aviation Corporation (parent company of American Airways) continued to refuse to sell back the only other Northwest stock still held by an aviation firm, Brittin went straight to Senator Hugo Black of Alabama, who had been named chairman (on September 26, 1933) of a Senate committee to investigate ocean mail contracts, and asked Black's help in convincing Aviation Corporation that interlocking ownership of airlines was unwise and probably unethical.

Brittin wrote Dick Lilly: "Senator Black commended our program for an independent Northwest Airways, devoid of interlocking interests with other lines." He added that he was working closely with A.G. Patterson, special investigator for the Black Committee, who was "sympathetic toward the aim of Northwest Airways to develop an independent transcontinental service." Neither the commendation of Black, nor the sympathy of Patterson, was to last.

Aviation Corporation, however, finally capitulated and sold back its 22½% stock holding to Northwest.

Senator Black's committee plodded along with little or no publicity at first. Then Fulton Lewis, Jr., a radio commentator and reporter for the Hearst newspapers, learned from a friend who had worked for the Ludington Line — a small airline in the east — that Ludington had bid an air mail contract at 25¢ a pound, but Walter Folger Brown awarded the contract to Eastern at 89¢ a pound. When the Lewis report, including a variety of other mail contract oddities, found its way into the hands of Senator Black, his committee immediately broadened its ocean mail investigation to include the airlines as well.

In cloak-and-dagger style, several dozen investigators for the Interstate Commerce Commission swooped down simultaneously on offices of the nation's airlines, served warrants and seized any documents they could lay their hands on that seemed to have anything to do with air mail contracts.

Dozens of witnesses were called to Room 312 in the Senate Office Building as Black sought to prove that many air contracts were excessive. The "spoils conferences" with Walter Folger Brown were exhumed, and evidence was produced that many big operators had attended them.

Ironically, Colonel Lewis H. Brittin — who had not participated in these conferences because his company wasn't even considered large enough to be invited — suddenly found himself in worse straits than the men who had.

The first step in this bizarre turn of events came when the Black Committee subpoenaed the client files of William P. MacCracken, Jr., an attorney and highly respected former Assistant

WOODEN-FRAMED LOCKHEED ORIONS filled the gap until Northwest's larger 10-A Electras arrived. They could do 200 M.P.H. The Orion's wheels had to be retracted by hand.

Secretary of Commerce, who performed legal work for half a dozen airlines, including Northwest. Brittin's own files were kept in MacCracken's office, because — to hold down expenses — most of his stenographic work was done there.

"If Colonel Brittin had a fault, it's that he was too thorough," in the words of Julian Baird, who was secretary of Northwest at the time of the Black investigation. "The Colonel put *everything* down in writing, including gossipy little facts about the idiosyncracies and weaknesses of the senators and congressmen he met."

If Brittin thought such-and-such an individual was asinine, or overbearing, or dumb, or a skirt-chaser, his notes reported it.

When the MacCracken files were subpoenaed, the colonel was aghast at the thought of his private papers falling into unfriendly hands, so he raced to MacCracken's office, hastily selected a few memorandums and letters, tore them up and threw them into the trash.

Unfortunately for him, paper shredders had not yet been invented. Investigators learned of his act, collected 300 sacks of waste from MacCracken's office building, and laboriously pasted together several of the colonel's papers.

The Black Committee subsequently learned Harris "Pop" Hanshue, president of Western Air Express, and his assistant, Gilbert Givvin, also had retrieved some of their documents after the MacCracken subpeona.

Then MacCracken moved the whole affair —which up to then had created no real interest —onto the front pages when he staged a comic opera hide-and-seek game for several days with Chesley Jurney, the Senate Sergeant-at-Arms, before being placed under arrest. Eventually, in what some observers called "a kangaroo court if there ever was one," all four men — MacCracken, Brittin, Hanshue and Givvin — were tried for contempt of the Senate, with that body sitting as a court for one of the few times in its history.

Brittin freely admitted he had torn up "purely personal papers," and challenged the com-

mittee's authority to try him — as did MacCracken.

While all this was going on, investigators had seized files at many airline offices including Northwest headquarters in St. Paul. ("How we hated those men," recalls Dorothy Metcalf Towne, later of Des Moines but then a Northwest switchboard operator. "The whole airline was like a big family — everybody took an interest in everybody else, from Colonel Brittin on down.")

February 6, 1934 — five days after Carl Leuthi inaugurated Northwest's new high-speed service to the Pacific Northwest in a 200-mile-an-hour Lockheed Orion — the Board of Directors authorized Croil Hunter to send a special message to Senator Hugo Black expressing regret for the destruction of letters by Colonel Brittin and adding: "We welcome the investigation by your committee and we know that Colonel Brittin was heartily in favor of it. We believe it will bring out forcibly the obstacles that Northwest Airways as an independent operator has had to contend with in the legitimate development of commercial aviation here in the northwest."

During the contempt trial, Senator Black (later named by Roosevelt to the Supreme Court during the 1937 "court packing" episode) dredged up the National Parks Airline discussions, but since nothing had come of those talks, he next showed Brittin several of the pasted-together letters that had been salvaged from office trash and asked him to identify them.

None of the letters introduced contained any important mail contract data, but the colonel again conceded he had torn up a number of personal papers that were under subpoena.

Voting in closed session with Vicepresident John Nance Garner presiding, the Senate freed Hanshue and Givvin because Hanshue had returned the documents they were charged with taking. But Brittin — who had resigned several days earlier in an effort to spare Northwest from involvement in his trial — and MacCracken, who hadn't even been present when Brittin obtained the papers he tore up, were sentenced to serve 10 days in jail for contempt of the Senate.

Senator Tom Schall of Minnesota called the verdict "a damn shame." He told reporters "there was nothing incriminating in any of the letters that agents claimed he destroyed. None of them they so laboriously pieced together indicted the integrity of Colonel Brittin."

There's a widely-believed story that Brittin spent his 10-day sentence as a guest in the home of a sympathetic sheriff, who felt the colonel had been "jobbed," but the facts are otherwise.

He began his term February 15, 1934, occupying cell No. 203. Interviewed in jail, Brittin told reporters he slept "between a bootlegger and a burglar" on a regulation prison cot, and spent his time working on files and prison records. Food was skimpy, but he had at least one nourishing meal because Julian Baird later recalled he and Croil Hunter had a special turkey dinner prepared at Washington's Mayflower Hotel and delivered it in person to the colonel's jail cell.

In addition to resigning from Northwest while his Senate trial was in progress, Brittin also resigned as chairman of the Minnesota Aeronautics Commission and as president of the National Association of State Aviation Commissioners. He was fired by the Democratic administration from his post as director of air field projects for the Civil Works Administration (CWA) in Minnesota.

He told reporters that after severing all connections with the airline industry, he was going to start immediately — at age 57 — to look for a job.

"I bear no malice against the Senate or the Black Committee," Brittin said. "That they were mistaken in this instance is unfortunate for me, but much good may result.

"Such unpleasantness as I have suffered is not to be weighed against the gains that may accrue to the industry if now the government will reorganize its air mail contracts in such a way that monopoly will not be fostered and independent lines will not be forced to make the kind of driven and desperate fight that confronted our line from the beginning against the large air mail operators.

"It is my hope that in any new arrangement that may be adopted, the government will not overlook the importance of preserving out there in the Northwest a northern transcontinental line owned by the people of the section it serves."

The colonel's resignation (he went on to many years of gainful employment as a private consultant and adviser on aviation matters) had been accepted by a shaken Northwest Board of Directors, who next found themselves faced with another and even graver crisis that rocked the entire industry.

10

National Turmoil

WHILE THE BLACK COMMITTEE hearings were in progress, President Roosevelt conferred with his advisers about implications of the airline "spoils conferences." Attorney General Homer Cummings said in his formal legal opinion: "There can be no reasonable doubt that the arrangements, understandings and agreements out of which the route certificates subsequently grew were highly irregular and interfered with . . . freedom of competition."

Roosevelt decided to do something dramatic. On February 9, 1934, he issued an executive order canceling all existing air mail contracts, and ordered the Army Air Corps to carry the mail.

Charles A. Lindbergh wired Roosevelt: "Your present action does not discriminate between innocence and guilt and places no premium on honest business. Your order canceling all air mail contracts condemns the largest portion of our commercial aviation without just trial."

Fortune magazine reported the president's precipitate action threw large numbers of men and women out of work, at a time when jobs were scarce, and "kicked the underpinnings of a $250,000,000 investment shared by 300,000 stockholders."

For ten days, the United States had no air mail at all. Then the ill-prepared Air Corps — flying obsolete and obsolescent planes — did its best to maintain 60% of the former commercial mail routes. Predictably, the service was woefully poor and — worse yet — Army fliers suffered a series of fatal crashes which Eddie Rickenbacker called "legalized murder." The public, and the press, revolted.

Many airlines closed up shop and laid off virtually all employees when Roosevelt's cancellation order became effective. Others maintained a skeletonized operation. At that time, 80% of Northwest's income came from mail contracts (about $50,000 per month) and only 20% from passenger service, but the Board of Directors gamely tried to continue passenger flights on a reduced basis.

Northwest was caught in a double financial squeeze, because the Board had just invested in three Lockheed Orions and shortly were to begin taking delivery on the half million dollars worth of 10-As which had been ordered in anticipation of the hard-won extension to Seattle-Tacoma — now suddenly a very hollow victory indeed.

"About one third of the 150 employees were furloughed, and most of the remainder stayed on at half wages," says retired captain Tom

59

Hillis, who at that time was a mechanic. "I worked for half my regular $90 a month, because this was in the depths of the depression and a job was a mighty precious thing." Bert Ritchie, a co-pilot at the time mail contracts were canceled, recalls that co-pilots continued to receive their normal pay of $112 a month.

A few days after the mail contracts were canceled, Croil Hunter issued this statement: "The cancellation of mail contracts prompted us to suspend part of our service in order to conserve our assets and protect the investments we had made. For civic reasons, we developed a Northern Continental route from Chicago to the Puget Sound country along the natural East and West traffic highway — the only one which will adequately serve this entire territory.

"At the loss of this service, a flood of protests developed by individuals and numerous civic and business interest in every community on this entire route . . . Urgent requests for the resumption of these flights have been received from the entire territory.

"We have therefore decided to continue this service and in addition to the present schedules from Chicago to Billings, will extend our run from Billings into Spokane, Seattle and Tacoma. This splendid service — without mail — can only be operated at a great financial loss, but this territory must be served . . . we know that our record is entirely clean, and we are sure the Post Office Department will find it so. We trust that very soon we will again be flying the air mail over this route under the direction of the government."

On February 14 Northwest Directors sent a "Valentine" to Postmaster General Farley in the form of a letter offering to carry the mail free until the army could tool up for the job.

"We heard with a great deal of concern," said the message, "that the army does not contemplate flying any mail on our routes for some time. We think it would be regrettable to have the public get out of the habit of using air mail and we believe it is highly important that there should be no interruption of air mail service over

TEN-PASSENGER LOCKHEED ELECTRAS became the backbone of the fleet in the Thirties.

60

the northwest routes that have been developed."

The letter went on to offer "such of our planes, personnel and radio equipment as would be necessary . . . Mr. Croil Hunter, our general manager, is now in Washington. We have instructed him to cooperate in accordance with this letter and he is at the Willard Hotel if you care to reach him."

The statesmanlike offer was ignored, but if Farley had known the troubles that lay ahead, he probably would have run — not walked — to the Willard Hotel.

In the same Farley letter, Northwest directors revealed this piece of startling news, which up to that moment had been a closely guarded secret: "We have offered the physical assets of the company (Northwest) on a basis of *actual cost less depreciation* to the Great Northern and Northern Pacific Railroads jointly. We believe that in their hands the line will develop and be a tremendous factor in transportation facilities of this region."

With the 20-20 vision of hindsight, it seems incredible — though true — that directors of the two railroads rejected the offer, but they suffered from a fairly common type of business myopia: they thought of themselves as being in the railroad business, when in fact they were in the *transportation* business.

Shortly after mid-March, to halt the growing number of Air Corps deaths, all Army planes were grounded for seven days, and U.S. air mail service again ceased completely while efforts were redoubled to install up-to-date instruments which already were in common use among the commercial airlines.

But the Air Corps could not be re-created in one week's time, and when mail service was resumed — by daylight only, in optimum weather — the crashes continued. Congressional hearings droned on, leading eventually to the Black-McKellar Act of 1934 which set up controls over the airline industry, but in the meantime the administration announced a plan was under way up to put mail back in the hands of private carriers "as soon as possible."

(The Army's own figures, as quoted in the New York Herald Tribune, showed the cost-per-mile to fly the mail under Army auspices was more than *four times* the average mileage paid to commercial operators.)

Time Magazine reported on April 9 that "after tortured weeks of criticism and recrimination, the Post Office Department was ready to hand the air mail back to private enterprise, thus relieving the Army of its ill starred postal duties."

Time's report continued: "Pending permanent air mail legislation, Postmaster General Farley invited private carriers to bid on three-month renewable contracts comprising some 18,000 miles of the 34,000 miles flown before the February 9 cancellation order."

Farley's specifications were that none of the 12 lines whose old contracts were annulled could

SHREVE M. ARCHER of Minneapolis took over as president during the troubles of 1934.

61

be eligible for new ones without reorganizing, and purging their ranks of any officials named by Farley (32 in all) who had attended Walter Folger Brown's "spoils conferences." He also specified bids could not exceed 45¢ per airplane mile.

The "reorganizations" that followed made it still mighty easy to tell the players without a scorecard. Transcontinental and Western Air became T.W.A., Inc.; American Airways became American Airlines, United Airlines merely divorced itself from United Aircraft, Western Air Express re-incorporated as General Air Lines (and in a few months resumed its old name), Eastern Air Transport became Eastern Air Lines, and Northwest Airways — even though it had not taken part in the "spoils conferences" — re-incorporated April 16, 1934, under Minnesota law as Northwest Airlines, Inc.

Next came what one disgruntled airline official described as Farley's "open invitation to all the crapshooters of 1929 vintage" — in other words, new air mail bids which were to be opened April 20, 1934.

"Had the operators played their cards right," says historian Henry Ladd Smith in *Airways*, "they might have skinned enough out of the Postmaster General to more than offset the losses of the cancellation period. The embarrassed administration was ready to eat humble pie, following the disastrous Army interlude, and the airlines might easily have emerged with more favorable mail contracts . . . (but) so desperate were the operators for mail payments that they played right into the hands of the harried Postmaster General."

Northwest Airlines — already bled white because of its efforts to keep passenger service operating without any mail income, not to mention heavy start-up costs on the new extensions to Spokane and Seattle — lost its original bread-and-butter line between Chicago and the Twin Cities, as well as the Twin Cities schedule to Fargo and Pembina. These routes were awarded to Hanford Tri-State Airlines.

Northwest managed to salvage the mail contract from Fargo to Seattle, but now found itself in the strange, and costly, situation of running an airline whose eastern-most terminal was 228 miles west of home base.

All hope of maintaining the Chicago service Northwest had pioneered was dashed to bits by the mail award to Hanford, so the airline reluctantly discontinued this route May 17, 1934, after maintaining two daily passenger flights for three months during the period of mail contract cancellation.

As 1934 wore on, the whole year seemed to fit that famous old expression: "Things are tough all over." The U.S. Navy dirigible Akron crashed off the coast of New Jersey, killing 73 persons; labor strife in many parts of the country flared into violence, including a bloody truck drivers' strike in the Twin Cities; the financial empire of Wilbur B. Foshay, builder of the first Minneapolis skyscraper, had collapsed, wiping out the investments of several thousand mid-westerners, bringing Foshay a 15-year prison

NEW LOGO ADOPTED IN 1934, using "Airlines" instead of "Airways."

sentence after his 1934 trial for using the mails to defraud; and now Northwest had lost its founder plus its original air route.

One of the few smile-producing events of 1934 came to light in Callander, Ontario, when a young father went to his local newspaper and asked if there was a special discount for running five birth notices simultaneously. His name, of course, was Oliva Dionne, and for years the Dionne quintuplets occupied the front pages as they helped a depression-weary world forget some of its day to day troubles.

Hanford Air Lines took over Northwest's old Chicago-to-Pembina route the first week in June, just as Congress put the final touches on a new Air Mail Act. This legislation reduced air mail postage to 6¢, provided for one-year mail contracts with rates fixed by the Interstate Commerce Commission, prohibited inter-locking directorates and holding companies, and permitted carriers whose contracts were canceled by President Roosevelt to sue for damages.

Northwest limped along until December, operating its Fargo-to-Seattle route from the office and overhaul base in St. Paul. Then word reached Dick Lilly — Chairman of the Board —and Shreve M. Archer, who had taken over the presidency, indicating Hanford officials had bid so low to get the Chicago-Fargo-Pembina contract that they were losing money.

Low mail rates or not, Northwest needed that route to put home base on line once more, so the two directors negotiated to buy the contract back from Hanford for $46,000, effective the final day of 1934.

Thus, after nearly a full year's delay caused by one crisis after another, Northwest finally set out to operate the Northern Transcontinental according to original plans.

11

Prelude to World Conflict

A FINANCIAL HANGOVER from the chaotic events of the two preceding years left Northwest still fighting a red ink battle in 1935, with a net loss of $161,119. But with the new Lockheed 10As adding more speed and carrying capacity, the airline began to make up for lost time.

Revenue passengers doubled (to 25,125) during the first 12 months of operating the Northern Transcontinental, and mail jumped from an anemic 91,000 to 648,492 pounds. From a high of 19 directors prior to the air mail cancellation troubles, only six persons had been elected to the Board at the time of re-incorporation as Northwest Airlines — Shreve Archer, H.H. Irvine, Croil Hunter, E.I. Whyatt, Fred Whittemore and Camille "Rosie" Stein. The latter four, of course, were all airline personnel.

Despite the interruptions and disappointments of 1934, Northwest became the nation's first airline to fly the highly regarded 10A Electra on August 11 that year, primarily because its own engineers had sat down with their counterparts at Lockheed and participated in the design of this new twin-tailed workhorse. Thirteen 10As and one 10B eventually carried the NWA emblem.

In mid-1935, Lewis M. Leffingwell — like Archer, an official of Archer Daniels Midland Co. in Minneapolis — was elected president of Northwest, and on October 10 the airline again became an international carrier when through flights to Winnipeg were reinstated.

This eliminated the previous government-required transfer of passengers and mail to Western Canada Airways at Pembina, N.D., for the remaining 67 miles to Manitoba's capital.

Elsewhere, millionaire Howard Hughes — far from being a recluse at that stage of his life — set a new world's land plane speed record of 352 miles per hour, and up in Point Barrow, Alaska, cowboy humorist Will Rogers perished with Wiley Post when their plane crashed on takeoff during a goodwill trip.

Finances at the growing airline returned to the black in 1936, the same year Roosevelt swamped Alf Landon in the U.S. presidential election, Margaret Mitchell published her Civil War classic, "Gone With the Wind," and Edward VIII assumed the crown of England, only to abdicate so he could marry "the woman I love" — divorcee Wallis Warfield Simpson of Baltimore.

One of the year's less publicized events was a token payment of $51,365 to Northwest by Uncle Sam, representing the government's settlement of NWA's claim for damages suffered through cancellation of its air mail routes in 1934. At the same time, Uncle finally returned securities worth $12,000, which had been posted as a surety bond when the routes were awarded originally.

Although the 10A had proved to be a highly serviceable airplane, Fred Whittemore persuaded Lockheed to build a larger, faster version (160-mile cruising speed, 14 passengers plus crew) known formally as the 14-H, but nicknamed the "Sky Zephyr." Newsweek magazine reported that "before a plate had been formed or a rivet driven, Northwest had sponsored the Lockheed 14 by working out initial specifications with Lockheed officials and consulting on each detail of design."

The first eight Zephyrs were contracted for at $80,000 each. Northwest announced they would cut the flying time between Chicago and the Twin Cities to 1 hour and 45 minutes, and the Chicago-Seattle time to 10 hours 15 minutes, despite five intermediate stops.

Newsweek reported the Zephyrs were counted on as "a telling blow against increasing competition from high speed train service between the Pacific Northwest and Chicago" and would give Northwest "a strong bid against the United Airlines service into Seattle by way of Salt Lake City."

While the Zephyrs were nearing completion in mid-1937, Amelia Earhart disappeared somewhere over the Pacific on a round-the-world flight, Japan stepped up its attacks on major cities in China, and Croil Hunter was elected president of Northwest — the first time an operating officer (rather than an investor) had held that office.

On the national scene, the U.S. Senate defeated Franklin Roosevelt's plan to "pack" the Supreme Court by increasing its membership with new appointees, and internationally there were rumbles of things to come when Japanese planes bombed and sank the U.S. gunboat Panay on the Yangtze River, Hitler repudiated the Versailles Treaty that ended World War I,

and Italy withdrew from the League of Nations.

Northwest introduced the new Sky Zephyr to U.S. air travelers October 1, 1937, and the following January announced the lowest "educational fares" in the history of commercial aviation, designed to create new customers by giving "a concrete demonstration of the advantages of flying," as the fare announcement stated.

In an effort to combat the annual wintertime slump in air travel, for a 60-day period all Twin Cities-Chicago and Winnipeg-Twin Cities flights were cut to $15, and the Chicago-Seattle fare was reduced to $141.50.

But only 10 days after the plan had gone into operation, fate intervened. One of the speedy new Zephyrs crashed 12 miles northeast of Bozeman, Mont., in an accident that was traced to a structural failure of the tail surfaces. The pilot lost in this accident was Nick Mamer, who had helped make history by flying the first Northwest plane into Seattle. Nick was so eager to fly the new aircraft that he had begged Frank Judd to switch schedules with him.

SKY ZEPHYR ad appeared in 1938.

All Zephyrs were grounded temporarily while Lockheed redesigned the tail surfaces under the watchful eye of the Bureau of Air Commerce, but although others had success with these planes (Howard Hughes flew one around the world in less than four days) Northwest continued to have its troubles. Fred Whittemore was killed when he hit a canyon wall while ferrying one Zephyr from Lockheed's California plant to the Twin Cities. A third was lost near Miles City. Three others were damaged in lesser incidents, and for two years Northwest was back in the red.

In the nation's capital, a brand new set of guidelines for U.S. commercial aviation was created when the Civil Aeronautics Act became law June 23, 1938.

Combining most of the aviation duties formerly spread among the Post Office Department, the Interstate Commerce Commission and the Bureau of Air Commerce, the act established a Civil Aeronautics Authority with an administrator and a five man board to establish policy, grant routes, determine tariffs, mail rates and business practices.

Existing airlines were granted permanent certificates for routes then held, and the old contract air mail system was discarded in favor of a plan to negotiate certificates for all future extensions. The new law also set up a three man Air Safety Board to cooperate with the C.A.A. but to operate as an independent body.

(Two years later, a further change resulted in creation of the Civil Aeronautics Board — C.A.B. — to take over the handling of policy, routes, tariffs, mail rates, business practices and investigative work formerly handled by the Air Safety Board. The C.A.A., however, continued to exist, with an administrator in charge of many important safety-related duties, including regulation of airways, air traffic, airports and navigation facilities. Both the C.A.B. and the C.A.A. were established as functions of the Department of Commerce during the 1940 changeover.)

Northwest Airlines was granted permission to add Portland, Ore., to its flight schedule May 23, 1938 — one of the nation's last route extensions under the pre-C.A.A. setup.

Hitler's army had occupied Austria earlier that year, after which Great Britain and France agreed to the dismemberment of Czechoslovakia — a move which British Prime Minister Chamberlain called a guarantee of "peace in our time." In the United States, thousands of jittery Americans panicked from a make-believe invasion, generated by a realistic "Attack From Mars" radio program that was the brainchild of actor-director Orson Welles.

As the specter of war stalked Europe, Northwest pondered the pros and cons of joining the parade of U.S. airlines to the "giant" new 21-passenger DC3, a Douglas creation that soon was to make all other planes obsolete.

"How will we ever fill them up?" asked some, who pointed to the fact that the 10-passenger 10As and 14-passenger Zephyrs often flew without a full load, because Northwest served many communities with comparatively small populations.

"How can we afford to operate without them?" was Croil Hunter's answer.

There was no question that filling the seats represented a distinct challenge, but the operating economies and quiet operation of the DC3 — plus its greater load capacity — made it a far more desirable airplane than the Sky Zephyr, not to mention the fact that virtually the entire personnel of the airline was eager to change aircraft as soon as possible.

One of many topnotch men to grace the ranks of Northwest Airlines over the years was George E. Gardner, whose lot it was to do something about that aircraft change near the close of 1938. During commercial aviation's early years, Gardner — a skilled pilot himself — had been Minnesota inspector for the U.S. Department of Commerce, and in that capacity issued transport licenses to many Northwest pilots. Later, as head of the inspection division of the Department's Aeronautics Branch, he attended the historic Washington meeting in which Colonel

Brittin received approval for Northwest to pre-empt service from Spokane to Seattle.

Just as the first Sky Zephyr arrived, Gardner — after leaving the Department of Commerce — was hired as a pilot by Northwest. The intention was to assign him to the Fargo-Winnipeg route, but at that same time, Bob Mensing resigned superintendency of the western division and returned to flight duty, so Gardner was chosen to replace him. He performed so efficiently that within a year, Gardner was named operations vicepresident.

In that capacity, he was assigned to find a buyer for the 10 remaining Sky Zephyrs at the best possible price. Gardner astounded everybody by working out a deal with Robert Gross, then president of Lockheed, to sell the Zephyrs back at their full original purchase price, after

which Northwest jubilantly ordered its first six DC3s at $110,000 each. To prepare for the arrival of these planes, the airline leased a DC3 for use in training flight and maintenance personnel.

Before 1939 ended, it proved to be an eventful year for the entire world as well as for NWA. Hitler invaded Poland, Britain and France declared war on Germany, Russia attacked Finland and all signs pointed to an ever-widening conflict.

With the growth of Northwest, employees based at the Seattle terminus felt a strong need for regular inter-communication among the airline's personnel, so they asked — and were granted — permission to originate a company newspaper. Prime movers in this grass roots project were Seattle's Bob Polhamus and Tom

FIRST DC3 TO ARRIVE IN 1939 created a big day for shutterbugs.

67

Hinman, who became roving editors of "The Northwest News" when it began publication in January, 1939, with Authur Rice as editor; Sara Ratcliff, publisher, and Les Theits, artist.

The second issue of this "granddaddy" of today's employee publication carried the news that with the arrival of the DC3, Northwest would begin stewardess service by registered

DOROTHY STUMP EATON, first NWA stewardess hired in 1939. Virginia "Ginny" Johnson was hired later the same day.

nurses, and that "the first of these charming young ladies are Miss Virginia Johnson, Minneapolis, and Miss Dorothy Stump, Chicago." Thus the old newsletter helps settle a friendly but long-ranging debate over the identity of the original cabin attendants. Miss Stump was hired only two hours before Miss Johnson.

Virginia Johnson (later Mrs. Victor Beck of Redmond, Wash.) confirmed that "Mal Freeburg hired Dorothy Stump and me the same afternoon." (Miss Stump, who became Northwest's first million-mile stewardess, flew for 13 years before retiring to become the wife of Dr. Samuel J. Eaton, Denver, Colo.)

"Our uniforms were dark brown worsted wool, with a pointed cap to match," recalled Mrs. Eaton. "Rosie Stein bought them at Field & Schlick in St. Paul, and they wore like iron. In fact, we kept hoping they'd wear out a little sooner than they did. To begin with, our meals were just cold box lunches, but the passengers never complained."

By mid-1940, with 11 DC3s in service, two more on the way and four Lockheed 10As still operating, traffic continued to zoom. This table shows the airline's resurgence since the dark days of 1934:

Calendar Year	Passengers Carried
1934	12,097 (year of air mail cancellation)
1935	25,123 (Lockheed 10As in service)
1936	38,022
1937	37,786
1938	46,323 (Sky Zephyrs in service)
1939	74,519 (first six DC3s arrived)
1940	136,797 (11 DC3s in use)
1941	149,212 (last pre-war year)

Abroad, "blitzkrieg" became a new and feared word as Hitler's armies surged across Belgium, Denmark and the Netherlands in 1940, attacked Norway, overran the Maginot Line and quickly forced France to surrender. Winston Churchill took over as England's prime minister shortly before the "miracle of Dunkerque," when 335,000 Allied soldiers were snatched from the jaws of defeat and evacuated from France by an impromptu armada of 900 British civilian and naval craft.

Next came the six-month "Battle of Britain." Clouds of Nazi bombers pounded London and many other targets across the English Channel in an overwhelming effort to win a quick victory with the sheer might of German air power. But somehow, the British held, thanks to their never-give-up spirit and the Royal Air Force. At the same time, Japan, fresh from several victories on the Chinese mainland, invaded French Indo-China.

In the United States, President Roosevelt signed the first peacetime draft law in the nation's history, and one of the top songs of the day was "Good-bye Dear, I'll be Back in a Year" — which turned out to be a king-sized piece of wishful thinking.

Still endeavoring to span the entire U.S. continent, Northwest Airlines again filed an application to serve New York City (by way of Toronto) in 1940 — which was denied — and early in 1941 petitioned for service to Fairbanks, Alaska. With prophetic vision, Northwest's application emphasized the importance of Alaska to national defense, as well as the route's value in saving 800 miles on all existing ways to reach Fairbanks from the nation's capital. But the C.A.B. took no action.

Among many "firsts" that dot the history of Northwest, one of the more unusual ones had its beginnings at a 1938 party given by Rochester's world-famous Dr. Charles Mayo, who later was to serve as an honored member of the airline's board of directors.

On social occasions, all of us are prone to take advantage of doctors by asking them about a mysterious little ache or two, and Croil Hunter was no exception to the rule. He knew Dr. Mayo was an aviation enthusiast, so during a chat with his host, Croil described in great detail the occasional drowsiness and woozy behavior of several NWA pilots who had flown the mountain routes near Seattle.

"At what height do you cross those mountains?" asked Dr. Mayo.

"Well, some of the passes are much lower, but as a safety measure, our planes observe a minimum altitude of 13,000 feet," replied Hunter.

"Sounds like an oxygen deficiency to me. I'll assign three of our top men to work with your people on this problem."

Dr. Mayo put together an all-star cast, consisting of Dr. William H. Lovelace, noted surgeon and a licensed pilot; Dr. Walter Boothby, well known physiologist, and Dr. Arthur H. Bulbulian, highly innovative doctor of dental surgery and winner of several honors from the American Academy of Surgeons.

SPARSE EQUIPMENT was available for cabin service in the DC3. This is Olga Loken at work.

In pressure chamber tests at the Mayo Clinic, where high altitudes could be simulated, the doctors experimented with Northwest personnel and verified that most individuals had slower reactions and many found it difficult to stay awake at 13,000 to 20,000 feet.

There was nothing new about the use of oxygen — such as in hospital oxygen tents — but the difficulty was to devise a simple method of administering it that would permit flight crews to talk into a radio transmitter, eat a meal or move about the cabin. Previous attempts to solve this problem were all crude and inefficient. One method had been for an individual suffering oxygen deficiency to hold a tube in his mouth and breathe straight oxygen, which was wasteful, and of course did not permit the desired mobility nor the ability to talk and eat.

Working together, the doctors sketched out this ideal: an extremely lightweight mask that would fit over the nose — leaving the mouth uncovered — and that would mix air and pure oxygen in the proper quantities with the aid of a small rubber "lung."

Dr. Bulbulian, who had perfected a high temperature method of making lifelike noses and ears from liquid latex (for victims of accidents, cancer and other diseases) made plaster casts of 150 different types of faces in order to develop a mask that would fit almost any facial dimension, aided by the "give" of the latex. This is the same material used to make surgical rubber gloves, and by adapting the techniques he had developed in re-making human faces, the doctor fashioned a 4½-ounce mask that met all specifications.

MAYO CLINIC TECHNICIANS teamed up with Northwest Airlines to develop the first practical high altitude oxygen mask. NWA made test flights in 1938 and 1939 to both coasts during this research. Left to right, preparing for a flight to Boston, are Dr. W.M. Boothby, Captain Mal Freeburg, Dr. A.H. Bulbulian, Dr. W.R. Lovelace and Mrs. Freeburg, who rode along in the "flying laboratory."

The next step required some tricky scientific work to devise a valve and meter to control the flow of oxygen and correctly proportion its intake with that of the surrounding air. A small rubber "lung" that would hold exactly the amount of air required for one breath was fabricated to hang around the wearer's neck, and this was hitched to an oxygen tank with a long flexible tube. Then the nose mask was connected to the lung, and in dozens of laboratory tests the new device worked perfectly at simulated altitudes as high as 40,000 feet.

After Dr. Bulbulian developed an assembly line method of turning out oxygen masks quickly, all was in readiness for a practical test in one of Northwest's Lockheed Sky Zephyrs.

Sure of success, NWA announced a special 10-man test flight to Los Angeles to demonstrate the new "B.L.B." (for Bulbulian, Lovelace and Boothby) oxygen mask. The flight took off July 27, 1938, and its results made headlines throughout the nation.

Dr. Lovelace went along to monitor the 1900-mile test at an altitude of 20,000 feet, and wore a "B.L.B." mask as did pilot Mel Swanson, copilot Bert Ritchie, engineer Ralph Geror, and a crew including "Big Jim" LaMont, L.E. Koerner, E.C. Heideck, Jim Buelow, Louis Marodi and Mal Freeburg, then superintendent of Northwest's Eastern Division.

The Minneapolis Tribune's front page headline summed up the results in five words: "CITY FLIERS WRITE AVIATION HISTORY." On landing in California, Dr. Lovelace told reporters that the respiration and heart action of the crew checked out perfectly throughout the flight.

Many newspapers reported that the mask-wearing fliers looked "like visitors from outer space" and the INS wire story said: "Conquest of the sub-stratosphere was greatly advanced here today."

The flight stirred up so much interest that NBC sent technicians and an announcer along on the return flight in order to broadcast a play-by-play report on the efficiency of the new mask.

They persuaded Dr. Lovelace to remove Mel Swanson's mask for a few minutes, and excitedly told the nation: "Without his mask, Swanson's lips and fingertips have started turning blue."

This, of course, is one of the classic telltale signs of oxygen deficiency.

After the demonstration's success, Northwest installed the new masks on all its Zephyrs, granted permission to two other airlines to adopt the same equipment for their flight crews, and eventually became the *first* U.S. airline to install individual oxygen outlets for passengers, as well. (Originally, the oxygen mask was viewed strictly as a flight safety measure, for pilots only.)

When Mayo Clinic staffers prepared to attend a Harvard conference on high altitude problems the following March, Northwest volunteered to stage another demonstration of its important new equipment, generating further national interest with what the Associated Press called a "record sub-stratosphere flight" to Boston on Northwest's "flying laboratory." The planeload of scientists ate chicken dinners at 23,000 feet while wearing B.L.B. masks.

The San Francisco Chronicle reported several experts considered the mask "suitable for military use" — a prediction that was only a trifle ahead of its time. With further adaptations and improvements by the Mayo doctors (including a need to make the device frost-proof) a direct descendant of the B.L.B. mask first used by Northwest made a giant contribution to victory in World War II by giving allied fighter pilots and bomber crews the precious advantage of efficient high altitude operation.

All this happened during the early stages of World War II, but in 1980 — though long retired — Dr. Bulbulian still maintained a laboratory in Rochester where he continued to experiment and develop new facial reconstruction techniques for the benefit of the human race.

Northwest achieved an operational milestone in the fiscal year ending June 30, 1941, when for the first time in its 15-year history, passenger revenue exceeded mail revenue ($2.34 million versus $1.852 million.)

MILITARY ADAPTATION of the Mayo-NWA oxygen mask played an important role in winning World War II.

The fleet then consisted of 13 DC3s, four Lockheed 10As and two service planes not in commercial use — an old Hamilton Metalplane and a Stinson Reliant. Passengers carried in 1941 totaled a record 149,212, but international events beyond the airline's control were to delay that growth pattern.

Another milestone occurred on Valentine's day, 1941, when Northwest common stock first was offered to the general public on the Chicago Stock Exchange. It was quoted on the New York Stock Exchange six weeks later.

After trading 50 U.S. destroyers to England for a lease on eight naval base sites in British possessions, President Franklin Roosevelt signed a lend-lease bill to help strengthen Allied resistance to the Nazis just a few weeks before Yugoslavia surrendered and German tanks rolled into Athens. Then on June 22, 1941, Hitler abruptly scrapped his non-aggression pact with Stalin and attacked the Soviet Union, shortly after the U.S. Ferry Command had been organized to fly warplanes across the Atlantic for use by Allied forces.

It was in this atmosphere of world conflict that Northwest Airlines prepared to observe a fifteenth birthday, with one of its 13 DC3s already commandeered by the government for defense purposes.

"It is hoped that the company will not be required to give up any more units from its fleet," said the annual report to stockholders.

This was a vain hope but Northwest performed gloriously in behalf of its country in the years just ahead.

PART III

The Wings of War
(1941-1945)

12

Lifeline to Alaska

WHEN JAPANESE BOMBS AND TORPEDOES blasted the U.S. fleet at Pearl Harbor December 7, 1941, the attack triggered a chain of events during which 21 of the nation's commercial airlines played significant roles in the eventual Allied victory.

They all performed with distinction, but none equaled Northwest Airlines in the variety (11 major government assignments) and the magnitude of its wartime tasks.

Despite the most critical manpower shortage in history, Northwest recruited and trained so many people that its personnel jumped from a pre-war 881 to more than 10,000 men and women needed to help carry out these vital projects.

After Pearl Harbor, Japan deployed part of its navy and troop carriers toward Alaska and the Aleutian Islands. This was the most vulnerable area on the North American mainland for three reasons: first, because at that time defenses were weak; second, because the outermost Aleutians are barely 2,000 miles from Japan, and third, because vast distances in the rugged "land of the midnight sun" created grave difficulties for the job of establishing strong U.S. military outposts.

With Japanese submarines roaming the sea route to Alaska, and the whereabouts of Tojo's aircraft carriers unknown, the military decided an over-land lifeline between U.S. supply centers and military posts in Alaska must be established across the forests, mountains and frigid trackless wilds of northwestern Canada.

There were no air routes on this "back door" entry to Alaska — no radio communication facilities, no landing fields, no fuel storage system, no hangars, no quarters for personnel. But General Robert E. Olds of the Air Ferrying Command believed Northwest's successful wintertime operation across the coldest northern states qualified it to create, virtually overnight, a much larger and much longer airline than it had been operating from Chicago to Seattle.

Northwest management quickly agreed, and signed a contract February 26, 1942, to "lay out routes, prepare range maps, provide radio contact, erect facilities . . . and then to fly military personnel and supplies "over what soon was nicknamed the "Flying Boxcar" line.

Next, one of NWA's most celebrated wartime achievements began with an incident that would have been laughable if it had not been for the war emergency. One day after the contract was signed, Northwest dispatched its first survey flight to study the logistics of setting up a route from Minneapolis-St. Paul to Alaska via Edmonton, Alberta.

"We were all gung ho to tackle the challenge of creating an aerial lifeline," recalled George Gardner — then operations vicepresident — "so the moment the contract became official, we rushed out to buy cold weather gear, and took off in a Douglas DC3 on the 1092-mile leg to Edmonton.

"Frank Judd, who had been chosen as superintendent of Northwest's newly created Northern Division, headed up the survey crew, which included Dale Merrick as his second in command; Tommy Nolan, cargo superintendent; Hank Olson, maintenance supervisor, and Lee Smith, operations manager."

But when the party landed in Edmonton, the events that followed were reminiscent of a comedic Gilbert and Sullivan operetta, minus the music.

FRANK JUDD led Northwest's first survey flight to set up the World War II Alaska lifeline via the Yukon. Ray Wiehe, then Director of Communicatons, snapped this in the DC3.

"The Canadian gendarmes met us," Gardner said, "marched the entire group to the McDonald Hotel and put us under house arrest, while one soldier with a rifle and long bayonet stood guard over our plane."

The catch was that local officials in Edmonton had received no approval for the flight from Canadian government authorities in Ottawa.

"It was a very sensitive day," said Judd later. "The telegraph wires hummed back and forth between Edmonton and Ottawa and between Ottawa and Washington, where quite a furor developed after Columnist Drew Pearson fired off a big blast on his nation-wide radio newscast.

"While a lot of high level negotiations were going on, we flew back to the Twin Cities, but just as soon as proper clearances had reached Edmonton, they welcomed us back with open arms. We learned to respect the Canadians totally — they were great to work with, and helped us overcome all kinds of obstacles."

Northwest leased Government House, one of Edmonton's showplaces at that time, to serve as Northern Region headquarters, with the airport there serving as the jumping-off point for Alaska by way of Grande Prairie, Alta; Dawson Creek, Ft. John and Ft. Nelson, British Columbia; Watson Lake, Whitehorse and Dawson in Yukon territory, and on to Fairbanks or to Anchorage, via Northway.

Eventually the "Flying Boxcar" route extended out to the tip of the Aleutian Islands, 3,986 air miles from the Twin Cities.

Battling temperatures as cold as 70 below zero in northwestern Canada, crews tackled the monstrous job of creating an "instant airline."

Giant fuel tanks were cut apart, flown in and welded back together; trucks and other heavy equipment also were sectioned, and then reassembled with a welder's torch; 25 buildings of varying sizes were erected; a network of radio stations was created, and a mountain of supplies hauled in to all way stations.

But to begin with, there were virtually no facilities at all beyond Edmonton. Flying reverted to the old "seat of the pants" method, maintenance crews worked outdoors in the bitter cold, and all hands agreed it was the ruggedest winter in history, as they surmounted one challenge after another.

On the route to Anchorage and Fairbanks, it was a case of "can do" and "make do." At Whitehorse, in Yukon territory, Arthur "Art" Petersen, later to become Western Region manager of flight operations, ran into severe difficulties while trying to set up a base as part of the military contract operation.

"When I picked out a location," he recalled, "I discovered it was impossible to buy any property in a hurry. This was no time to quibble, so I simply took squatter's rights to about 50 acres of Canadian government land.

"Croil Hunter and a group of company officials arrived a short time later on an inspection trip and Croil asked me: 'Pete, do you have a lease on this property.' "

"Sure," replied Petersen.

"Let's see it," said Hunter.

Petersen "walked into the john, ripped off an armload of toilet paper, walked back to Croil, slammed it down on the table," and laughed:

"Here's your lease."

In one of its periodic reports, the Office of War Information (OWI) called NWA's Alaska operations "one of the most difficult and graphic of (all) the airlines' war activities."

Air Transportation magazine added: "Winter problems were almost beyond belief. On occasion the temperature went down to 70 below and ground crews working on engines and parts could only put in a few minutes before they had to stop to warm themselves.

"FLYING BOXCAR" being loaded with materiel for Alaskan troops.

"Bare hands doing delicate work could stand the icy winds and the silent cold for no more than a few seconds at a time on the coldest days. Rubber hose shattered into pieces like glass. Fingers quivering with cold tried to fix a nut to a bolt and succeeded after possibly an entire hour of trying. Three men had to work in shifts to change one sparkplug. Workers wore scarves over their mouths to keep their lungs from freezing and engines had to be kept running for fear that once shut off they could not be started again. But the work went on."

Northwest had operated 13 DC3s on its regular stateside routes before six of them were taken over by the government for war needs, but by the time the Alaska operation was fully operative, the "Flying Boxcar" line received double that many planes from the military, mostly C47s (military version of the DC3) and several C46s, another twin engine monoplane known as the Curtiss Commando.

The first northward-bound cargo flight left the Twin Cities March 15, 1942, less than three weeks after the original survey trip, and within two weeks supplies were being carried on a scheduled basis, even though some landing fields still were being hacked out of the wilderness.

When time and equipment permitted, mechanics built small nose hangars to protect them from the cold while they worked on their engines.

"The first year was really rough," recalled Eric Linden, retired manager of flight testing and one of a great many men who spurned their exempt seniority rating to volunteer for service in the Northern Region. "Quarters to sleep in were skimpy or non-existent. Sometimes the men used sleeping bags along the edges of runways. Engine maintenance was outstanding, but I don't know how in the world those guys did it. They had to warm their tools on a hot stove every few minutes during wintertime, and at some bases the mosquitoes drove everybody wild in the summer."

As part of the massive project, Northwest set up special training classes for mechanics in

Edmonton, and the first maintenance instructor was Clarence Magnuson, who was on his way to becoming one of the nation's top aircraft engine specialists and later made many key contributions to Northwest as Superintendent of Power Plant Engineering.

The long-debated Alcan Highway (later renamed the Alaska Highway), proposed as a means of connecting Alaska with populated areas of Canada, was given top priority as a defense measure when the Canadian government approved construction of this 1,523-mile artery by U.S. Army engineers in March, 1942. While working on the segment between Fort Nelson and Ft. St. John, a large work party was marooned when a spring thaw took out the winter road, leaving them short of food and much needed construction supplies.

Judd diverted several C47s for a round-the-clock ferrying operation to bring in supplies and food that kept the Army crews working, with night landings made by the flickering light of oil-soaked rags.

In the midst of this extra-curricular project, a new emergency arose when a 24-bed military hospital in Nome burned to the ground. Two

AT 70 BELOW ZERO in Alaska, hot air was blown into the engines of military transports to help get them started. This snap by Tom Winn.

Northwest crews were dispatched immediately for St. Louis, and within 48 hours a complete new hospital — from beds to bed pans — was winging in to Nome. On another occasion, when construction materials for a radio station were lacking, a complete sawmill was flown in to produce the needed lumber.

Communications posed a special problem in Alaska, because the aurora borealis — one of many splendors in this unspoiled land of glaciers, volcanoes, wild game, king salmon and majestic snow-clad mountains — sometimes made radio signals unusually clear, and sometimes blocked them out entirely.

By pirating equipment from some of their own stations, Northwest communications experts — including W.D. "Hippy" Inness, Harry Morton, Ray Wiehe, Carl Swanson and Robert Glischinski (later the airline's Vice President — Communications and Computer Services) — first set up 3,000-watt transmitters at Edmonton, Regina, Fort St. John, Fort Nelson, Watson Lake, Whitehorse, Northway and Fairbanks. Eventually other stations were added at Anchorage, Cold Bay and Shemya.

MAKE-DO GAS STATION operated in Alaska by W.D. "Hippy" Inness, left; Ray Wiehe and Dale Merrick, Frank Judd's second-in-command of the Northern Region.

"When the northern lights started blocking out our radio signals," reported Glischinski, "we solved the worst of the problem by installing low frequency equipment that operated at 130 kilocycles, but we still had occasional fading problems that made some trips a real adventure."

The race to fortify Alaskan military bases went into high gear in May, 1942, as Northwest's flying boxcars carried a steadily growing stream of soldiers, guns, ammunition, dynamite, food and that greatest of military morale builders — mail — along the Alaskan lifeline.

One month later Japanese forces struck at the Aleutians.

Carrier-based planes bombed the U.S. naval installation at Dutch Harbor on rocky Unalaska Island June 3, 1942, keeping American forces occupied while attack troops swarmed ashore and seized the outer islands of Kiska, Attu and Agattu.

It marked the war's *only* invasion of the North American continent, thanks in large measure to the buildup of U.S. strength by Northwest's day and night shuttle of men, supplies, munitions and aircraft.

With B17 bombers urgently needed for defense of the Aleutians, Colonel Harold L. George — who had succeeded General Olds as head of the Ferrying Command — asked Northwest to organize a special task force to fly in more planes and bombs, just as elements of the Japanese fleet steamed toward Dutch Harbor.

Nine other airlines were named to assist, with NWA — as the "grandfather operator" in that war theater — in charge of briefing flight crews and handling all radio-weather contact, major maintenance, loading and fueling.

Everybody got into the act — chiefs as well as Indians. Frank Judd pitched in because "we were so short of pilots that many of us flew almost around the clock, just catching a few winks in a chair while our planes were being loaded and unloaded."

"Everything was in a mess after the Dutch Harbor bombing," added Judd. "They handed us a chart and said: 'You are going to haul

DOG SLED TEAM took over to deliver urgently needed medical supplies flown to Burwash Landing in the Yukon by a Northwest crew on March 23, 1942. Photo is one of Ray Wiehe's souvenirs.

reinforcements to Umnak, beyond Cold Bay. Be sure to stay close to the clouds.'

"When we asked why, they said: 'Because there are Japanese out there'. "

Frank fueled up and took off with a load of 21 GIs plus all the ammunition, dynamite and guns that could be crammed aboard. He made seven round trips — 1,000 miles each way between Anchorage and Umnak — before going to bed.

An Office of War Information report said: "On one hop with a plane load of military personnel, the pilots were alarmed by strange vibrations that shook the ship periodically. They finally discovered the source — the passengers were stamping their feet to keep warm."

To eliminate duplication of effort, General Hap Arnold ordered all Army air transport services to be unified and merged into the A.T.C. (Air Transport Command) in June, 1942, and this new "airline to everywhere" became world famous for its efficient development of a new military tactic — strategic air supply — on a global basis.

Interestingly enough, the man who was named G4 (in charge of operations) for the A.T.C. was Colonel George Gardner, who — like several fellow Northwest officials — had left the airline for military service.

"I was lucky enough to inherit as my executive officer a young Lieutenant Colonel who was the greatest man at getting things done I've ever known," said Gardner later. "His name? Donald W. Nyrop."

Neither man had any way of knowing then that some years after the war both of them were destined to be airline presidents — Gardner of Northeast and Nyrop of Northwest. The practical experience both gained as key men operating the famed "airline to everywhere" contributed to their later successes.

While men and materiel were being assembled under rigid A.T.C. priorities in preparation for re-taking the outer Aleutians, Army tactical flight crews totaling more than 2,000 men were given special briefings by Northwest personnel on instrument procedures and other navigational aids that had been developed to permit day and night operation despite fog, mountains and tricky winds.

Two Northwest captains — Roman Justiss

TRACTOR HELPED LOAD this "flying boxcar" in Minneapolis-St. Paul, then went along to Alaska to help unload dozens of other planes bringing in wartime supplies.

and Lloyd Milner — were awarded the Air Medal for their work in teaching instrument techniques to Army fliers, a rare honor since normally this medal is strictly for the military.

The Army's citation said Justiss and Milner "materially aided the accomplishment of military operations on a 24-hour all-weather basis."

Air medals also were awarded posthumously to another pair of Northwest captains — Frank Christian and Raymond Dyjak — who lost their lives while hauling supplies during the Alaskan campaign.

In Edmonton, an ancient warehouse was leased by Northwest to serve as an in-transit cargo depot, and a frequent visitor to that facility was Donald H. Hardesty, who had been hired as chief military accountant when — in the urgency of "getting the job done" — Northwest officials suddenly discovered that documentation was lacking on $12 million worth of services performed under government contract.

Hardesty worked the problem out to everyone's satisfaction — just the kind of competence one might expect of a man who eventually

became the airline's top financial vicepresident and a member of the Board of Directors.

On the night before Christmas, 1942, Northwest sent out its own Santa Claus in the form of a C46 that took off from Edmonton for all remote way stations on the route to Alaska, with a cargo of turkeys, ice cream, candy and all the trimmings for Christmas dinner. Santa's assistants were Dale Merrick, Tom Nolan and Don King, who later served as superintendent of the Northern Region during the final year of the war.

"At our first stop," Nolan related, "the ground crews took one look at all that food and started singing and dancing until their rickety cabins shook as if there had been an earthquake. The ice cream was frozen solid as a brick wall, but the boys had a solution. They put it on the stove and warmed it up.

"Another base had been living on Army rations for weeks, and those fellows rolled out of their sleeping bags and started baking the turkeys to a steaming sizzle right then and there."

By spring of 1943, a 100,000-man U.S. and Canadian force had been assembled in Alaska, and on May 11 allied forces, led by the Seventh Infantry Division, annihilated 2,350 Japanese defenders on Attu. Three months later Kiska and Agattu also were secure, and the Aleutians once more were totally in the hands of the United States.

The O.W.I. said re-taking of the Aleutians would have taken "many months longer" if air transport provided by Northwest had not been able to fly in men and cargo "quickly and in great quantities."

Eventually, Northwest set up regularly scheduled service to continue supplying key bases in Alaska and the Aleutians, from Seattle as well as from the Twin Cities, with daily flights to Adak and Attu, way out the long Aleutian chain.

The airline also helped fly in 14,000 troops to occupy Shemya, 1,461 miles out the Aleutian chain from Anchorage — an inhospitable, foggy little rock four miles long by two miles wide, buffeted on one side by the North Pacific Ocean and on the other by the Bering Sea.

But Shemya, however barren and windy it may be, was to play an important role in the postwar future of Northwest Airlines.

There is no record of the monumental man-hours piled up — often in 18 and 20-hour days — during the Northern Region operation, but Northwest crews flew a total of 21,559,469 miles on Alaskan missions, moved 44,977,183 ton-miles of cargo and amassed 164,814,621 passenger miles while transporting the military.

SNOWSHOES WERE INCLUDED among the emergency gear carried on all flights to arm and supply forces in Alaska. Left to right are E.K. Nelson and L.M. Horner.

13

The "Mod"

AT THE SAME TIME Northwest was establishing its flying boxcar route for Alaska's defense and recapture of the outer Aleutians, the airline tackled 10 additional war projects, including what Washington's O.W.I. report called "one of the most spectacular contributions" to victory.

It was known as the "Mod" — short for Bomber Modification Center — and here is how it came into being.

Just as the pinch of a nationwide manpower shortage set in, NWA was visited by officers of the U.S. Army and the British War Mission on February 18, 1942. This was the problem they outlined:

America's industrial might had roared into high gear, turning out critically needed bombers on an assembly line basis that the Axis Powers could not match. But it was not practical to slow down these fast moving assembly lines in order to incorporate sophisticated new scientific improvements being created almost continuously. Nor was it practical to slow down production by pausing to customize a portion of the output for special missions or for service in different climates.

The Army's question was: "Will Northwest create a huge bomber modification plant in St. Paul to update these planes for combat, so we

can keep the assembly lines going at top speed?"

Northwest's Board of Directors quickly said "yes."

Two days later, the Mod barely existed on paper when a squadron of B25s — urgently needed by the British in their desperate stand against Rommel in northern Africa — arrived at St. Paul's Holman Field to be outfitted for desert warfare.

Starting from scratch, with no extra facilities and no personnel except those stolen from other jobs, Northwest gradually built a force of 6,000 "Mod" employees. Many of them worked outdoors in the rigors of winter until more hangar space could be constructed.

Under the direction of Superintendent Ralph Geror — who had flown as Speed Holman's mechanic in Northwest's early days — NWA launched what amounted to a giant technical school. They trained housewives, teachers, shoe salesmen, cab drivers, secretaries, retirees and other volunteers to become qualified specialists in a variety of tasks involving everything from machineguns, carburetors, automatic pilots, communications equipment and triple-lensed cameras to super-secret radar, which keyed the growing superiority of Allied air power.

In its early months, the Mod used a small

amount of available space in Northwest's own Holman Field building and leased the nearby 109th National Guard hangar. This facility had not been built for aircraft as large as the big 4-engine B24 Liberators NWA prepared for battle during the war, so Northwest set up an ingenious open air production line, with tarpaulins as the only protection from snow, ice and wind.

Planks were laid across the grass, power lines and compressed air hoses were run out to the work areas, overhead lights were strung and telephones installed for this open air "factory." Temporary shelters were built, and construction of a 600-foot-long hangar was started at once, with a second one begun before the first went into use December 7, 1942 — exactly one year after Pearl Harbor.

A broad corridor connecting these two hangars contained a variety of work shops, offices, storerooms and a modern cafeteria

GUN MECHANICS Arlene Ziemer, top, and Evelyn Burke helped outfit bombers with .50 caliber machine guns.

where 6,000 employees were served daily at the height of the war effort — with meals at cost that ranged from 25¢ to 50¢ each.

The Mod became a self-sufficient city. In addition to the cafeteria, it operated a fire department (needed because all bombers had to be test flown by NWA personnel before being turned over to the Air Force), employed several hundred armed guards, ran a jitney bus service to carry workers from one facility to another, its own post office, and a newspaper known as the "Field and Hangar."

One of the war's popular tunes celebrated women's contribution to victory by singing the praises of "Rosie the Riveter," but the Mod boasted of "Gussie the Gun Moll," because many of its gunsmiths were women.

Automatic pilots produced in the Twin Cities by Honeywell were included among dozens of technical improvements installed by Northwest at the Mod. Radar at that time was so hush-hush that it was referred to only by a code name — H2-X. Northwest was the only civilian organization in the United States chosen to install this equipment, which enabled Allied airmen to bomb with accuracy day or night, unhampered by overcast or clouds.

In addition to destroying enemy war plants, fuel tanks, rail centers and submarine bases, radar-equipped bombers drove the once-feared Nazi sub fleets to cover, opening sea lanes for the transport of men and materiel.

E. Ben Curry, who succeeded Geror as superintendent of the Mod midway through the war, recalled: "Radar equipment came via baggage cars under armed guard. The manufacturer (Bendix) was able to produce only 82 units per month, and we installed 82 units per month. Two days after each radar installation was completed, the plane would be in Great Britain, because that's how fast they needed them."

Government secrecy regulations, however, were so strict that guards hovered over workers and made it difficult for them to maintain that 82-per-month quota.

84

In this dilemma, one NWA official telephoned a Bendix vicepresident and asked for advice.

"So far as I'm concerned," came the reply, "I wouldn't be alarmed if someone took one of the H2-X sets and put it in Hitler's lap. It would take the S.O.B. six months to figure it out, and by that time there will be so many improvements that it wouldn't do him any good anyway."

"After that," Curry reported, "we just took with a grain of salt any regulations that stood in the way of fast production, and kept on meeting our quotas."

On August 1, 1943, 177 B24s equipped at the Mod helped drain Hitler's gas tank when they made one of the war's most celebrated missions by bombing the Ploesti oil refineries in Roumania. Two years later, Brigadier General Leon W. Johnson, who led that Ploesti raid, visited the Mod to extend his personal thanks for the center's many contributions to victory.

Innovations developed at the Mod included the "flying gas tank" — a special project in which B24s were stripped of all armament and fitted out with extra gas tanks to a point where — fully loaded with gasoline and critically needed war supplies — they were unable to fly on three engines, as a standard B24 could.

Most of these aircraft were used in the famous "hump" operation, carrying materiel from India across the Himalayas to China.

Some of the Mod's bombers were camouflaged in shades of dull pink, for use in the African desert campaign, while others were specially winterized for Alaska service, with added heat exchangers, carburetor and propeller de-icing equipment, plus cold weather hydraulic and engine oil systems.

Bombers came off factory assembly lines with only one .30 caliber machine-gun in the nose, which the Mod replaced with three heavy .50 caliber guns. Scanning windows were provided for side gunners, oxygen outlets were installed for use with an adapted version of NWA's "B.L.B." oxygen masks, flexible guns were

THE NORTHWEST "MOD" CENTER resembled a giant air base at the height of the war. John Kern and Gordon Mensing are shown towing a B24 ticketed for installation of radar equipment.

incorporated at each waist gun window, heated suits were put in for the gunners, along with interphones, ammunition boxes, communication and navigation equipment.

A number of B24s were equipped with batteries of newly invented "super eye" triple-lensed cameras, giving Allied fliers the most up-to-date photo reconnaissance of the war — one of the little-known keys to victory. An Associated Press story from the western Pacific February 4, 1944, reported: "Two Marine photo planes (outfitted at the Mod) pried the lid off one of Japan's most precious secrets today when

they became the first foreign aircraft to fly over Truk, principal enemy sea and air fortress in the South Pacific."

Information gleaned from these Mod-installed cameras paved the way for a "turkey shoot" in which U.S. squadrons raised havoc with Japanese ships and planes deployed at Truk's big concentration of air fields, forts and warship anchorages.

Many workers at the Mod wound up flying B24s turned out by their old buddies, and took time to write back a word of thanks. One of these was Lt. Daniel L. Otten, an employee in the

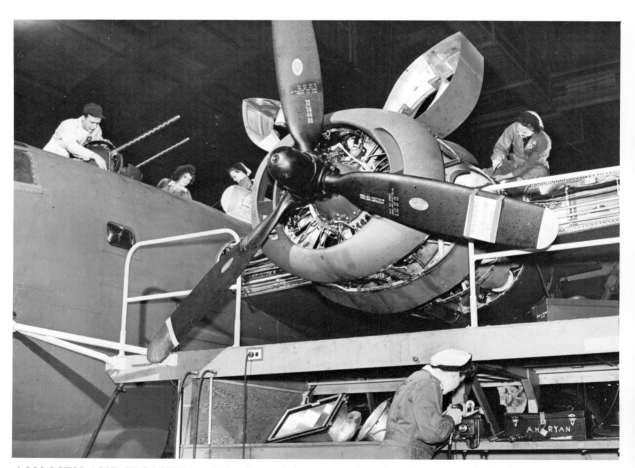

6,000 MEN AND WOMEN kept Northwest's Bomber Modification Center in St. Paul buzzing with activity during World War II. Many worked outdoors until shelters could be built.

sheet metal department before he enlisted, went to flight training and became a B24 pilot. He wrote:

"I got a little surprise when my own 'baby' arrived and found out that the brand new plane came from you guys. We are a radar crew and this is a radar plane. It sure is a good one, thanks to you men. You don't realize what a great job you do. I never realized when I worked there how great it would feel to get a plane from the Mod."

In its never-ending search for wartime personnel, Northwest proved that neither size, nor sex — nor eyesight — had any bearing on the quality of work many individuals could perform. The Mod's smallest mechanic was 20-year-old Bob Bailey who stood only four feet one inch, and its largest guard was Ray "Babe" Phelps, a 240-pound six-foot-four ex-pitcher for the Chicago White Sox and the old St. Paul Saints.

Nine employees were blind.

First of the blind workers was Joseph DeBeer, then president of the United Blind of Minnesota. His contributions proved so valuable that eight of his friends were added shortly.

Prior to that time, metal sweepings from the workshop floors had been thrown out as waste, and many a small carburetor part or other item in short supply vanished forever. From that point on, sweepings were poured through a series of four screens to separate the larger and smaller metal pieces. Then they were spread out on tables for the blind workers to examine with their sensitive fingers. They sorted out nuts, bolts, washers, rivets, screws, tiny machine parts, and made savings far beyond the salaries they earned.

Said Ben Martin, their foreman: "Just one variety of bolt might come in 27 different sizes. To sort this out would be delicate work even for one with full sight, but our blind workers did it perfectly."

During the first five months of the Mod's employee suggestion system, more than 1,000 ideas were stuffed into the open mouths of Hitler, Mussolini and Emperor Hirohito, whose caricatures adorned the various suggestion boxes — and four of the Suggestion Pin winners were from the crew of blind workers.

Even "language pollution" was harnessed by the Mod on behalf of fighting men overseas. Somebody in the sheet metal shop started it, and soon most areas of the sprawling modification center featured a "swear box," into which anyone caught uttering a cuss word tossed one cent. These fines were combined into a cigaret fund for the military.

By June, 1944, growing Allied successes made it possible to relax part of the tight security which had surrounded the Mod. Famed commentator H.V. Kaltenborn brought an NBC crew with him to St. Paul and devoted an entire program to the Mod's accomplishments, which included outfitting 3,286 aircraft for war service. (Because the Mod prepared numerous B25s for the British, a myth has arisen that it also outfitted the 16 B25s Jimmy Doolittle and his carrier-borne raiders used to bomb Tokyo on April 18, 1942.)

"Not true," says Ralph Geror, then the Mod's superintendent. "We were so busy on planes already sent to us that those 16 aircraft were prepared at the hangars of Mid Continent Airlines."

After General Dwight D. Eisenhower's combined forces invaded "fortress Europe," Brigadier General E.M. Powers, deputy chief of staff of the Army Air Force, sent a special message of commendation to Northwest Airlines in which he said:

"Many more gold stars would be in windows of American homes if it had not been for the supply — in time and enough, instead of too little and too late — of the B24s modified at your center and used on D-day to clear the Normandy beaches."

Later that same year, Mrs. Clara Decker — a radio mechanic at the Mod and mother of six sons in military service — was chosen by Mod employees to represent them at a civic ceremony when NWA was awarded the Army-Navy "E"

87

3,286 U.S. BOMBERS WERE OUTFITTED at the Northwest Airlines "Mod" during World War II, and this was the final B24. (St. Paul Pioneer Press-Dispatch Photo.)

for carrying out what Colonel Nelson S. Talbott of the Army's mid-central procurement district described in glowing terms as "a heroic chapter, scarcely less glorious than those of battle."

It was a proud day for Northwest, but the Mod and Northwest's lifeline to Alaska represented only a fraction of the airline's continuing wartime service on government assignments.

14

Action on the Home Front

THE NATION WAS BESET with food rationing, gasoline rationing, tire rationing and shortages of almost every description, as Northwest struggled to maintain service between Chicago and the Pacific Northwest with its seven remaining DC3s while meeting constant government requests for more wartime help.

For many weary months, both before and after Pearl Harbor, the front pages carried one long parade of bad news for the free world. While Hitler's blitzkrieg paralyzed Europe, Japanese forces occupied many Pacific strongholds including the American base at Wake Island. The Japanese seized Hong Kong on Christmas day, 1941, captured Manila a week later and staged the Bataan "death march" April 9, 1942, after gallant U.S. forces in the Philippines finally succumbed to superior numbers.

Under orders from President Roosevelt, the War Department established a tight priority system governing travel on all U.S. airlines. Northwest was forced to eliminate its air link between Seattle and Portland, as well as the one between Duluth and the Twin Cities, while Chicago-Twin Cities schedules were cut from seven to three trips per day. Only two daily flights remained to Seattle-Tacoma.

With many pilots leaving for the military and scores of others siphoned off by still more projects undertaken for the government, Northwest recruited and trained 250 fliers during the war — chiefly at schools established in Billings and Rochester, because the Mod's bombers had congested air lanes around the Twin Cities. Instrument training also was carried out at NWA facilities in Chicago, Fargo, Winnipeg and Seattle.

At the same time, a flood of government assignments turned Northwest into one of the nation's most unusual "defense plants."

VANDALIA TEST CENTER: Success of the Mod in St. Paul led Army officials to approach Northwest late in 1942 with a request that the airline undertake another technical operation at Vandalia, Ohio, to be known as an Accelerated Service Testing Center. By January, 1943, the Center was open for business.

Its principal mission was to "de-bug" all new aircraft models produced for the military by test-flying them, running lab tests, writing engineering reports on malfunctions, and rushing these reports back to the manufacturers so production-line aircraft would be in tiptop operating order.

89

"We got the first three planes of every new model produced for the military," explained E. Ben Curry, superintendent of the facility. "Many of them were fighters, but the center also tested bombers, reconnaissance planes, fighter-bombers — even gliders used in the Normandy invasion."

Some "bugs" in the new aircraft were easy to find, such as when the landing gear came up through the wing of one plane being checked. But at other times, the center's activity was more like detective work, involving micro-photography and a wide variety of mechanical tests.

At the height of its activity, Vandalia's test center employed more than 1,000 men and women, with the difficult manpower recruitment in the hands of a rising young employee named Robert A. Ebert, who worked his way up the ladder to become Vice President-Personnel during his long service with the airline.

As war continued making vast changes in the daily business operations of Northwest Airlines, security regulations did not permit a full explanation to stockholders of this war work. Most of it was disguised under the phrase "various training, experimental, research and other aviation activities for the Army and Navy" in the annual reports to shareholders.

One of these unpublicized projects was designed to lick the airman's mortal enemy — ice.

FLAMIN' MAIMIE": Even on flights crossing the equator — as well as those in more northerly climates — icing conditions had cost the military numerous bombers, fighters and cargo planes. K.O. Larson, NWA's chief engineer, proposed that Northwest establish a flight test laboratory under auspices of the Air Transport Command, with the airline providing both ground and flight personnel to carry out de-icing experiments on wide ranging flights all over the North American continent.

The A.T.C. snapped up the offer in June, 1942. Northwest assigned 100 engineers, pilots, mechanics and other support personnel to this project, which made basic contributions to the safety of flying, not only for the military but for commercial aviation as well. Walter Bullock, A.E. Walker and A.F. Becker were selected as lead pilots for the de-icing program, which involved many aircraft including an experimental B25 nicknamed "Flamin' Maimie."

Maimie served as the principal research vehicle for scores of aerial laboratory experiments.

"She was a basic B25," Captain Walker explained, "but rather than having standard short exhausts terminating in tail pipes, she had collector exhaust rings in order to accommodate heat exchangers. Maimie got her nickname from the fact so much heat was generated through the four exchangers that ice removal was almost instantaneous — even when so much ice had accumulated that our cruising speed was cut by 50 miles per hour."

During latter months of the war, when security measures had been eased, Time magazine carried this report from Dayton, Ohio, on one of Flamin' Maimie's flights into a freezing rain — once considered unflyable weather:

"When the plane landed safely at the field, its wings almost as clean as a dentist's fingernails, the plane and crew were greeted by a group of cheering flyers and engineers.

"For three winters this field has served as an ice research laboratory for the Army Air Force's Wright Field Air Technical Service Command. Said one of the waiting experts: 'The day is in sight when we will have an airplane in which pilots can just forget ice.'

"The research station, operated by NWA under the supervision of two Army airmen — Major Al Olsen (a former Northwest pilot) and Lt. Myron Tribus — had enlisted the help of top notch scientists, among them the famed physicist, Irving Langmuir, of General Electric Company. They began with a fundamental study of water drops. Their newest gadget, designed to show how well a heated wing repels ice at various temperatures, is an odd looking plane with a vertical wing section, like a shark's fin, on its back. High speed cameras, mounted in a special plastic turret, photographed water drops as they hit this upright wing, and recorded the speed of ice formation.

"Raindrops in the air, for reasons which scientists do not completely understand, remain liquid in temperatures far below water's freezing point, but turn to ice when they hit a solid, such as dust particles or a plane wing. Then they freeze fast.

"Big drops hitting a plane wing form a smooth, uniform coat known as glaze ice. It does not change the wing contours, but its weight may eventually make the plane crash. Small droplets make a rough, pebbly surface called rime ice, which is more dangerous than glaze because it quickly changes the plane's airfoil (the shape of the wing) on which the plane's ability to fly depends.

"The Minneapolis researchers have found that the most efficient wing de-icer is an exhaust gas heating system for wing edges, which is now standard on B24 Liberators. But this method could not be applied to a propeller, which is just as vulnerable to icing as the wings. That problem was finally solved by electrical heating; a small generator, mounted on the hub of the propeller, supplies current to the heating filaments inside the propeller blade."

Long before war's end all B24 Liberators bound for Europe and the Far Pacific had "hot wings" and "hot tails" as a result of the long experiments conducted by Northwest personnel.

Walter Bullock recalled: "We tested everything — propeller icing, wing and tail icing, cabin heating, even several different types of propellers — including some that were hollow — and our missions went as far as Alaska. It was on a flight to Edmonton that we made the final tests before heat exchangers were put into assembly line manufacture for the B24. We also made dozens of flights to New Hampshire, because the military maintained a mountaintop laboratory on White Mountain, near Berlin, N.H."

Many commercial and technical organizations contributed their talents to the ice research studies, including General Electric, Hamilton Standard, Boeing, Douglas, Lockheed, Convair and the Massachusetts Institute of Technology.

HONEYWELL RESEARCH: Development of massive bombing armadas which pulverized

WARTIME BOARD OF DIRECTORS — Seated, from left, Shreve Archer, Croil Hunter, Camille "Rosie" Stein and E.I. Whyatt. Standing, from left, John Parker, William "Bill" Stern, R.M. Hardy, Lewis Leffingwell, Edward White, Tom Irvine, and A.E. Floan, secretary.

enemy defenses both in Europe and in the Pacific was speeded up by a pair of hush-hush research projects in which Northwest cooperated with Honeywell engineers, when Army officials decided their own pilots did not have enough experience to fly experimental military aircraft during a long series of scientific tests.

One project involved the Honeywell-developed C-1 Autopilot which, with its companion Norden bombsight, was credited with much of the U.S. Army Air Corps' success in the European and Pacific theaters. "George" — as the Autopilot was nicknamed — dramatically improved bombing accuracy, because it held bombers precisely on course during the crucial run at designated targets.

Northwest personnel also participated in scores of flights during perfection of Honeywell's B-3 Turbo Supercharger Regulator system, which improved engine performance to a point where U.S. bombers often were able to fly higher than enemy antiaircraft fire could reach. In addition, this system minimized the problem of stragglers, which had been easy prey for enemy fighter planes.

The C-1 Autopilot and B-3 Regulator became standard equipment on all U.S. heavy bombers — notably the B17, B24, B32 and B29 — and of course both of these developments became a continuing boon to peacetime aviation, as further adaptations and improvements were made by Honeywell technicians in the post-war years.

HELP FOR THE MARINES: In the fall of 1942, the U.S. Marine Corps asked Northwest for assistance in training pilots sorely needed to fly multi-engine transport planes carrying supplies to far off Pacific bases.

Most of these young Marine officers were brand new flight school graduates, with no experience beyond single engine SNJs, so Northwest devised a highly successful on-the-job training program by assigning Marines as extra members of the crews on all DC3 commercial flights between Chicago, the Twin Cities and Seattle.

With this practical training in navigation, instrument flying and all-weather operation, the Marine graduates swiftly picked up the experience needed for their military assignments. Actor Tyrone Power was one of them.

NEXT, THE NAVY: Early in 1943, Naval Research Laboratories asked Northwest to join a research program aimed at eliminating electrical interference caused by precipitation of all types — even airborne dust over deserts — which was slowing the war effort by blocking voice communications and radio code signals.

Rain, snow, sleet and electrical storms were the prime villains in creating precipitation static, so Northwest's assignment included scores of flights into violent weather while research scientists rode along to monitor various experimental static suppressors. Flights to Mexico, Alaska and Labrador were common. On one occasion Captain J.R. Galt and co-pilot L.F. Knudsen took a research plane to Greenland and back.

For two years, Twin Cities residents wondered what was going on inside a big half-million-dollar Navy hangar at Wold Chamberlain field, never dreaming that a million-volt lightning generator developed at the University of Minnesota was creating man-made storms indoors so preliminary experiments could be made before actual flight tests were undertaken.

Results of this lengthy program included the development of static elminators and a new type of antenna, which enabled planes to fly through weather that previously had made radio navigation either impossible or far from reliable.

BILLINGS A.T.T.P.: At the same time the precipitation static research began, Northwest established an Airmen's Transition Training Program in Billings, Mont., for the Air Transport Command, to develop personnel for the operation of multi-engine transports needed to keep military supply lines filled.

Courses began February 18, 1943, one month after NWA had been asked to organize the project. Fifty Northwest mechanics were flown to Billings, and a 107-man faculty included 30 pilots, 13 radio operators, five radio mechanics and various other personnel needed to conduct ground schools, flight training and specialized maintenance courses for 700 military students. Part of the Billings high school was converted into a radio training unit, and an aging municipal hangar at the Billings airport doubled as a classroom and storage base.

Even with these facilities, it was necessary to hold many classes outdoors because space was at a premium.

THE O.T.U.: Co-incident with the Billings training program, Northwest tackled another project for the A.T.C. by establishing an Operational Training Unit (O.T.U.) to serve as a "graduate course" teaching *complete crews* to work as coordinated teams in the operation of Army transports. Each team included two pilots, one radio operator, a navigator and a flight engineer. One hundred of these five-man teams were graduated by Northwest's O.T.U.

FLIGHT CONTROL: As U.S. manufacturers turned out hundreds, then thousands of planes for military use, the Air Force urgently needed trained men to carry out the same kind of flight control procedures used by commercial airlines. In December, 1943, Army officials asked Northwest to set up such a school, and NWA's first flight control course opened in Seattle January 3, 1944.

Specially selected Army officers were indoctrinated in all phases of civil air regulations and flight operations, even to the point of receiving instruction in a Link Trainer so they would be familiar with the problems of pilots flying on instruments.

Graduates of the school — limited to eight students per five-week session — were given followup training in the Twin Cities, where Northwest again used on-the-job training

methods by assigning the men as special assistants to its own supervisory personnel. Finally, these trainees were assigned to duty at 23 different Army flight control centers scattered across the United States.

ANOTHER JOB FOR THE NAVY: As the Navy's officer procurement program escalated, many of its new college-trained ensigns were long on theoretical instruction but short on practical experience. Naval headquarters called on Northwest to organize a series of 12-week courses preparing officers to superintend engine and propeller maintenance on aircraft carriers and at naval land bases.

The University of Minnesota Aeronautical Engineering Department, then headed by Professor John D. Akerman, contributed several members to the school's faculty. Northwest's "professors" were headed by Joe Schuster — widely regarded as the leading propeller expert in the United States — and Stanley Malachway, for several decades one of Northwest's top aircraft maintenance specialsts.

FARGO JOINS IN: Brigadier General Dale V. Gaffney, commander of the A.T.C.'s Alaskan Wing, was so impressed by the success of Northwest's Flying Boxcar route that in the winter of 1942-43 he issued another contract to NWA for establishment of a special service in Fargo to modify and maintain all A.T.C. aircraft headed for cold weather duty in northwestern Canada and Alaska.

Northwest personnel was spread so thin because of its many war activities that an additional employee training program was set up in a frame building at the Fargo airport, with 276 newly hired men and 200 "old timers" manning the base to install oil dilution systems, wing ice-indicator lights, cabin heaters, oxygen lines and a variety of other equipment, including the much-heralded pressurized ignition harness.

Invented by one of Northwest's leading engineers — Carl E. Swanson — the harness utilized air pressure to keep moisture away from

ARMY-NAVY "E" FOR EXCELLENCE for Northwest's outstanding wartime service was accepted by President Croil Hunter from the Navy's Captain Harris and the Army's Colonel Nelson Talbott.

ignition wires, materially increasing the efficiency of engine operation.

FLIGHT TO INDIA: In addition to a variety of war contracts carried out by NWA for the military, on many occasions Northwest pilots were assigned to special ferrying jobs for the A.T.C., moving everything from B17 Flying Fortresses to small photo reconnaissance planes.

The most remarkable project of this type was carried out in April, 1943, in response to the A.T.C.'s call for help to bring 30 Curtiss Commandos — laden with 90 tons of urgently needed war materiel — from Miami, Florida, to Karachi, India. The 30 C46s were ticketed for duty over "The Hump," bringing supplies across the Himalayas to help China battle the Japanese invaders.

Northwest contributed 15 pilots to this 4½-day 15,000-mile odyssey — the longest mass flight of transport aircraft ever undertaken up to that time — while the A.T.C. provided five of its own captains and TWA the other ten.

Taking part in this history-making voyage were Frank Judd, C.L. "Les" Smith, H.M. Barnes, C.P. Wheelock, C.L. Wright, Warren Schulz, Earl Hale, Lyle Strong, Willis Strong, E.E. LaParle, Joseph Osowski, Robert Ashman, Walter Bullock, R.O. "Jack" Bain and Jerry Thompson, who was mentioned in news reports as the "youngest airline captain in the world" because he celebrated his twenty-first birthday during the flight.

Six of the Northwest group — including Captain Judd — remained for a time to train Army airmen in operation of the C46, and on a flight to Chungking, Judd quickly learned how wartime shortages can drive prices sky high.

"An ordinary cigaret lighter could get you $75 in American money," he reported, "and a pen and pencil set would bring $150. Gasoline was $7 a gallon, and eggs were $1.50 each."

Wartime operation of commercial airlines had one plus to go along with the inevitable minuses.

Before Pearl Harbor, U.S. domestic and international carriers operated 434 aircraft, but 244 of these had been purchased or leased by the Army and Navy before the end of 1943. Despite this attrition, the clamor for travel space created unusually high passenger loads, with an industry load factor of 68% in 1942, while Northwest reached an astounding 85.17% for the year ending June 30, 1944.

By that time, Allied forces had seized the initiative in virtually all sectors of the global war. The sparse victories of 1942 — notably Tobruk, El Alamein, Guadalcanal and the Coral Sea naval battle — were followed in 1943 by Italy's surrender, Russia's recapture of Kiev from the Nazis and more Pacific successes at Tarawa, Makin and Bougainville.

The tempo picked up in 1944. Russia broke the siege of Leningrad, Pacific forces captured Kwajalein, raided Truk and landed at Hollandia, New Britain, shortly before General Eisenhower's combined armies swept across the English Channel June 6, 1944, and began the march toward Berlin.

That same month, U.S. Marines captured Saipan, establishing a base for long range B29 bombers to strike at the heart of Japan's war effort, and on October 20 MacArthur landed on Leyte — the first step in recapture of the Philippines.

Despite Northwest's multiple wartime tasks — under government contracts totaling $63,350,000 — the airline began to prepare for inevitable post war changes in a variety of ways.

Thirteen different route applications were sent to the C.A.B. in 1943, including renewal of earlier bids for New York and Alaska plus a new request to add several Orient destinations, followed by a 1944 filing to serve Honolulu.

Next, hot meals replaced cold box lunches on all domestic flights, shortly after Northwest — in common with many other airlines — eliminated the requirement that stewardess candidates be registered nurses. (Applicants still had to be college graduates, weigh no more than 120 pounds, stand 5 feet 2 to 5 feet 5, and be 21 to 28 years old.)

95

Another preparation for the competitive era that lay ahead saw R.O. Bullwinkel named "acting sales manager" in June, 1944. This marked the beginning of a specific sales organization. Prior to that time, Northwest had operated with a traffic department, advertising department, mail and express department and a passenger service department, but they had not been coordinated — partly because the chief salesmanship required in wartime was to convince would-be passengers that no space was available.

By mid-1944, a personnel department checkup showed the airline had lost 2,045 employees to military service. This made all the more remarkable NWA's successful recruitment and training of men and women to swell the pre-war payroll from 881 to a peak of 10,439, before lessening government demands helped reduce the employment roster to 3,051 by war's end.

Even with Allied forces gaining the upper hand over Axis powers, the U.S. War Production Board was in no hurry to ease restrictions on commercial construction projects, but finally approved two much-needed Northwest communications projects — a PLT (private line teletype) system between all stations, and a new high powered radio telephone and telegraph facility in Billings.

Christmas came a little early for Northwest Airlines near the end of 1944, and an employee named Ben Blenner — stationed on Adak Island near the end of the Aleutian chain — first got the good news from Japan's infamous Tokyo Rose, whose broadcasts were designed to undermine the morale of U.S. fighting men.

Blenner's morale, however, went sky high.

"We are so far from home," he wrote in a letter to Northwest's General Office (which had been moved in mid-war from St. Paul's airport to a University Avenue location between the Twin Cities) "that we get most of our news from Tokyo Rose, who just told us via Japan radio that NWA has received an OK on its New York run. Is it true?"

Happily for Northwest, it was indeed true that the long campaign to become the nation's fourth transcontinental carrier had succeeded — even though continuing shortages of aircraft and equipment meant service to New York was still nearly half a year in the future.

PART IV

Reaching Out
(1945-1950)

15

Coast-to-Coast at Last

IN THE GREATEST TOTAL of airline extensions since 1929, the C.A.B. granted 24 new routes to 13 carriers (8,435 miles in all) several months before the end of World War II, to ease growing pressure on the nation's overloaded transportation lines.

One of these routes was Northwest's long sought authority to serve New York City, which was approved via the Twin Cities, Milwaukee and Detroit, eliminating — for the time being —requested service to Cleveland. Pointing to NWA's remarkable wartime record, the New York Times editorialized: "New York welcomes this additional air carrier not only because of the practical conveniences which its service will provide, but because of the self-reliant Northwest spirit."

Growing Allied successes helped Northwest get a head start on its postwar ambitions when Uncle Sam returned six DC3s to replace aircraft commandeered three years earlier, and made similar returns to other airlines as well.

In the spring of 1945, U.S. Marines captured Iwo Jima in Japan's "front yard" shortly before Franklin D. Roosevelt — who had been re-elected to an unprecedented fourth term — died April 12. Berlin fell on May 2 and Germany capitulated five days later, while the last great battle of the war was nearing a crescendo on Okinawa. After this key base in the Ryukyu Islands was secured, President Harry S. Truman made the decision to unleash the world's first tactical atomic bombs on Hiroshima and Nagasaki, bringing a sudden Japanese surrender August 14.

Northwest was in the midst of hectic preparations to launch its newly won coast-to-coast route when the airline accepted one final military assignment, by creating still another "instant airline" for the government. It was needed to rush many of Europe's re-deployed troops from Newark and Buffalo to west coast embarkation points for the final push on Japan.

For this impromptu transcontinental line, the Air Force provided a fleet of 15 transports while Northwest supplied flight crews, maintenance and all operational services on a regular schedule of four round trips per day from Newark to Seattle via Buffalo, the Twin Cities, Fargo, Billings and Spokane. This temporary airline continued to operate for six months, because after Japan's surrender, it helped speed returning GIs to separation centers in the east. More than 30,000 military passengers were carried in all.

June 1, 1945, became one of Northwest

Airlines' red letter days when New York-Seattle service was celebrated at the eastern terminus with special ceremonies, during which Governor Thomas E. Dewey of New York received a frozen great northern pike from Minnesota's Governor Ed J. Thye and Mayor Fiorello La Guardia was presented with a totem pole from the citizens of Seattle.

Motioning toward it for photographers, roly poly La Guardia joked in his distinctive, high-pitched cackle: "*This* is the totem pole. *I* am the mayor."

The original schedule included three coast-to-coast flights daily, plus an additional round trip between New York and the Twin Cities. A second Twin Cities-New York flight was added shortly, and service to Portland, Wenatchee and Duluth — interrupted by the war — was resumed when the government reduced air travel priorities in September and abolished them altogether October 15. Round trips between Rochester, Minn., and Chicago also were restored.

Gasoline and tire rationing were in their final stages, but did not disappear completely until year's end.

In common with other airlines, Northwest eagerly awaited an opportunity to fly the 4-engine 44-passenger DC4, which had been allocated solely for military use during the war. (It was known as the C54 by the Army and as an R5D by the Navy and Marine Corps.) To prepare for the anticipated post-war travel and shipping boom, NWA leased a surplus Army C54 so maintenance and flight crews could begin training with this much larger aircraft at once.

The original DC4 was brought in by John Woodhead and Joe Kimm, with Kimm, Bill

NWA'S FIRST TRANSCONTINENTAL FLIGHT landed in Minneapolis on June 1, 1945, on its way from Seattle to New York, with 20 returning servicemen and one civilian aboard. (Minneapolis Star-Tribune photo) By then the military had begun to return the company's DC3s.

100

Richmond and J.J. Corrigan — all of whom had flown these 4-engine jobs as members of the A.T.C.'s "Brass Hat Squadron" carrying government and military leaders during the war — named as chief flight instructors.

SEATTLE'S GIFT TO FIORELLO La Guardia then mayor of New York City, was a totem pole as tall as "hizzhonor" at a ceremony observing the fact that Northwest Airlines had become the nation's fourth transcontinental air carrier June 1, 1945. Stewardess Rose Oedbauer made the presentation to "The Little Flower."

The price tag on just one DC4 was $430,000, so to prepare for the financing job (an eventual 36 were purchased) Northwest issued common stock rights (at $23 per share) raising slightly more than $4 million in late 1945.

Even without DC4s, Northwest's passenger travel — which had dropped to a wartime low of 93,494 in 1943 — leaped to 330,489 in 1945.

That was only the beginning, because with Northwest now established as a coast-to-coast airline, there were more worlds to conquer, both domestically and internationally.

One of the most indefatiguable workers on behalf of Northwest during the Washington infighting frequently associated with the spirited battle for new routes was William "Bill" Stern, president of the Dakota National Bank in Fargo and a member of the airline's Board of Directors.

Bill Stern spent so much time on company business that he was appointed a special assistant to President Croil Hunter, with a permanent office at his disposal.

A genial, slightly built man with a shrewd look and ready smile, Bill was reputed to have more close friends — and a wider acquaintanceship — than any of his contemporaries in public life. He was known to some as "Mr. Republican," but his friendships crossed party lines. Adorning the walls of his office were autographed pictures of President Harry Truman, Herbert Hoover, Douglas MacArthur, Wendell Willkie and many others.

A world traveler, Stern was as much at home in the shadow of the Egyptian pyramids as he was in his native Fargo. He loved Fargo with a passion but enjoyed kidding his home town every now and then. As proof, his business card carried this statement: "The three most overrated things in the world are home cooking, home loving and Fargo, North Dakota."

On one of his trips to Egypt, Stern was part of a tourist lineup clamoring loudly for rooms at a hotel in Cairo.

"All rooms are taken," shouted the manager.

From the back of the line, a voice spoke up:

101

BILL STERN of Fargo, N.D., long time member of Northwest's Board of Directors, spent so much time on behalf of the airline that he was named a special assistant to President Croil Hunter and officed at the G.O.

"Do you have a room for Bill Stern of Fargo, North Dakota?"

"Certainly," came the reply. "Step right up and register."

A veteran of World War I, Stern was a co-organizer of the American Legion. While he never married, he believed deeply in helping young men get ahead, and sent more than a dozen of them through college. Among those he befriended were several young people from the Orient.

Interestingly, another veteran Northwest Board member — Alonzo Petteys of Brush, Colo. — founded the Petteys Memorial Foundation, enabling a number of young Chinese to attend United States colleges and universities in the immediate postwar period.

This interest in the Orient and its people was shared by the entire airline, because next, all eyes were turned to the not-so-Far-East.

After the grueling long distance campaign to help fortify Alaska and the Aleutians, Croil Hunter was convinced that Northwest was ready to spread its wings on to Japan and China. But once again there was a "battle of Washington" to be fought in the halls of Congress.

16

"Northwest Passage"

NORTHWEST'S JOY at becoming the fourth transcontinental carrier in the United States was accompanied by deep concern over a long-ranging controversy involving national policy governing air service to foreign lands. The eagerly awaited NWA authority for an Orient route via Alaska hung in the balance.

Most airlines, and most members of Congress, urged a system of regulated competition among U.S. carriers, but a vociferous few insisted on a "chosen instrument," under which foreign routes would be awarded to a single airline.

To all appearances, this idea was laid to rest in mid-1945 when the C.A.B. recognized the right of domestic airlines to enter the international field by awarding North Atlantic routes to TWA and American Export, as well as to Pan American, which — with Atlantic authority already in its possession — had battled for the single "American Flag line" policy.

Montana pioneers used to claim that if they killed a rattlesnake in the morning, he'd wriggle until sundown, and — like a rattler — the "chosen instrument" philosophy continued to wriggle long after many considered it dead.

Everything looked like smooth sailing when a C.A.B. examiner recommended that Northwest be certified from New York and Chicago to the Orient by way of the Twin Cities, Edmonton and Anchorage, although his report created momentary consternation when it failed to include Alaska-Orient service from Seattle. The C.A.B., however, approved both routes, and when President Truman signed the certificate August 1, 1946, N.W.A.'s victory seemed complete.

But in the spring of 1947, barely three months before Northwest was ready to begin its shortcut to the Orient via the Great Circle (or Polar) route, the entire operation was in jeopardy.

Senator Pat McCarran of Nevada introduced a bill that once again resurrected the "chosen instrument" policy, saying it was "necessary to avoid destructive rivalries between American companies abroad and to present a united American front against the competition of foreign air monopolies."

Opponents termed it a "monopoly bill," and Croil Hunter — appearing before the House Committee on Interstate and Foreign Commerce — called McCarran's legislation "a serious threat to the American system of free enterprise that would lead to government ownership of all transportation."

He added: "It is contrary to the best interests of the people, who are weary of paying heavy taxes and subsidies. Why should this government set up a subsidized air service and join a complete monopoly . . . when long established enterprises and companies with outstanding records in the domestic and foreign field are already launched on an international air service program that conforms with the American way of progress."

Hunter called the legislation "just another in a long series of attempts by one carrier, Pan American World Airways, to grab complete control of all United States international air transport operations.

"Taxpayers of the nation would be forced to carry a new burden because the McCarran bill calls for four separate and distinct subsidies, including a subsidy to offset subsidies."

Turning his guns on Juan Trippe, president of Pan Am, who had testified as a witness in behalf of the bill, Hunter declared Trippe and his airline "do not, as they claim, really fear foreign competition. They are afraid of the competition they are getting, or about to get, from the domestic airlines of the United States."

"I cannot share his pessimism," Hunter continued. "The airlines carrying the flag of the United States in the international field are superior to their foreign competitors in every phase of operations and routes. These airlines, representing this nation, will become stronger through fair and regulated competition among themselves."

Finally, McCarran's bill died and so — it seemed — did the "chosen instrument" idea. It even stopped wriggling — but not for good.

For several hundred years, seafaring explorers from the old world had sought a shortcut to the Far East by means of a "Northwest Passage" across the top of the North American continent.

And in 1931, when Charles and Anne Lindbergh made their famous "north to the Orient" flight, they demonstrated a fact appreciated only by students of global geography — that a Great Circle route across the top of the world brought New York approximately 2,000 miles closer to Japan than the conventional warm weather passage through the mid-Pacific.

No other carrier showed the slightest interest in tackling a chilly route over the Pole, but Hunter was convinced the resultant saving of many hours on the long and tiring trip to the Orient would give Northwest a powerful new "plus" in the battle for overseas passengers.

When the anxiously awaited authority for this service was approved in Washington, newspaper editors from coast to coast hailed it as the beginning of a "Northwest Passage by air."

Said the Minneapolis Morning Tribune: "Minneapolis now is sitting on top of the world — literally. Authorization by the Civil Aeronautics Board of Northwest Airlines routes to the Orient puts the Twin Cities on the Great Circle route, a shortcut around the world. Mid point of the transcontinental route of this airline, the Twin Cities now also are the mid point of this world operation."

The St. Paul Pioneer Press added: "Northwest Airlines established its claim to the Great Circle Route largely by virtue of its excellent wartime performance as a military transport agency during the Alaskan and Aleutian campaign."

Only one month after the certificate had been authorized, Northwest began flights to Anchorage September 1, 1946, from Seattle-Tacoma on the "outside" coastal route, and on January 2, 1947, launched the "inside" overland passage by way of its familiar wartime operation from the Twin Cities via Edmonton, Alberta.

But getting ready to serve the Orient was a far more complicated matter. The first survey flight took off New Year's Day, 1947, followed by another one a few weeks later, to begin a mountain of preparation required to establish service in the war-torn Far East, where little or no supplies were available.

Just as the airline had tackled its wartime trail blazing job in Alaska, so did a host of top and middle management officials go to work setting up maintenance bases, stocking parts and equipment at key points, acquiring and furnishing staff houses, work shops, setting up their own electric generating plants, radio bases,

DOUBLE-CHECKING ALL DETAILS before post-war service to Alaska began, Frank Judd, left — then Vice President of NWA's Western Region — and John Woodhead, right, Operations Manager, met with noted Alaskan bush pilot Bob Reeves at Elmendorf Field, Anchorage, in August, 1946.

offices and indoctrinating necessary personnel. Don J. King was named Orient Region vice-president and 242 other Americans were transplanted to new bases in the Far East.

In all, NWA moved nearly 1,000 tons of materiel to the Orient, much of it by air but with some of the larger items going by ship, including 10 diesel generators, 200,000 pounds of aircraft parts and supplies, several complete electric light plants, three 42-passenger buses and a fleet of passenger cars and trucks.

Three DC4s and two DC3s took part in the air supply project, while a major maintenance base was set up in Tokyo and a smaller one in Manila. Only one month after its initial survey flight,

Northwest inaugurated charter flights to Tokyo carrying materials needed by the U.S. occupation forces.

Robert Ebert, a graduate of the arduous wartime manpower procurement job, was named Orient personnel director. He was assigned added duties that included making sure employees received instruction about Far East customs, traditions, history, business relationships, government backgrounds and economic conditions — not to mention recruitment of Asian young women for training to serve as stewardesses on flights between Tokyo, Shanghai, Manila and Seoul, Korea.

American style food was virtually non-

SCHEDULED ALASKA SERVICE via Seattle began September 1, 1946. With a bit of help, President Croil Hunter holds the key to Anchorage.

existent in the Orient, so Northwest flew in 25,000 pre-cooked frozen dinners from the Maxon Kitchen in New York, with 11,000 of them stored under refrigeration in Tokyo, 3,000 in Manila and another 11,000 divided between Anchorage and the Twin Cities for use on Orient flights.

During this preparatory period, Wayne W. Parrish — editor of the American Aviation Daily — wrote: "A debit angle (on Northwest's Orient service) is the educational campaign required to convince the public that the Great Circle route is the shortest and fastest to Tokyo and Shanghai . . . that going north to Alaska is *not* out of the way but is really the direct route over the globe.

"Most people shudder at the thought of Alaska and the Aleutians, yet on the second NWA survey flight in February, temperatures were above those in Washington and Chicago, and sunshine prevailed most of the time."

Then, as now, passengers traveling via Anchorage marveled at Alaska's magnificent scenery — including that overlord of all U.S. mountains, 20,270-foot Mt. McKinley — plus dozens of other snow-hooded summits sparkling in the sun, herds of caribou, active volcanoes and an occasional brown bear scooping his dinner of king salmon out of the picturesque fish-laden streams below.

Paul Benscoter, originally Northwest's station manager in Shanghai and later a vice president of the Orient Region, had this to say about the first survey flight: "It was a beautiful day when we circled Fujiyama before settling down on Haneda Airport, but all of us were horrified by conditions.

"The Japanese had no food, and block after block of homes were in irreparable condition. One of the first commercial places to be reestablished in the post war period was the Takashimaya department store, which was then the Marshall Field of Tokyo. They had practically nothing — a few fish in the basement, postcards, carved wooden dolls and — strangely — shelf after shelf of Kiwi shoe polish.

"I've often wondered about that. A land starving for food had more shoe polish than it knew what to do with. In fact, very few persons in Tokyo had shoes to polish.

"In contrast, Shanghai during the immediate post war period was a bustling city with a festive air. British, French and American businessmen had gotten things back in shape. The city was gay and there was plenty of food and entertainment."

Unfortunately, these conditions in China were not to last.

Time magazine, commenting on Northwest's successful application to serve Alaska and the Orient, said: "Northwest pilots know more than the Eskimos do about Alaska and the dismal Bering Sea . . . Pan Am could no longer claim a monopoly on the knowhow of overseas flying. Since Pearl Harbor, Pan Am's competitors had learned the hard way how to navigate the ocean's airways."

Governors of every state on the NWA route structure sent congratulatory messages, many of which echoed this thought offered by Governor Sam Ford of Montana:

"Too much credit cannot be given Northwest Airlines for its magnificent accomplishments during the relatively brief period of one score years. The unique record of being the only carrier to become a transcontinental line and then an international operator through its own natural growth and expansion — without any form of merger — is something for the books."

At the time the route award was announced, Chairman Lloyd Welch Pogue of the C.A.B. suggested Northwest should merge with Pennsylvania-Central Airlines to put it on a better competitive footing, but the airline ignored this proposal and went ahead to organize plans for its Alaska-Orient service, which had come as a slightly premature twentieth birthday present.

In addition to overseeing the physical job of setting up a totally new operation via Anchorage to Tokyo, Seoul, Shanghai and Manila — with a necessary fuel stop at barren Shemya island 38 miles from the tip of the Aleutians — one of Don King's first projects was to negotiate for landing

DON KING was named Northwest's first Orient Region vice president in early 1947.

rights with the governments of China, the Philippines and Korea, as well as with the occupation army's General Douglas MacArthur in Tokyo.

The second NWA survey trip was participated in by three Board members — Bill Stern, Alonzo Petteys and another highly regarded veteran director, Joseph T. Johnson of Milwaukee, who took his directorial duties so seriously that he personally held a weekly station inspection in Milwaukee to make sure everything was up to snuff.

Also aboard was Dr. Jan Tillisch of the Mayo Clinic — an aviation medicine pioneer — who went along to check on sanitation problems and living conditions of the airline's Orient-based employees.

When the survey party reached Shanghai, a group of Chinese civic and business leaders hosted the Northwest group at a dinner which was such a large affair that two adjoining banquet halls were required to seat everybody. Frank Judd, then manager of NWA's Western Region, was asked to serve as master of ceremonies in one of the rooms, while Croil Hunter and Bill Stern took charge of the other.

"Suddenly we heard roars of laughter coming from the adjoining room," Judd recalled later,

NORTHWEST'S FIRST ORIENT FLIGHTS begin July 15, 1947, with a throng of Twin Cities well-wishers on hand, including Mayors John J. McDonough and Hubert H. Humphrey.

108

"and this was hard to understand because we knew our people could not speak Chinese and very few of the hosts could speak English. We peeked through the doorway, and there were Croil Hunter and Bill Stern directing their audience in that time-honored American school children's game called rock, scissors and paper.

"It didn't take our hosts long to learn that scissors cut paper, paper covers rock, and rock dulls scissors."

Although the U.S. government did not approve opening Japan to tourism for a full year, Northwest launched a three-times-a-week schedule to the Orient July 15, 1947. The DC4s to be used on this route were christened at public ceremonies in New York, the Twin Cities, Seattle-Tacoma and — because NWA had high hopes of adding Washington, D.C., to its route structure — in the nation's capital.

Minnesota's Governor Luther W. Youngdahl had named July 13 through 19 as "Northwest Passage" week, in honor of the new service, as did Mayors Hubert H. Humphrey of Minneapolis and John J. McDonough of St. Paul.

General Carlos P. Romulo, one of the Philippines' great war heroes, and Madame Wellington Koo, wife of China's ambassador, participated in the christening of three DC4s named Manila, Shanghai and Tokyo.

These planes, and many to follow, made transpacific fuel stops at rocky, desolate Shemya, where Northwest remodeled abandoned Army Quonset huts into a staff house, crew quarters, commissary, laundry, mess hall, recreation lounge, maintenance shop, fuel depot and living quarters.

Nicknamed "Schmoo" by its inhabitants, Shemya housed 55 NWA volunteers (one year per hitch) and even though a perennial ping pong tournament was one of the few local excitements, a number of employees ignored the rain, wind and fog to volunteer for three hitches in a row because "this is a great place to save money — no place to spend it."

In Tokyo, Northwest's first Orient office was two blocks from the Daichi Building, where MacArthur made his headquarters.

"When the general strode out each noon," recalls Bob Ebert, "thousands of Japanese gathered every day to bow and pay him homage."

Military restrictions originally required Far East travelers on nongovernment business to stay aboard the aircraft in Tokyo and proceed to Seoul, Shanghai or Manila, so Shanghai became NWA's prime source of revenue operations in the early months of Orient service.

By August, 1947, Japan-bound air mail and cargo were permitted for the first time. The initial Tokyo pay load included photographic plates used to print Newsweek Magazine in the Orient, and the next flight carried a shipment of artificial limbs consigned by a Twin Cities factory.

HUBERT H. HUMPHREY, then mayor of Minneapolis and later Vicepresident of the United States, keynoted the civic celebration of Northwest's extension to Orient destinations.

While Northwest was extending its routes north to Alaska and the Orient, a variety of changes marked the early postwar era. Even the stewardesses began to get taller.

Arrival of the much larger DC4 led Rosie Stein to alter the old five-feet-four maximum height for cabin attendants, and Elizabeth Stoery — at 5 feet 8½ inches — became the first to prove tall girls had their place in the scheme of things.

Longer runways, too, were required by the DC4. In Spokane, Felts field proved inadequate for the new equipment, so Northwest negotiated with the Army for use of Geiger field — known ever since in airline parlance as "GEG." In Detroit, the airline moved out to Willow Run airport, and preparations also were made in New York to transfer from LaGuardia to spacious new Idlewild (now J.F. Kennedy airport.)

In common with many other employers, Northwest adopted the 5-day 40-hour work week at the start of 1946, the same year an employee pension plan was established.

Less than a month after the start of Alaska service, a plane load of Twin City business and civic leaders made a good will tour to Anchorage, where a young sales representative named Robert J. Wright had been sent to open a ticket office. Later that same Bob Wright became one of Northwest's numerous "home grown" management executives, when he took over as Vice President-Sales (in 1961.)

Late in 1946, A.B. "Cot" Hayes — former mayor of Juneau, who had been named Northwest's Alaska traffic manager — messaged Twin Cities headquarters for help when employees could not find homes in Anchorage, because a lengthy maritime strike made it impossible to bring in building materials to alleviate the housing shortage.

Once again, the Northwest spirit of "can do" and "make do" came to the rescue, in a performance that vividly dramatized the lifting power of the DC4.

Twenty prefabricated six-room houses were built in sections at Sheboygan Falls, Wis. — plus 20 garages — and a DC4 converted into a freighter made round trip after round trip, hauling not only the house and garage sections but refrigerators, washing machines, stoves, laundry tubs, oil heating systems and all other household necessities — complete even to the doorbells.

Foundations were built in advance on a plot of land near Bootlegger's Cove, and the homes were set up and occupied as fast as they arrived.

Housing was a problem in Tokyo, too. The city's first postwar home construction permit granted to a non-Japanese company was issued to Northwest for a 20-house compound in the suburban Shibuya area to help provide quarters for locally based personnel.

When Orient service began, elapsed time from the Twin Cities to Tokyo was 36 hours 35 minutes, with actual flight time of 33 hours 5 minutes. But more and faster planes were on the assembly lines.

NEW "NWA" LOGO ADOPTED IN 1946

17

The "Red Tail Fleet"

SLIGHTLY MORE THAN A YEAR after the end of World War II, Northwest's aircraft included 23 DC3s — then becoming obsolescent despite this plane's great contribution to aviation — and 18 DC4s, 15 of them converted from military C54s, with only three built since the war.

About the same time Northwest took a major step toward all-weather flying by adopting ILS (Instrument Landing System) equipment January 1, 1947, the airline moved to update its fleet by ordering 10 huge double deck Stratocruisers (the 83-seat Boeing 377) and the first 10 of an eventual 25 Martin 202s.

The 300-mile-an-hour Stratocruiser — a luxurious peacetime version of the B29 bomber — provided 69 first class seats on the upper level and space for 14 passengers in the lower deck cocktail lounge.

Northwest's engineering personnel had made a careful study of the projected Martin 303, and recommended its purchase rather than the Convair 240, but in a fateful decision, Martin decided to produce the smaller, unpressurized 202 first, and persuaded Northwest management to accept this plane instead. With an announced cruising speed of 245 miles per hour, the 202 was a low altitude, short range aircraft with a capacity of 40 passengers — later reduced

to 36 in order to provide for more cargo space.

Meanwhile, the postwar boom had simmered down. The aviation industry was faced with sharply rising costs for labor and equipment at the same time public use of air transportation began to slacken. Northwest's revenue passengers nearly doubled (to 631,398) in 1946, but leveled off at 663,352 in 1947, with a net loss of $1,141,340 for the year, followed by another loss in 1948.

To help take up the slack, Northwest pioneered the idea of space-available air freight — particularly attractive to international shippers — when air mail shipments showed an alarming drop, and also offered a few all-cargo flights plus several combination passenger-cargo schedules.

Eventually, when massive construction delays on the Stratocruiser left Northwest in a desperate competitive position with its aging DC4s, the airline pioneered another "first" by launching the nation's original transcontinental all-coach service March 24, 1949.

Coast-to-coast fares were cut to $97 versus $157.85 for first class. While competitors griped this would steal from first class revenues, the Oregon Journal cited figures showing Northwest's cross-country coach service running at a 91% load factor, while first class occupancy on rival lines showed little or no change.

The paper's conclusion: Northwest was developing new customers for air travel. Other airlines had proved short haul coach flights were practical, and eventually, the gripers followed suit on both short and cross-country service.

The speedy Martin 202 — whose new features included two self-contained hydraulic ramps for passenger and freight loading — could carry a 3,600-pound greater payload than the DC3, in addition to its other advantages. It was hailed in the press as "the plane of the future" and "the plane that cuts operating expenses 35%," at the time it passed all CAA tests and was certificated for passenger service August 13, 1947.

By the end of November, Northwest's first ten 202s were on the line.

Domestically, Northwest added six cities to its route in 1947 — La Crosse, Wis. (a resumption of prewar service), Jamestown, N.D.; Aberdeen, S.D.; Bozeman, Mont.; Eau Claire, Wis., and Great Falls, Mont. Shortly before Princess Elizabeth of England married her Prince Charming — Philip Mountbatten —

Northwest also added Okinawa as a new destination in the Orient on September 25, 1947.

One of the airline's most frequent passengers at that time was William "Big Bill" Lyons, a disabled Minnesota war veteran with a unique claim to fame. Wounded at Pearl Harbor and hospitalized for 13 months, he had passed the dreary hours by learning to crochet with his feet. His many flights were occasioned by the fact that — in a one-man war against hospital boredom — he made 53 trips to veterans' hospitals all over the U.S. so he could give foot-crocheting lessons to other bedridden GIs.

As things turned out, the only lasting contribution the Martin 202 made to Northwest Orient Airlines — as the company became known in the late '40s — was its participation in events that led to adoption of the distinctive red tail which makes Northwest planes recognizable instantly, all around the world.

Origin of the red tail has been the subject of friendly argument for many years, and a careful study of the facts reveals a logical reason for the dispute.

SOLID RED TAIL, which became Northwest's permanent identifying mark, was introduced in 1948. This Martin 202, painted in new color scheme adopted that year, is shown over Washington, D.C. (Original version included red wing tips and nose, but these were eliminated as being "too busy.")

112

Many veteran employees remember that during the last half of Northwest's wartime Alaskan operation, the Army repainted a number of its olive drab aircraft, making the tails and wing tips red so they could be located more easily if forced down in the snow. (It had taken 31 days to find one downed plane only 1½ miles from the Watson Lake runway.)

Some old timers used to claim this was the start of NWA's "red tail fleet," but the war-born idea vanished completely after the end of hostilities. Two years later — in the fall of 1947 — Donald O. Benson of the airline's maintenance and engineering department was assigned to consult with industrial design firms on a new paint job for the Martin 202.

One of the companies he talked with — a well known eastern firm — offered four different experimental designs, each featuring one dominant color — green, red, yellow and blue.

Charles "Bud" Morgan — then and for more than 30 years employed in the Northwest paint shop — says: "We experimented with several of the color schemes that had been suggested, not only on some of the 202s but also on an least one DC4."

Benson adds: "Three or four planes were put in service to check out public reaction, but apparently most people felt the designs were too busy. Then I retained Charles Butler Associates of New York. It was Butler who came up with a drawing that featured a solid red tail, plus red wing tips and nose. We flew four 202s out on the line to demonstrate this design and everybody loved it — including Croil Hunter.

"We did our own paint job on the first ten 202s already in service, and the factory did the next 15, which began arriving in May, 1948."

The red wing tips and nose soon were eliminated, but from that time forward the solid red tail became a permanent Northwest identification mark.

In the minds of several men who go back to the war years, this question still remains: is it possible that one of the designers on Charles Butler's staff in New York just happened to have remembered from his military service the sight of a red-tailed C47 operated by Northwest as part of its Alaska lifeline?

Just as the red tail was becoming a permanent fixture, two more route awards of major importance were granted to Northwest in 1948.

With air traffic to Tokyo still primarily governmental or military in nature, the airline's Orient service urgently needed a long-requested access to Washington, D.C., which was granted

GLENN MARTIN, builder of the Martin 202, helps Croil and Mrs. Hunter celebrate the fact that the nation's capital became a Northwest port of call March 15, 1948.

by the C.A.B. and inaugurated by Northwest March 15 via Cleveland and Pittsburgh — both important markets in NWA's plans for the future.

This key service was launched with impressive ceremonies at the nations's capital but — as frequently happens in C.A.B. route awards — it was a case of "the Lord giveth and the Lord taketh away," because Capital Airlines was given an extension from Milwaukee to the Twin Cities, thus paralleling Northwest's entire route from Minneapolis-St. Paul to Washington.

A similar "give and take" marked the next important route award a few months later.

From the day it was organized, Northwest Airlines had needed warm weather destinations to ease the annual winter slump in business. In mid-war, its application to serve Honolulu from Seattle-Tacoma and Portland was tabled. In 1946 the C.A.B. turned the request down as "not necessary at this time."

Marshaling support from the entire Pacific Northwest, when the C.A.B. again re-opened the case, NWA presented these arguments:

Passengers from Seattle to Hawaii would save 415 miles on Northwest's proposed *direct* route, rather than going by the then-necessary detour via California (2672 miles versus 3087 miles.)

Portland travelers would save 354 miles.

Comparable mileage savings would apply to passengers coming from all the northern tier of states across which Northwest flies.

National defense would be served by the more direct route.

Residents and business interests in Hawaii would be given *direct* service to another important sector of the mainland.

Once the Pacific Northwest-Honolulu case was reopened, Pan American — which already was serving Hawaii by way of the heavily traveled California gateway — and the Matson Steamship Company also submitted applications.

Then, in the fall of 1947, a C.A.B. examiner surprised everybody by recommending United Airlines, which had not even filed for the route. Eventually, the C.A.B. granted Pacific Northwest-Honolulu routes to both Pan Am and NWA and the certificates were signed by President Truman. Hawaii's addition gave Northwest a 20,433-mile route structure — fourth largest among U.S. domestic airlines at that time.

Mixed emotions marked the Northwest inauguration of Honolulu service December 2, 1948, because the airline was competing against newer and larger Pan Am aircraft with DC4s, which had to operate with reduced seating capacity so they could carry an adequate reserve of gasoline.

"The opposition jumped the gun by one day and beat us into Honolulu," Frank Judd reported, "but we had the last laugh. On their first arrival from the Pacific Northwest, they sought out Duke Kahanamoku — Hawaii's famous Olympic swimming champion — to christen their plane with a coconut. The Duke was a strong man, and swung the coconut so enthusiastically that it bashed in the plane's cowling. It took a couple of days to get it fixed.

"In the meantime, our DC4 came in, and it would have been foolish to choose a lesser celebrity than the Duke for our own ceremony, so we took a hacksaw and carefully scribed a coconut so it would open at the slightest touch. That's why our return flight to the mainland was the first from Hawaii to the Pacific Northwest."

While Northwest was sweating out the arrival of its 10 double deck Stratocruisers — already more than a year behind the planned delivery date — a fierce internal struggle in China between Communists and Chiang Kai-Shek's Nationalists once again brought war to a destination served by Northwest — Shanghai — in late spring, 1949.

One of the airline's employees in this bustling Chinese city was a young flight superintendent named Reginald C. Jenkins, who later rose to vice president in charge of the Orient Region. In

1948 BOARD OF DIRECTORS. Top photo, from left, Dr. Charles W. Mayo, Joseph T. Johnson, Alonzo Petteys, A.E. Floan (secretary), Thomas Irvine and E.I. Whyatt. Bottom, from left, Croil Hunter, W.T. Gardiner, Edward White, Bill Stern, R.M. Hardy and Malcolm S. Mackay.

all, he served more than 30 years in the Far East.

With Communist forces encircling Shanghai, Don King — then Orient Region vice president — elected to stay behind with J.P. Farrell, district traffic manager, in an attempt to rescue as much Northwest equipment as possible, and ordered the few remaining U.S. personnel to evacuate on May 15, 1949.

"Our last flight brought $10,000 in U.S. greenbacks for King," Jenkins remembers, "because by that time inflation had grown until local money was worthless. Even in late 1947, it took a bundle of Chinese paper money seven inches square to buy a package of cigarets. Six months later it took 20 bundles.

"From time to time they replaced old money with new on a basis of 10 or 20 to one. It took a fair sized suitcase full of Chinese currency to pay a one-week laundry bill. Soon the rate of exchange had reached, 30,000 to one. People burned money for fuel because it was not as expensive as coal. Eventually, with paper money accepted by no one, the exchange shifted over to silver only."

Oddly, with gunfire clearly audible inside the

COMPASS SYMBOL ADOPTED in 1947-48

city, the evacuation from Shanghai was a model of orderliness.

"There was no panic and it was difficult to persuade many Americans to go," Jenkins continues. "The U.S. Navy had removed its vessels from the Yangtze River, so the only way to get people out was by air. We scheduled three or four extra flights. One plane went out so overloaded that it was necessary to pull up the arm rests so three people could sit in a double seat, but the rest of the aircraft were not even full.

"We had moved out all of Northwest's American dependents three or four months earlier, at the time Nanking fell. Those people were flown down to Manila, so there were only six management men left in Shanghai.

"During the evacuation we had so much space that Wally Greer — then chief Shanghai mechanic and later a Northwest pilot — moved his piano out on one of our DC4s.

"Almost as soon as we took off from Lungwha airport, we could see where the battle lines were. The Communist armies had surrounded the city, but strangely enough, inside that perimeter everything was orderly."

Warren "Avie" Avenson, a retired 747 captain who was John Denman's co-pilot during the Shanghai evacuation, agrees that "an unreal quiet" had descended over Shanghai when its capture was imminent.

Not long after China ceased to be a Northwest port of call, Northwest's glamorous double deck Stratocruisers began arriving in August, 1949, a year and a half after the promised delivery date. At long last, the equipment pinch appeared to be over, and — with the fleet of Martin 202s already in operation — Northwest looked forward to a rosy 1950, with all its tired DC3s soon to be phased out, and the aging DC4s assigned primarily to hauling cargo.

But things didn't work out that way, even though 1949 showed a record profit of $1,357,679, with new coach revenues representing 15% of the total system passenger income — a small harbinger of the future.

PART V

Rough Air
(1950-1954)

18

Crisis

FEW PLANES IN THE HISTORY of piston engine aircraft developed as many devoted fans as the Stratocruiser, and few were as costly to operate. As one NWA official wryly commented: "It took a 110% load factor to break even."

This inside joke stretched the truth only moderately, because the actual breakeven load was estimated at between 75 and 80%.

But while the big double-deckers continued to win friends and guzzle gasoline, a far more crucial turn of events overtook the airline in 1950.

Although one Martin 202 had been lost two years earlier, a structural deficiency in the wing spar was corrected by the manufacturer and these swift planes soared in popularity, setting new speed records almost daily. Then Northwest was stunned by a series of four more accidents involving the 202 in a space of less than 10½ months.

By early 1951, the entire Martin fleet was out of service because nobody — neither the public nor crews — wanted to fly them. Instead of being able to offer passengers the newest in post-war equipment, the airline — which had sold off its aging DC3s and several DC4s — was reduced to scrounging for the very same type of elderly aircraft it had been shedding. It was a grim silver

anniversary for Northwest — and conditons were due to get grimmer.

The whole United States had its own share of bad news in 1950 when — less than five years after defeat of the Axis powers — it found itself again at war, in a long and frustrating conflict which President Truman initially termed a "police action." Communist North Korean forces crossed the 38th parallel and invaded South Korea June 25. Two days later, Truman dispatched U.S. air and sea units to aid the South Koreans.

American involvement quickly escalated, and once again Northwest airlines was called on by the government — this time as prime contractor in the famous Korean air lift — to carry men and supplies over NWA's Great Circle shortcut and help pave the way for an eventual armistice three years later.

The Korean War was exactly one month old when heavy fighting roared into the outskirts of the capital city of Seoul at 7 a.m. July 25, 1950. A local employee of Northwest's sales office pounded on the door of Bill Hansen — then district sales manager in Seoul — shouting "The North Koreans are attacking!"

Hansen dressed, rushed to the city ticket office, turned on his intercom to alert station manager Ed Krunsky at Kimpo airport, then hurried to the American embassy and offered Northwest's services to U.S. Ambassador John J. Muccio.

Hansen's next call to the airport was made just as Krunsky rolled under his desk when a swarm of Yak fighters peeled off overhead and strafed the field. Hansen could hear the gun bursts over his intercom. An old Army C54 was raked by the flying bullets, but there were no NWA ships on the field because they had been flown out the day before as a precautionary measure.

After burning his ticket stock, Hansen turned over the keys of Northwest's four vehicles to several Korean employees, instructing them to head south for Pusan, then packed a small grip with several thousand dollars in company funds, a tooth brush and a silk dress recently purchased in Seoul as a gift for his mother back in Long Island. He hastily joined Krunsky at the airport and — under a screen of American fighter escorts — the two men joined dozens of other Americans who were flown to safety in Japan.

When United Nations forces, under the command of Douglas MacArthur, re-took Kimpo some weeks later, it had been blasted so continuously by gunfire and bombs that one of the few items found still intact was a Northwest Orient Airlines sign which had hung near the airport ticket counter.

Northwest added Taipei — Nationalist China's capital on the island of Taiwan — to its Orient ports of call that summer on June 3, although an application for eight other destinations in the Far East was denied. When British authorities failed to grant landing rights at Hong Kong, the airline arranged for initial service to that picturesque city from Taipei by means of a charter contract with Hong Kong Airways.

While the Korean War dragged into its second year, Northwest — with the blessing of the U.S. government — played a key role in reviving

COMFORTABLE DOUBLE-DECK STRATOCRUISER, well liked but costly to operate, helped Northwest battle its equipment shortage for several rugged years in the 50s.

KOREAN WAR BATTLE left Seoul's Kimpo airport in shambles in 1950. But when the airport was recaptured from the communists, these two U.S. Marines found a Northwest sign which was one of the few objects that survived the shelling. Northwest soon resumed service to Kimpo.

Japanese commercial aviation by providing the knowhow, the aircraft, the maintenance and operational personnel needed to establish a domestic airline known as Nippon Koku Kabushiki Kaisha. Today this carrier is one of Northwest's tough international competitors under the more familiar name of Japan Air Lines.

Under a one-year contract, Northwest supplied the new line with flight crews plus two twin-engine and one four-engine aircraft, while the Japanese handled all sales activity and related ground services. The first flights between Tokyo and Sapporo, on the northern-most island of Hokkaido, required only 2½ hours, versus 36 hours by train and boat.

The original three flights a week were expanded to daily 67-passenger flights on DC4s before long, and service was added to Nagoya, Osaka, Hiroshima and Fukuoka. Reg Jenkins recalls that "the local ticket agents were so enthusiastic about their work that to begin with, they sent planes out with standees, until we explained to them that strap-hangers are not permissible in aircraft."

As part of its service, Northwest trained Japanese pilots, stewardesses, pursers and mechanics, created operational and training manuals, and brought a number of Japanese personnel to the Twin Cities for advanced flight instruction before turning the total operation over to Nippon Koku at the conclusion of the

VICEPRESIDENT ALBEN BARKLEY, right, welcomed Northwest's first Stratocruiser to serve Washington, D.C., in 1951, piloted by twins Lee and Les Smith. Lee is at the left — or it that Les?

agreed 12-month period of intensive training.

Because of the critical equipment shortage, a number of planes operated during the Korean Air Lift were leased from other carriers — plus five from the U.S. government — but NWA's most remarkable aircraft was a DC3 known as UN 99, which Northwest purchased for the United Nations and operated as a "one ship airline" between Korea and Japan.

UN 99 carried VIPs, evacuated wounded and performed a variety of battle zone missions for the United Nations, which had assumed overall direction of the multi-nation force opposing Communist aggression, with General MacArthur as field commander. Bob Chernich, later to become a district sales manager, reported he was shot at more while a purser on UN 99 than when he served in World War II.

Dwight D. Eisenhower, America's hero of World War II, was elected President in the fall of 1952 and took office January 20, 1953. The Korean War ended with an armistice signed in late July that same year. The New York Times, calling Northwest's contribution to victory "an achievement important to the nation and to the world," pointed out that much more was involved than the 13,779,853 revenue plane miles and the 66 million ton-miles of priority military traffic compiled by the airline. In its editorial, the Times declared:

"As the end nears with victory in Korea, there should be a memorial some place for the man and the organization that saved and made efficient the airlift along the Great Circle route to Japan and the battlefields. The man is Croil Hunter, its president, and his organization is Northwest Airlines.

"It will be remembered by many that (at one time) it seemed inevitable that the great air bases in Alaska, which make the route possible,

122

SILVER ANNIVERSARY CLASS of Northwest stewardesses graduated in September, 1951.

were to be closed in the interest of so-called economy. Mr. Hunter rushed to Washington. Almost single-handed and with the vigor for which he is famous in the airline industry, he induced the authorities to keep open the huge base at Shemya, necessary for refueling and weather guidance for the planes of his line. Three months later the blow fell across the Thirty-eighth Parallel. Northwest became the prime contractor for the lift of the men and the vital materials so critically needed. The Shemya

route is 2,500 miles shorter than that through Hawaii . . ."

Even the great New York Times can make an occasional error — the saving is really closer to 2000 miles, which is still a major improvement, because that's about as far as from Cleveland to Seattle.

However well deserved, the heartening salute from the Times did not alleviate Northwest's growing equipment and financial crisis.

19

Decision

WHILE THE UNITED STATES aviation industry was making a 42% gain in available seat-miles during 1951 and 1952, Northwest Airlines showed a seat-mile loss of $1^1/_3\%$.

The irony of NWA's equipment pinch is that the fleet of Martin 202s — all sold off by early 1952 because too many people considered them jinxed — had been modified and improved to a point that they gave their new owners (mostly in South America) years of excellent performance.

Service to Duluth, Eau Claire, La Crosse, Wenatchee, Aberdeen and — eventually — Miles City was suspended as a result of the aircraft shortage. Striving desperately to provide more passenger capacity, Northwest added eight seats to all Stratocruisers and contracted to operate an Eastern Airlines Super Constellation between Chicago and Seattle.

To reduce the competitive disadvantage on Orient flights, Stratocruisers were assigned to two of the three weekly Tokyo flights, cutting nearly eight hours off the DC4 flight time.

But even though operating revenues improved by $6.8 million in 1952, expenses rose $8.4 million, so the profit squeeze worsened.

Adding insult to injury, Mother Nature went on a rampage that spring, when the Mississippi River overflowed its banks and completely flooded St. Paul's Holman field. In addition to indirect costs from interrupted service and damaged equipment, the battle against this flood took another $200,000 out of the NWA coffers.

In the midst of these problems, directors of Northwest and Capital Airlines made a preliminary agreement to merge into what, if consummated, would have given the consolidated firm the largest domestic route structure in the nation — 8,089 miles compared to United's 7,800 and American's 6,515.

"On paper, the merger looked good at first," says Malcolm S. Mackay, a long time Northwest director. "But we began to cool off because the more we studied the route structures and the different types of aircraft used by the two airlines, the more we began to feel Capital and Northwest were not compatible."

Local pride, and deep concern about Twin Cities jobs entered the picture too. Capital would have become the dominant survivor and it was considered an absolute certainty that headquarters of the consolidated airline would have been moved to the east.

Less than the required two-thirds of Northwest's shareholders approved the merger, and negotiations ended. Several years later Capital disappeared forever when it was absorbed by United Airlines, after Capital's big gamble on a fleet of short range Vickers Viscounts proved unsuccessful.

Northwest's problems multiplied in a "domino effect" as the months went by. Public confidence had been shaken, combination cargo-passenger flights did nothing to improve the airline's image, employee morale sagged, financial lenders were frankly dubious about the company's future, and competitors could better any planes Northwest had to offer except the Stratocruiser.

Not surprisingly, the deeply concerned Board of Directors did not see eye to eye on a solution to these problems. Everybody agreed economy was a must, with expenses growing faster than operating revenues. But beyond that, there was little unanimity, except an agreement that the lack of common stock dividends should be corrected as soon as possible.

Croil Hunter — deeply impressed by the businesslike record of Donald W. Nyrop, first as administrator of the C.A.A. and then as chairman of the C.A.B. — had approached Nyrop and urged him to accept the Northwest presidency. Albert G. Redpath, a long time Northwest director, said later: "Don told him he had a commitment to the C.A.B. and it wouldn't be right to leave it."

Redpath added, "We had a couple of dissidents in the east who wanted to take over board operations. They threatened a proxy fight, even hired an accountant to check the books, but everything was in order. Finally they got an executive committee appointed to find a new president."

"The Board hired Booz, Allen & Hamilton — at a $20,000 fee — to survey the field and recommend a man," explains Malcolm Mackay. "They finally narrowed 200 names down to 10, then to five, and eventually recommended General Harold R. Harris — formerly of the Army Transport Command and a vicepresident of Pan American Airways."

General Harris, as the selection of what one Board member (James H. Binger) wryly referred to as "the wise men from the east," took over as president and chief executive officer in January, 1953, with Croil Hunter becoming chairman of the board.

Mackay — whose fellow directors had pressed him into double service as executive vicepresident — met Harris at the airport, and was surprised to note the new president showed no interest in buying or renting a home or automobile, but simply moved into a suite at the posh Minneapolis Club. The reason became obvious later.

Harris — whose favorite saying was "we've all got to spend more time thinking" — instructed Mackay: "If you see me do anything wrong, be sure to come in and tell me."

After making a tour of the Orient Region, Harris signed a contract to buy six triple-tailed Super Constellations from Lockheed, and shortly thereafter announced executive offices of the airline would be transferred to New York City, occupying three floors of office space he had rented at 535 Fifth Avenue.

Rumors flew about the Twin Cities that Northwest's main overhaul base — one of the area's largest employers — would be the next to go, because Harris had appointed a committee to look into this possibility.

Mackay, reminding the general of his earlier request, told him: "I think you have just made a mistake."

Harris' only reply was a gruff "Thank you."

In the tumultuous weeks and months that followed, a rift grew between Harris and the directors — including those who had backed his hiring — because the Board insisted on economy, and Harris, as he told reporters, believed "you've got to spend money to make money."

A year after taking over, the general departed on a two month "leave of absence," after which his contract with Northwest was terminated. The directors persuaded Mackay to take charge until a new chief executive could be secured.

One Twin Citian deeply concerned by the

you meet such interesting people when you fly

NORTHWEST
AIRLINES

EXCLUSIVE STRATOCRUISER SERVICE COAST TO COAST AND TO ALAS

NEW YORK, WASHINGTON, PITTSBURGH, CLEVELAND, DETROIT, CHICAGO, MILWAUKEE, MINNEAPOLIS-ST. PAUL, WINNIPEG, SEATTLE-TA
EDMONTON, SPOKANE, PORTLAND...HAWAII...CANADA...ALASKA...JAPAN...KOREA...OKINAWA...FORMOSA...CHINA...PHILI!

FIRST MAGAZINE COLOR AD in 1952 used costumes to "telegraph" Northwest's many
destinations in the U.S., Canada, Hawaii, Alaska and the Orient.

FLOODS INUNDATED HOLMAN FIELD in St. Paul in 1952, adding to Northwest's already difficult operating problems after the 25 Martin 202s had been sold.

goings-on at Northwest was Lyman E. Wakefield, Jr., then with First National Bank of Minneapolis and president of the Minneapolis Chamber of Commerce.

"Everything was in a state of flux, and it looked as if things were headed in a radical direction," he recalls. "There was even talk of selling NWA's Orient route to Pan Am. The company had been going through a traumatic period, and Croil Hunter was at his wit's end.

Few in the Twin Cities financial community seemed to care what happened to the airline. Its stock had gone down to eight or nine dollars a share and — with no common share dividends — there weren't many takers.

"It was one of those 'bird in the hand' situations, because it made more sense to keep Northwest than to go looking for new industry, so when Joe Johnson of Milwaukee alerted me to a block of 40,000 shares that were available in

Boston, I formed a small group of purchasers to buy up those shares for about $350,000. We bought considerably more shortly afterward, because a few responsible investors sensed two opportunities — a chance to aid the community, and to make a worth while investment.

"A number of local people joined in buying stock because they agreed that keeping the airline here was vital to the Twin Cities."

Two of those local businessmen were Donald G. McNeely, now Chairman of Space Center, Inc., who was to be elected to Northwest's board some years later, and James H. Binger, then a vicepresident of Honeywell, Inc., and later president, a director and chairman of its executive committee.

Says Binger: "We didn't think of becoming directors then — simply looked on the stock purchase as an investment in our home town airline. But Lyman Wakefield was elected to the board at once."

"Shortly afterward," continues Wakefield, "Jim Binger also was added, and the balance of power began to swing back to the middle west."

"The real trigger of the situation occurred when Harris was fired by the men who were instrumental in hiring him. That shook up the financial community in the east."

John Bliven of New York's Bankers Trust Company — for more than two decades the lead bank in Northwest's equipment financing —said later: "there was deep concern then about Northwest in financial circles — it was a real confidence problem."

The next few months were anxious ones. In keeping with the board's economy program, employment rolls were cut from 5,709 to 4,900 by Mackay, working with Linus C. Glotzbach, personnel vice president, and William C. Eiden, Treasurer. Weekly meetings were held to go over finances and "count the cash" while the search for a president continued.

Several of his fellow directors urged Binger to accept the presidency, "but when it looked as if we had a chance to get Don Nyrop, that settled the matter," says Binger, "because he was so eminently qualified — a natural for the job."

"Croil Hunter had never given up on getting

BOATING TO WORK at the Northwest main base was par for the course in April, 1952, when the Mississippi River staged an uprising near downtown St. Paul.

Nyrop," added Albert Redpath, "and neither had Joe Johnson or I. We knew of George Gardner's high regard for him and of course his record spoke for itself."

Nyrop's roots, like those of Northwest Airlines, were in rural mid-America. Two 747s would just about carry the entire population of his native Elgin, Neb.

He had graduated from Doane College at Crete, Neb., during the Great Depression, taught school for a year, then worked days as an accountant in the nation's capital while earning his law degree by attending night classes at George Washington University (which years later named him to its board of trustees.)

In 1942, Nyrop became special assistant to the chairman of the C.A.B., then spent four years in the Air Transport Command, during which he rose to Lieutenant Colonel and was awarded the Legion of Merit. After the war he joined the Air Transport Association, but soon was called back to be deputy administrator of the C.A.A. In 1950, Harry Truman appointed him administrator. A year later, his effective no-nonsense record as an administrator brought him chairmanship of the C.A.B. at an unheard-of youthful 39.

"He was the only executive in Washington who made a crusade out of saving money for the taxpayer," reported a former C.A.A. official. One example: when Nyrop's research showed C.A.A. automobiles were driven less than 8,000 miles a year, he promptly sold 69 of them and canceled a predecessor's order for 25 new ones.

After two years as head of the C.A.B., Nyrop resigned to enter private law practice and "thought they wanted some legal work" when a committee of Northwest directors — Croil Hunter, Joseph T. Johnson and Frank Reavis of New York — called on him in mid-1954.

Nyrop, of course — with his C.A.A. and C.A.B. background — was fully aware of Northwest's equipment, management and financial dilemma. He asked for 60 days to study the pros and cons of leaving a highly successful law practice for an airline neck deep in problems. In a subsequent meeting with the Board — at which an earlier proposal to sell the Orient and Hawaiian routes (plus the Stratocruisers) was brought up — he made it clear he would have no interest in the presidency if such a sale were made.

His 60-day study convinced Nyrop that Northwest had a future as well as a past, and he also had a deep-seated feeling that the midwest was an ideal place to raise a family. So at the age of 42, Donald William Nyrop became the youngest president of a major air carrier in the United States when he took over the reins of Northwest Airlines September 27, 1954.

"There was no difficulty whatever in obtaining a unanimous vote of the Board," appends James Binger, "even though it was quite clear at the start that Don Nyrop was going to be his own man and operate as he felt necessary to get the job done."

Thus, even before he took office, the new president had contributed to an important accomplishment — his election marked the first time in many a moon that the Board had been unanimous about *anything*.

129

PART VI

Uphill Struggle
(1954-1976)

20

A Busy Year

WHEN BOYISH-LOOKING Donald W. Nyrop first strode into the old Northwest Airlines General Office at 1885 University Avenue in St. Paul — "early sod hut without air conditioning," as a long time veteran remembers the venerable G.O. — a rubbernecking employee whispered to one of his buddies:

"Looks as if they've sent us a boy to do a man's job."

He lived to eat those words.

No abrupt changes were noted by outsiders, because Nyrop is the kind of man who does his homework before acting. Unlike his predecessor, he did not take off on an immediate trip to the Orient, but buckled down to digging for facts, asking pointed questions, listening carefully to answers.

As soon as time permitted, the new president traveled the airline, station by station, meeting people, studying each installation intently.

"Later, when I made a trip with him," says Don Hardesty, "it was nothing short of amazing to see how many people he could call by name, and how much he remembered about each person — not only about the man's job, but how many kids he had in school, whose wife had just had an appendectomy, or whatever.

"I once read that the difference between a genius and an ordinary guy is that a genius has the ability to absorb intricate detail, and that's something Don Nyrop always did unbelievably well."

When department heads came in for their first budget sessions with the new president, they quickly discovered two facts: cost control was going to become a way of life at Northwest Airlines, and one of life's great virtues is *precision*.

While Hardesty was waiting his turn, another officer presented a budget covering 3,000 employees in all.

"Have you gone over all this material carefully?" asked Nyrop.

"Yes I have — I'm sure my figures are 99% correct."

"Does that mean there could be an error of 1% one way or the other?"

"Yes, I suppose so."

"Then if the budget is 1% high or 1% low, that could amount to a total fluctuation of 2%, and 2% of 3,000 employees would be 60 people. Why don't you go back over these figures and show me which 60 you intend to eliminate — then come back and see me."

Hardesty was next, and Nyrop asked: "How many people does your budget cover?"

"It covers 250 employees."

"All right. Two per cent of 250 is five, so if your budget is 1% high or low, that means you can take out five people."

"No," replied Hardesty, "four at the most, because if I've made a mistake, then the first name to come out would be mine."

"Do you mean you are willing to bet your job I can't take five people out of your department?"

"No, because anybody can take five people out of it, but according to my figures, we need every person covered by this budget."

Nyrop smiled, checked the figures carefully, then OK'd them. Hardesty picked up his papers and turned to leave.

"If you walk out that fast," chuckled Nyrop, "everybody will think I'm too easy. Sit down — let's have a cup of coffee."

DONALD W. NYROP began his 22-year presidency of Northwest Airlines in 1954.

The following year when Hardesty came in with his budget, Nyrop grinned: "Now are you going to be reasonable and discuss this, or are you going to get mad and threaten to quit again?"

Thus was a long and ideal working relationship born.

Over the years, the precision of Northwest's figures became legendary in the financial community.

"Their projections were always the most accurate in the industry," according to Roy Dye, retired vicepresident and senior loan officer of Bankers Trust Company.

"But to begin with, of course, Don Nyrop was not known to us. We checked on him thoroughly, and got nothing but fine reports. Even so, it was only normal prudence to go easy on loans until a new president could prove himself."

Nyrop's first discussion with the banks in New York didn't last very long. They were still concerned about Northwest's financial condition, so his No. 1 problem was to produce results that would justify borrowing additional capital for much needed new aircraft.

Directly related to this problem were several others:

1. The absence of common stock dividends had undermined investor confidence.

2. Never in its history had Northwest shown a first quarter profit, so warm weather destinations were a pressing need to ease the wintertime doldrums.

3. Northwest was still the only transcontinental line denied access to the high density traffic between Chicago and New York.

4. An improvement in the ratio of operating revenues to operating expenses was a "must."

5. As a foundation for future aircraft planning, NWA needed permanent certification of its routes to Honolulu and to the Orient.

134

The fleet at that time was a mongrel mixture of seven tired DC3s, 18 aging DC4s, the 10 gas-guzzling Stratocruisers and three DC6s — two of them leased.

While no abrupt changes had been noted on Nyrop's arrival, the airline hummed with activity as he established priorities and began tackling one key problem after another. A careful study had convinced him that the economics of the situation dictated increasing the fleet of DC6Bs and — as soon as it became practical — eliminating the Super Constellations that were on the way.

The DC6B — a reliable 260-mile-per-hour plane with a capacity of 64 to 76 passengers — was highly acceptable to the traveling public, and cost less per unit, so emphasis on this aircraft helped accomplish this twin need of economy and more up-to-date planes. It was too

DONALD H. HARDESTY, FORMER treasurer and financial vice president, also served on the Board of Directors.

late to cancel four of the Connies ordered by General Harris, so when these four arrived in early 1955 they were assigned to NWA's international flights, then later were sold at a profit to help build the growing fleet of Douglas aircraft.

Another important plus resulting from this action was that fewer *types* of aircraft enabled great savings through a reduction in spare engines and parts, as well as in personnel training and day-to-day maintenance costs. This was just one of the first in a long series of ways in which Northwest's management team has demonstrated the value of *standardization*.

One of Nyrop's first moves as president — before rapidly growing lender confidence enabled him to order aircraft in quantity — was to buy two DC6Bs from Mexicana airlines and, with another pair added shortly afterward, Northwest soon was flying seven of these much needed planes.

Another of his early actions was to officiate at a "mortgage burning." On April 1, 1953, General Harris had mortgaged the 10 Stratocruisers and 10 DC4s, putting them up as security on a $21,800,000 loan, $15 million of which was intended for the purchase of six Constellations. Twenty small metal plates that said "Mortgaged to Banker's Trust Co." were affixed to the bulkheads of the 20 aircraft. These plates came off for good when Northwest worked out a new credit agreement November 1, 1954, for $18 million on an unsecured bank credit to finance four Connies and the start of a DC6B fleet. By mid-1955, the credit limit was extended to $29½ million and in 1956 to $38½ million. (Turning the clock ahead for a moment, Northwest's line of credit had reached $350 million by 1972.)

Voluminous applications for 10 new domestic routes were filed in 1955, including service to Los Angeles, San Francisco and Miami.

In the meantime, Northwest worked out a way to participate in Florida travel on a limited basis by means of an interchange agreement with Eastern Air Lines. Under this plan, launched December 10, 1954, Stratocruisers made daily trips to Miami with Northwest crews handling the Twin Cities-Chicago segment and Eastern crews taking the plane on to Miami. This also permitted better utilization of Stratocruisers during NWA's slack winter season, with Eastern's Constellations replacing them in the summertime.

Another move that impressed the financial community came nine months after Nyrop's arrival, when directors were able to vote the first NWA common stock dividend (20¢ per share) since 1946. (Northwest has established an all-time industry record by continuing quarterly dividends without fail ever since, through good times and bad.)

Adding to the optimism generated in 1955 — the first year Northwest exceeded one *billion* passenger miles — was the electrifying news that after 16 years of trying, the airline had been granted approval for flights between Chicago and New York, including nonstops, Detroit stops and "turn around" or shuttle service between New York and Detroit.

Welcome though it was, the news came at a time when Northwest desperately needed more planes to serve this fiercely competitive route on which four airlines already were firmly entrenched — one of them offering flights every hour on the hour.

Another key Nyrop policy that was to contribute mightily to efficiency over the years involved *centralization* of effort wherever feasible. One of his early steps in this direction was to change from an eastern advertising agency to a Minneapolis firm "that can get out here in 15 minutes when we need them." The only real plus Northwest had to offer the public between Chicago and New York was the Stratocruiser — no other carrier flew this aircraft domestically — so he challenged his new agency to devise some novel ways to spotlight the Stratocruiser.

Out of this came the "Fujiyama Room," in which the plane's lower level lounge — formerly known to airline personnel as "the basement" —was transformed into a glamorous bit of the Orient, plus a series of unusual television commercials that quickly helped the sales force change Northwest from an unknown to a well known competitor on the Chicago-New York run.

An Oriental gong sound effect created for the TV commercials made them so memorable to the traveling public that the gong became a continuing *audio* symbol of the airline, just as the red tail had become a permanent *visual* trademark.

For a few anxious moments, however, the gong flirted with oblivion. Donald Nyrop is an unpretentious man who doesn't mind telling an occasional story on himself, and despite his canny judgment on other airline matters, claims he doesn't know much about advertising. Here's his recollection about the origin of the gong:

"It was a hot July day when the agency came over to the old G.O. on University Avenue and played four singing jingles, asking us to pick the one we liked best. I said I couldn't do it that way, so let's just eliminate one at a time, starting with the worst one.

"Things got awfully quiet when I said let's throw out that one with the gong, because that's the one the ad boys were counting on. After some discussion, I told them it doesn't cost any more to put that one on the air than any of the rest, so let's go ahead and use the gong for a few months and then evaluate results. In addition to doing a great job for us, the gong commercials won all kinds of awards. I guess a Gold Disc is still hanging on a wall at the Campbell-Mithun agency as a reminder that I'm no ad genius."

While Nyrop, like all successful men, is a strong personality, his agreement to permit a test of the gong idea demonstrated an important point — he did not close his mind to the deeply held beliefs of others if they were backed by logical reasons. In this case, he bought the reasoning that the gong was a unique attention-getting device which instantly emphasized the airline's stature as an international carrier.

In 1954, Northwest had been reducing its international mail subsidy payments from the

PRECEDENT-SETTING two page four color newspaper advertising helped kick off Northwest's long-awaited Chicago-New York authority in 1955. Checking the first ad proof, left to right, are Ken Ruble, then vicepresident of Campbell-Mithun advertising agency; President Donald W. Nyrop and James Mariner, NWA's Vice President-Sales at that time.

government faster than any other U.S. airline (to a total of $3,035,000 for the year) and on January 1, 1955, voluntarily became the first U.S. carrier to operate with no government subsidy on its transpacific and States-Alaska routes.

As Nyrop explained later, subsidy — like a cost-plus contract — undermines efficiency, and his insistence that Northwest should "stand on its own two feet" was not lost on the bankers whose loans were needed to update the fleet.

Elimination of subsidy was (and is) a boon for the U.S. taxpayer and — at least in theory — meant that an airline capable of operating without it should be a logical choice of the

powers-that-be when it came to awarding new routes. But the ways of Washington are sometimes hard to understand, and suddenly Northwest found itself faced by a serious threat to important routes the airline already served.

One of these involved service to Hawaii. While Northwest was still receiving a modest mail subsidy in late 1954, Nyrop offered to operate Northwest's Honolulu flights from Seattle and Portland *without* subsidy if Northwest were made the sole operator on that route.

The C.A.B. delightedly recommended approval of the offer by a unanimous vote. But President Eisenhower vetoed it, and then on February 21, 1955, announced he would ap-

Now... Northwest flies y[ou]
in world's largest airliner

Effective Sunday, Oct. 30

Roam its spacious double decks, relax in its fabulous new Fujiyama Room! Luxury that's yours only on NWA Stratocruisers!

Starting Sunday, Oct. 30, Northwest Orient Airlines offers you a memorable new experience in non-stop service to New York.

For the first time, *and only on NWA*, you can fly this route in the world's largest airliner, the Stratocruiser.

Already famed for its clubroom comfort, quiet flight, spacious double decks, the Northwest Orient Airlines Stratocruiser is now more luxurious than ever with its fabulous new Fujiyama Room symbolizing the other lands we serve beyond the Pacific.

When you step down the stairway from the main deck of the NWA Stratocruiser into the Fujiyama Room, you enter another world—tasting the charm of the Orient.

Here (or wherever you're seated), you will enjoy delicacies from our Fujiyama tray. Cocktail service, too, of course. At tea time, Oriental jasmine tea, if you wish. *And such meals*—juicy steaks, seafood ocean-fresh, salads crisp and cool as salads ought to be.

And before you leave, perhaps you'll accept a memento of the special experience that *only* an NWA Stratocruiser flight represents—regardless of how often you repeat it. And you will.

So don't delay *your* discovery of the Stratocruiser. Next time you're New York-bound, go Northwest Orient Airlines. And wherever you fly—coast to coast, Hawaii, Alaska, Canada, the Orient—call NWA. It's 1,923 miles shorter to the Far East!

NO EXTRA FARE: *One way, first class to New York, $45.10; round trip, only $85.70 (plus tax).*

You're a *special* guest when you fly Northwest!

NORTHWEST *Orient* AIRLINES

Ticket Offices: 100 So. Michigan Ave. and Conrad Hilton Hotel.
Evanston Ticket Office: 1649 Orrington Ave.   Phone: FINANCIAL 6-4900 or your Travel Agent

Step down into another world . . .   **. . . . into the fabulous**

on-stop to New York
e Stratocruiser

どうぞ富士山ルームで

Fujiyama Room

yama Room .... exclusive on NWA Stratocruiser fleet!

LONG SOUGHT CHICAGO-NEW YORK authority was kicked off October 30, 1955, with TV, radio and newspaper advertising featuring the newly created "Fujiyama Room."

prove renewal of Pan Am's certificate on the same route, but not Northwest's. This not only jerked the rug out from under NWA, but eliminated one-airline service to Honolulu for travelers all across the system.

Northwest's consternation was matched by that of governors, mayors, congressmen, senators and chambers of commerce by the dozen. Even the state legislatures of Minnesota and Wisconsin joined the outcry, adopting resolutions denouncing Ike's order.

It developed that presidential advisers had based their recommendations to him on erroneous information about subsidy receipts, and just as Minnesota's congressional delegation prepared to carry its objections directly to Eisenhower, he reversed his ruling and ordered the Pacific Northwest-Hawaii certificates of *both* airlines renewed for three years.

In a forthright statement, the President said: "Information came to my attention that convinced me I had been in error, so I tried to correct it as soon as possible."

Presumably the information included C.A.B. figures showing Pan Am had received twice as much Pacific mail subsidy as Northwest during the 12 months ending September 30, 1954, and that Northwest had offered to fly without subsidy as the sole carrier on its Hawaii route.

There was no time for Northwest to mourn the "half a loaf" it received when its offer was rejected, because an even more complicated "battle of Washington" was going on at the same time — a struggle that jeopardized its transpacific routes and dragged on into years of recommendations, decisions, reversals and re-reversals.

Before examining this strange chain of events, a look at figures from NWA's calendar year of 1955 shows this remarkable financial resurgence: the 1954 net operating income after taxes and before property disposals totaled $2,203,144, with the help of $3,035,000 in Pacific mail subsidy.

Nyrop's 1955 net was $2,027,319 with *no Pacific mail subsidy* whatever.

21

Transpacific Muddle

BACKGROUNDING the peacetime "war" over the Pacific were these facts: Pan American's long-held routes to the Orient from California via Hawaii consistently brought in about 75% of all transpacific revenue, while Northwest's Great Circle route accounted for the other 25%.

When Northwest requested a permanent certificate to replace its expiring seven-year authority, Pan Am filed for the right to duplicate NWA's North Pacific route and compete for the remaining 25%.

From then on, the struggle resembled a see-saw boxing match.

Round 1: December 15, 1954 — The C.A.B., after a careful study of Pacific traffic figures, recommended permanent certification for Northwest's Great Circle route and opposed the Pan Am request to duplicate it. The C.A.B. reasoned that available traffic did not justify two carriers, and that giving Pan Am duplicate authority would destroy any semblance of balanced competition in the Pacific. This report went to President Eisenhower. (All *international* route awards require presidential approval, because matters of foreign policy or national defense might be involved.)

Round 2: February 1, 1955 — Eisenhower disapproved permanent certification of NWA,

saying it was "premature as long as subsidy payments are necessary for its operations." (As in the Honolulu case, his advisers had their facts on backward — Pan Am was still receiving subsidy, Northwest was *not.*)

The President also set aside the C.A.B's rejection of a duplicate Great Circle route for Pan Am, and decided to "hold in abeyance" this request "pending further study."

Round 3: February 8, 1955 — In accordance with Eisenhower's direction, the C.A.B. re-issued 7-year temporary certificates for NWA's "outside" route (via Seattle and Portland) to Tokyo, 5-year certificates for Okinawa, Taiwan, Manila and Hong Kong (the latter still blocked by the British), plus 3-year rights to Korea.

Round 4: January 18, 1956 — The President directed the C.A.B. to reconsider the Pan Am Great Circle request "in the light of any new and relevant circumstances that it finds to exist." Thus, the transpacific Certificate Renewal Case was reopened once more.

Round 5: February 6, 1956 — Deciding that sauce for the goose was sauce for the gander, NWA filed a motion asking that the case be confined to Pan Am's request for a Great Circle route *from California,* or else that it be opened to three other issues:

(a) Allowing Northwest to fly the Great Circle to Japan *from Los Angeles and San Francisco.*

(b) Allowing Northwest to serve between *Honolulu and Tokyo.*

(c) *Permanent* certification of Northwest's current Orient routes.

Round 6: March 1, 1956 — The C.A.B. agreed only with the inclusion of Northwest's request to fly the California-Orient Great Circle, and to its request for consideration of permanent certificates on existing service to the Orient.

Round 7: March 3, 1956 — The President nullified the C.A.B.'s recommendation, ordering Northwest's motion to be denied, and confined the case solely to another hearing on the Pan Am application to compete on NWA's Pacific Northwest Great Circle to the Orient.

Round 8: May 3, 1957 — After extensive hearings, the C.A.B. again decided North Pacific traffic did not warrant the Pan Am duplication of Northwest's route, and unanimously recommended against it.

Round 9: August 2, 1957 — President Eisenhower approved the Board's findings, granted Northwest a *permanent* certificate on its Great Circle route to Japan (which it had operated for 10 years), but also awarded Pan Am a *permanent* certificate to fly the north Pacific from Los Angeles and San Francisco —a route it had not flown in the past.

Round 10: September 3, 1957 — At the risk of sounding like a broken record, it is necessary to report that the White House again reversed itself by directing the C.A.B. to "hold in abeyance" a final ruling on Pan Am's additional request for rights duplicating Northwest from Seattle-Portland over the Great Circle.

The chief reason given was that "there may have been substantial increases" in U.S.-Tokyo traffic (there had not — NWA passenger load factors remained at slightly over 50%). Northwest's rebuttal included these facts: (1) Pan American was still claiming $14,000,000 a year in subsidy (to zero for NWA); (2) Pan Am already was operating 13 weekly flights over three transpacific routes from four West Coast gateways (versus Northwest's seven weekly flights from the two smaller gateways), and (3) in the last year alone, Pan Am had been awarded more than 18,000 miles of new routes — more than Northwest's *total* domestic and internatonal system.

Obviously, a struggle of this magnitude is not conducted in a vacuum. Senators, congressmen, editors and columnists across the nation were concerned, too. Some of them seemed to feel the "chosen instrument" idea had begun to wriggle again. For example:

"Northwest Orient Airlines originally was given this (northern transpacific route to the Orient) at a time when Pan Am could have got it but didn't apply. Instead, it took what looked like the more lucrative route across the Pacific via Honolulu . . . Since last year's failure (to be authorized to fly Northwest's route) Pan Am has hired Ike's own nephew, plus the former assistant secretary of the Air Force, plus former Undersecretary of Commerce Murray, the man who intervened at the White House so effectively in favor of Pan American a year ago."
— Columnist Drew Pearson.

"I pay tribute to them (Northwest Orient Airlines) for getting off subsidy and for trying to reduce their costs and to make of themselves an enterprise which can stand on its own feet. Northwest Airlines deserves much credit . . . I only wish that some of the other airlines, which seem to enjoy great favors . . . could show a similar record."— Sen. Paul Douglas, Illinois.

"Both Northwest and the U.S. cities it serves have a right to ask just what goes on in Washington in this (transpacific) case . . . *If there is justification for 'competition' that Pan Am now chants, it is in Pan American's territory, not Northwest's.*"
— Wisconsin State Journal.

"Northwest carried the burden through the hectic days of pioneer operation, searching for

76-PASSENGER DC6B became the prime "work horse" in Donald Nyrop's early moves to improve the airline's severe shortage of up-to-date equipment.

the business that would make it pay for itself and convincing shippers and travelers that the northern route was safe, feasible and comfortable.

"It is only because the northern route has proven to be what Northwest, and Alaskans, claimed it to be that Pan American now wants in." — Anchorage Daily Times.

"In view of its (Northwest's) difficult job pioneering the short route to Tokyo by way of the Aleutians, this (no Federal subsidy since 1954) is a major accomplishment. The line now is established so successfully, in fact, that another airline which received heavy U.S. subsidy last year wants a chance at the route." — Cleveland Press.

"The central Pacific route carries about three times as much business for Pan American as does the north Pacific route for Northwest. *It surely isn't fair to require competition on the less important run and to allow no competition on the more lucrative route."* — The Minneapolis Star

Round 11: December 16, 1957 — A unanimous C.A.B. opinion informed President Eisenhower its studies showed no significant change in the Pacific traffic pattern — approximately 75% carried by Pan Am, 25% by NWA — and recommended no duplication of the Northwest routes from Seattle-Portland.

(By congressional action, Northwest's "inside route" via Edmonton was made permanent in 1957.)

Round 12: February 4, 1958 — The President approved the C.A.B.'s recommendation that Pan Am be denied North Pacific traffic rights out of Portland and Seattle, but requested the Board to furnish him Pacific traffic statistics for the full year of 1958.

Round 13: January 18, 1959 — The C.A.B. reported to the President that 1958 showed no significant changes. Its figures showed a slight *reduction* in overall Pacific traffic, so the Board saw no need to revive the question of additional Pacific authority.

The President, however, requested the Board to "immediately initiate a proceeding consolidating all Pacific route matters into a single record" and to "present its recommendations to me at the earliest possible moment."

Round 14: January 19, 1961 — *All* airline applications for new routes in the Pacific (including NWA's request for a Central Pacific route from Los Angeles and San Francisco, as well as Pan Am's application for authority from Portland and Seattle) were denied by President Eisenhower. At the same time, Northwest's certificates to serve Korea, Okinawa, Taiwan, the Philippines and Hong Kong (the latter *still* not concurred in by the British at that time) were made permanent.

Summing up: at this stage, Northwest finally had permanent authority over the same Pacific routes it had been flying since 1947, while Pan Am had been granted a *new* permanent Great Circle certificate from Los Angeles and San Francisco in addition to its long held (since 1935) mid-Pacific routes from Los Angeles and San Francisco via Hawaii.

But this was not the end. More rounds were to come, as we will see in later chapters of this book.

Northwest's one cause for satisfaction at this stage of events was that *all* of its routes now were permanently certified, while only 21% of the route miles had been under permanent authority six years earlier.

Centralizing in Earnest

TWO IMPORTANT DECISIONS involving geography — one right at home and the other nearly 4,000 miles away — faced Northwest in the mid 1950s.

While the airline was "between presidents" in early 1954, the United States government closed its Army base on Shemya — far out the foggy Aleutian chain — and removed all G.C.A. (Ground Controlled Approach) equipment, along with its weather station and trained personnel.

As a result, Northwest had discontinued using Shemya as a refueling base for transpacific flights and moved its fuel stop 900 miles toward the mainland where G.C.A. and weather services were available at Cold Bay, Alaska.

Adding 900 miles to each over-water flight segment meant a large increase in fuel requirements for these nonstops, and a corresponding decrease of nearly 40% in the pay load that could be carried in either direction between Cold Bay and Tokyo. After studying the logistics of this problem, Donald Nyrop decided on a bold move that saw Northwest become the only U.S. airline to purchase a G.C.A. unit and operate its own airport, when he leased Shemya from the government and reopened it with NWA personnel.

At the beginning of 1956, this $225,000 investment enabled Northwest to balance its payloads across the Pacific and to put these intercontinental flights in the black once more.

Another key geographical decision of the Fifties involved the entire Twin Cities area, as well as NWA. The airline had outgrown its facilities at St. Paul's Holman field, and recurring spring floods added to operational problems at that location, so a new maintenance and overhaul base was a must. Several cities — notably Chicago and Seattle — coveted the Northwest payroll and made a determined effort to lure the airline away from its traditional home area.

After long and careful evaluation of the various alternatives, NWA adopted a history-making plan that included far more than a new maintenance and overhaul base, and made Northwest the only major airline in the United States to centralize its total operation — General Office, maintenance and overhaul facilities, communications, flight operations and all related services — under one roof. The locale chosen was Wold-Chamberlain airport, where the airline had launched its career 30 years earlier.

Twin Cities officials breathed a sigh of relief at

the news, because this meant retaining an annual Minnesota payroll of $16,600,000 (which had grown to more than $336 million by 1985, not to mention another $323 million spent annually in Minnesota by Northwest for supplies, services and taxes for a grand total of $685 million.) And the figure grows every year.

Paving the way for this move toward an integrated operation that enhanced efficiency and reduced costs was an agreement reached with the Metropolitan Airports Commission under which the M.A.C. issued bonds to finance the $17.5 million base, with Northwest paying off the entire cost by retiring these bonds over a 30-year period.

The new system headquarters became the largest single building in total floor space (1,114,307 square feet) and the costliest structure ever built in the Upper Midwest up to that time, not counting millions of additional dollars invested in new equipment. (Originally budgeted at $15 million — with considerably less floor space — plans for the combination headquarters were enlarged, with a revised price of $18 million. Construction was brought in $500,000 under budget.)

"Sentimentally, we wanted to choose the Twin Cities for this giant project," said Nyrop's announcement, "for here is where Northwest was born 30 years ago. But no business decision can be based on sentiment alone. With the welfare of so many people involved, it took time

PRESIDENT DONALD W. NYROP receives lei at Hawaiian-themed affair celebrating Northwest's 30th birthday in 1956. Next in line are Byron Webster, the airline's first passenger; Dan A. Williams, president of the St. Paul Area Chamber of Commerce, and Croil Hunter, NWA chairman.

146

and study to decide whether to expand here or in one of the several other cities which made a strong case for selection of their sites.

"We're pleased — and we hope you'll be too — that facts, sentiment and a sense of responsibility to our employees and the public here in our home neighborhood, all pointed to the same final decision. Three of the principal reasons for the decision were these:

ONE — Our faith in the Twin Cities' future as a hub of world air commerce.

TWO — Our responsibility to our Twin Cities employees, now numbering 2,933 with a payroll of some $16,600,000 a year — including 1,000 at our present St. Paul overhaul base with a payroll of about $5,500,000 a year.

THREE — The knowledge that we would inevitably lose many of our key personnel by moving — and that we could not readily rebuild a corps of experienced employees as capable as the men and women for which this area is nationally known.

"Northwest has always been proud to call the Twin Cities 'home' for the entire 30 years of our steady growth. The new base emphasizes Northwest's determination to continue as a partner in the development of this community as one of the world's major air centers."

While Northwest engineers studied the pluses and minuses of other airline facilities across the country, a scientific work measurement program was launched at Holman Field base. These "time studies" were aimed at preparing for the best possible utilization of manpower, equipment and floor layout before blueprints of the new base were finalized.

Seven employees, chosen from 65 volunteers, carried out many studies with the aid of stop watches, measuring group work output — rather than individual output — to help in planning for a smooth and continuous production level at the new headquarters then on the drawing boards. Crew chiefs, mechanics and shop superintendents were consulted frequently, to make sure no practical considerations were overlooked in arriving at a workable floor plan.

Nearly four years were to elapse before maintenance and overhaul facilities of the novel base were ready for occupancy, because construction was delayed until the M.A.C. resolved several legal obstacles to the expansion of Wold-Chamberlain field. The attached General Office — finished a year later — was a departure from conventional design, air conditioned and sound-proofed against airport distractions with the aid of a windowless exterior.

In addition to work measurement studies that helped organize the new headquarters layout, President Nyrop also made use of scientific techniques to help him get better acquainted with the abilities of his own executive personnel, in order that — as a comparative newcomer — he could evaluate them better when considering promotions.

A number of middle management men went "back to college" for aptitude and IQ tests at the University of Minnesota — a fact which so impressed Roy Dye of Bankers Trust Company that for years he cited these tests as an example of the airline's businesslike approach back in the days when such management guidance tools were the exception rather than the rule.

By the start of its 30th anniversary year (1956) Northwest employment had risen to 5,452 — an increase of 552 since the depths of the post-war slump — and the employee suggestion plan had paid out $10,000 to 303 employees for ideas that resulted in savings of $183,000.

Shortly afterward, two men — Christian Lorsung and Ernest A. Jorgensen — split the highest suggestion award ever made up to that time when they received $12,000 for a mechanical improvement that reduced the maintenance work required on Stratocruiser engine cases.

Unfortunately, before their improvement could be applied to one of the airline's 10 Stratocruisers — named the "City of Tokyo" — this plane wound up in Puget Sound when, after a skillful ditching in which Northwest personnel used a life raft aboard to rescue 32 passengers and crew, the plane sank in 96 feet of water.

As vice president of operations and engineering, Frank Judd felt he could not ask his subordinates to tackle any job he wouldn't do himself, so he rented a deep sea diving suit and a tugboat, then descended to the sunken aircraft and determined that an open cowl flap had caused the severe buffeting which led to the ditching.

As he was hauled back to the deck of the tug, its captain handed Judd a ship-to-shore phone, saying: "Mr. Nyrop's calling you from the Twin Cities."

After Judd had reported on the cowl flap discovery, carefully omitting any mention of his personal underwater inspection trip, Nyrop commented drily: "By the way, I understand you've been fishing."

"Why, er, no, not exactly," stammered Judd.

"Just remember this," rejoined Nyrop, "I can't have any of my vice presidents risking their lives on the bottom of Puget Sound. There are too many important things to be done elsewhere."

Years later, at Judd's retirement party, both men led the assembly's gales of laughter when Frank was presented with a giant cartoon which depicted Judd in a diver's suit, just coming up from the briny deep, and Nyrop in a rowboat, shaking his finger at the underwater explorer.

By the time Northwest was preparing a special observance of its thirtieth birthday in the fall of 1956 — the same year actress Grace Kelly became Princess of Monaco and Eisenhower was re-elected president — the airline had

NORTHWEST'S THIRTIETH ANNIVERSARY in 1956 was highlighted by this crew's coast-to-coast goodwill tour in a rejuvenated Ford Tri-motor. Left to right, Walt Kollath, mechanic; Captains Deke DeLong and Joe Kimm, and Coral Yahr, cabin attendant. Their itinerary began in New York and ended in Seattle after visiting an even dozen cities on the way.

committed $52 million for DC6B and DC7C equipment, with another $37 million ticketed for the purchase of jet aircraft in the early Sixties. (An order for 21 jet engines was placed in advance. This assured a better delivery schedule when decisions were finalized on which type of aircraft was to be purchased, and it also meant a considerable saving on price.)

While needs of the coming jet age were being studied, the highlight of Northwest's birthday celebraton was a nostalgic coast-to-coast odys-sey featuring one of the famous "tin goose" Ford Tri-motors which the airline had flown a quarter century earlier.

The last Tri-motor had been sold off in 1934, so it took a bit of detective work to locate one of the original brood — old No. 8419 — which had spent part of the intervening years with Wien Alaska Airlines, and then wound up carrying "smoke jumpers" in anti-forest-fire patrols operated by the Johnson Flying Service of Missoula, Mont.

REPRESENTING EXOTIC DESTINATIONS served by Northwest, these cabin attendants took part in ceremonies launching the Ford Tri-motor's thirtieth anniversary odyssey. From the left, Coral Yahr, U.S.; Lulu Pedrosa, the Philippines; Alberta Chow, Hong Kong; Marilyn Atwood, Alaska; Tokiko Yosa, Okinawa; Irene Wang, Taiwan; Alicia Kawaza, Japan; Kym Choi, Korea, and Leolani Blaisdell, Hawaii. All nine also were featured on TV broadcasts from New York.

The old girl proved to be just as reliable as ever during her east to west itinerary, and attracted huge crowds and reams of publicity in New York, Washington, Pittsburgh, Cleveland, Detroit, Milwaukee, Chicago, Madison, the Twin Cities, Rochester, Minn., Spokane, Yakima, Portland and Seattle.

Captain Leon S. "Deke" DeLong — then Northwest's senior pilot — who had flown the first night mail plane from the Twin Cities to Chicago in 1929, was named skipper for the cross country flight, with Joe Kimm as co-pilot, Coral Yahr as stewardess and Walt Kollath traveling along as mechanic. Walt reported later: "All I did was gas and oil her — she performed perfectly at 200 feet or 10,000. The old tin goose had a wonderful temperament."

The transcontinental tour was kicked off with a big civic event at the New York airport, covered by a host of television and newspaper cameramen who were amazed at the Tri-motor's ability to take off after an unbelievably short run and climb like the proverbial homesick angel.

Prior to takeoff, DeLong, Kimm, and eight young flight attendants dressed in their costumes of the many lands served by Northwest — plus executive vice president Malcolm S. Mackay — were featured by Arthur Godfrey as guests on his national network TV and radio program "Arthur Godfrey Time."

Godfrey was so enchanted with his guests and the story of Northwest's 30 years that he devoted more than 45 minutes of his one hour show to the airline's anniversary.

One of the biggest chuckles of the day resulted from this conversation between Godfrey and "Deke" DeLong:

"As senior pilot, what route are you flying for Northwest now?" asked Godfrey.

DeLong replied: "Just the daily hop from Minneapolis-St. Paul to Winnipeg and back again."

"There must be something pretty good about that route if the senior pilot flies it when he could have his choice of glamorous destinations all the way to Hawaii and the many colorful wonders of the Orient," suggested his interviewer.

"There sure is," laughed DeLong. "I leave at eight in the morning, have an hour off for lunch, return at four and sleep in my own bed every night."

In Detroit, where the ancient Tri-motor made one of its cross country stops, an unusual problem had seriously hampered sales efforts by the start of the thirtieth anniversary year when — through an unaccountable oversight — the telephone company failed to list Northwest's number in the yellow pages.

To complicate matters, a local newspaper strike made it impossible to feature the phone number in printed advertising, so District Sales Manager Robert J. Wright — later to become the airline's vice president-sales — asked the telephone company to put a sticker on its bills, informing subscribers about the missing number. The request was denied.

In the absence of newspaper advertising, a competing airline had tried radio, but gave up when sales didn't improve one iota. This did not discourage Wright.

"See if you can come up with something just a little bit different," he suggested to NWA's advertising representatives. "The important thing is to make sure people know what our phone number is."

The number was Woodward 3-3500, and after a lengthy brainstorming session, it developed that WO 33500 could be dialed by spelling out the word "yodel," plus two zeros.

This suggested the "something different" Wright was seeking. A professional country western yodeler was hired to sing the opening and closing of a series of spot radio commercials, presenting messages like this:

(Singer: yodels "YODEL-ZERO-ZERO")

Announcer: There's a handy new way to remember the telephone number of Northwest Orient Airlines — route of the Stratocruiser fleet. Just dial the word "Yodel" followed by two zeros — like this —

(Singer: yodels "Yodel Zero-Zero.")

150

ENTERTAINER ARTHUR GODFREY devoted 45 minutes of his network TV-radio simulcast to Northwest's thirtieth birthday, interviewing the Tri-motor's crew and flight attendants from the airline's overseas destinations. Here Godfrey greets Captains DeLong and Kimm as Malcolm Mackay, representing the Board of Directors, waits his turn.

and when you yodel for Northwest Orient Airlines, you're set to fly east or west; coast to coast, Canada, Alaska, Hawaii or the Orient. Northwest features double-decked Stratocruisers — world's largest airliners. For your special pleasure, the lower deck of each Stratocruiser has been transformed into a glamorous Fujiyama Room, symbolizing the lands we serve across the Pacific. You're a special guest when you fly Northwest, so yodel for Northwest Airlines. Just dial Yodel-zero-zero."

Other commercials in the series featured specific flights to key destinations — New York, Chicago, Washington, Seattle and the Twin Cities.

Demonstrating that the *way* an advertising medium is used often has more to do with success than the medium itself, the "yodel" radio campaign in Detroit — corny though it may

have appeared — stirred up so much action that frequently the Woodward exchange was jammed, much to the displeasure of the telephone company.

Many of the calls represented amused curiosity on the part of the public, of course, but many others meant business.

Sales improved almost immediately, and even with 20% fewer seats available out of Detroit than were offered one year earlier, business showed a 10% gain during the first month of "Yodel Zero Zero," versus a comparable period the previous year.

One sales agent commented at the time: "The phones rang right off the wall, and that's the name of the game."

As Northwest moved into 1957 — the year Russia launched the world's first man-made satellite (Sputnik I) and Ford produced the

151

SEATTLE WELCOMERS braved a rainy day to salute Northwest's Tri-motor crew at the end of their nostalgic cross-country journey. Note "big brother" Stratocruiser at right.

Edsel — great strides were being made to alleviate the equipment problem that had plagued the airline for six years. Seven more DC6Bs and eight of an eventual 17 DC7Cs were placed in service, and by February Northwest became the only airline using pressurized aircraft on all flights to — and through — the Orient.

Radar had been added to every unit of the fleet, bringing more reliable operation during all weather conditions, and nonstop transcontinental service began from New York to Seattle and Portland in the DC-7C — longest range aircraft yet owned by NWA — with a cruising speed of 322 m.p.h. and a passenger complement of up to 82 persons.

On flights with dual configuration, first class passengers rode in the rear of the 7C rather than at the front.

The airline made a major step forward in the care and feeding of passengers in the spring of 1957 by launching "Imperial Service" on most first class flights, featuring complimentary champagne, reserved seating, superb food, and a "Fujiyama tray" of exotic snacks, which had been introduced originally in the Fujiyama Lounge of the New York-Chicago-Seattle Stratocruisers two years earlier. Faster ticketing and check-in procedures also added to passenger satisfaction.

In mid-year, shippers were pleased to note a resumption of coast-to-coast all-freighter service, for the first time since a shortage of aircraft had forced discontinuance of these cargo flights in 1950.

Despite substantial increases in passengers and revenues, all United States airlines experienced tough going in 1957 because of rising costs. The *combined* net profit of all 12 major domestic trunk carriers fell from $57.7 million to $25 million that year.

Northwest's operating expenses rose, too, with the inevitable extra drain caused by introducing new aircraft, but a system-wide cost control program helped cut expenses to 27.43¢ per available ton mile, and enabled Northwest to move against the industry trend by posting a net profit of $4.8 million.

newest members of the

GREAT NORTHWEST FLEET

Some already here! More on the way! In all, 24 magnificent, new DC-7C's and world-proven DC-6B's are joining Northwest Orient Airlines to give you the most modern, dependable fleet in the skies.

For the first time (and only on Northwest) you'll be able to fly luxurious DC-7C's—America's fastest, finest, long-range airliners—coast-to-coast.

And wherever you fly on Northwest's 18,000 miles of routes, you'll fly smoother, faster and with more assurance than ever. For all Northwest's new planes are equipped with all-weather radar. All have Northwest's amazing, new integrated instrument system that makes perfect instrument landings almost automatic under all conditions.

If you are planning a trip anywhere coast-to-coast, to Hawaii, Canada, Alaska or the Orient, fly the modern fleet. Fly Northwest. Call Northwest Orient Airlines or your travel agent now.

31 years of superior Airmanship **NORTHWEST** *Orient* **AIRLINES**

COAST-TO-COAST · HAWAII · CANADA · ALASKA · THE ORIENT

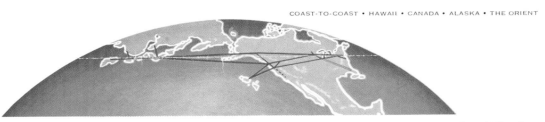

GROWING FLEET of up-to-date Northwest planes was highlighted in this 1957 advertisement featuring the addition of 24 DC7Cs — then "America's fastest, finest long range airliners." 153

23

Sunshine and the Jet Age

AS NORTHWEST CONTINUED its resolute climb toward the triple goal of better aircraft, better service and more profitability, Florida played an important role in the events of 1958.

After a C.A.B. examiner recommended against the airline's renewed application for its long sought Florida route, NWA countered with figures supporting its contention that he had failed to consider the needs of 90,000 air travelers who journeyed annually to Tampa and Miami from points on Northwest's system west of Chicago.

In addition to denying these passengers through-plane service to the "sunshine state," the examiner's recommendation would have deprived Florida residents of one-carrier service to important domestic cities west and north of Chicago, as well as to Hawaii, Alaska and the Orient.

Senators, congressmen and civic leaders of five states supported these arguments before the C.A.B. which — after a re-study of the case — finally awarded Northwest a Chicago-Miami route (nonstop and via Atlanta and/or Tampa). A few months later, Florida service from the Twin Cities and Milwaukee, either direct or via Atlanta, also was approved.

As we've noted before, quite frequently "the

Board giveth, and the Board taketh away." This proved true once again when the C.A.B. also announced two other airlines would be allowed to compete with Northwest on its long time bread-and-butter segment between the Twin Cities, Milwaukee and Chicago.

Delta and Eastern were firmly entrenched in the Chicago-Miami market, and before Northwest could inaugurate service on that route, Eastern petitioned a Federal Court to delay NWA's scheduled December 1 inaugural.

On December 4, the court ruled in Northwest's favor, and just two days later a Stratocruiser took off from the Twin Cities in three below zero temperatures, landing at Miami International Airport on a balmy 80-degree day to launch a north-south service NWA had needed since its founding 32 years earlier.

Competing with two established Florida carriers on this route posed a major challenge to Northwest's sales personnel if they were to achieve their hoped-for goal of balancing the airline's year-round traffic pattern.

As a first step, two new District Sales headquarters were set up, with four offices established in the Miami area and others opened to serve Tampa and its sister cities of St. Petersburg and Clearwater. Next, the "product" was improved.

With comfortable Stratocruisers chosen to launch Florida service, special blue-carpeted check-in areas were created, music was played over the Stratocruiser's loud speaker system before takeoff, all seats were reserved, copies of the Wall Street Journal were placed aboard for business-minded travelers and in-flight telephone service was offered to those who wished it. (Remember — this was in 1958.)

The airline's food service people got into the act, too, pampering their north-south clientele with coffee and Scandinavian delicacies shortly after takeoff, followed by beverage service, hot or cold Oriental style oshibori towels, curried shrimp and other hot hors d'oeuvres, lobster cocktail, salad, consomme, choice prime beef, champagne, after-dinner beverages and exotic desserts. (North-bound passengers were offered lime coolers instead of coffee.)

Once again, "something new" was needed to help gain the public's attention and make these Florida-bound pluses known to the traveling public. Famed pantominist Buster Keaton was enlisted for the job, starring in a series of hilarious television commercials that established a new high in the *effective* use of humor.

As viewers know, TV commercials that get laughs are often guilty of obscuring advertising messages in the process. The Keaton spots avoided this problem because their humor was built *directly into* the key objective — spreading the news of Northwest's new service to Florida — and *always* involved the Oriental gong that had become NWA's audio "signature."

For example: when seven huge letters spelling

NEW FLORIDA DESTINATIONS in 1958 were given a rousing sendoff by Buster Keaton's TV antics which were so successful that they launched the veteran comedian on a new career.

155

"FLORIDA" — suspended individually from above — hung unevenly, frozen-faced Keaton pulled down two of the letters in an attempt to straighten things up, whereupon another pair of letters rose simultaneously.

His frantic efforts to correct this added to the fun, and drove home NWA's new destination. When Buster whammed a large Oriental gong at the end of each commercial — breaking his mallet in the process — every listener in town knew that Northwest Orient Airlines had started flying to Florida.

Northwest's total sales effort surprised bystanders and shocked competitors when the airline captured 38% of the business from Chicago to Florida in the first three months of operation — just about double the expectation of impartial observers.

Atlanta service was launched September 27, 1959, on the Florida route, and flights to Ft. Lauderdale were added January 1, 1960.

Considerably north of Florida, two more rulings affecting Northwest were handed down by the C.A.B. in 1958, with good news outweighing the bad.

Previous restrictions on the airline's service between Detroit, Cleveland, Pittsburgh and Washington, D.C., were eliminated, allowing NWA to add immediate shuttle flights between Detroit and Washington. Another route case — in which federally subsidized local carriers had sought to take over several of Northwest's Montana destinations — was concluded with a decision allowing NWA to retain six of its seven cities in that state. Service to Kalispell, however, was ordered suspended.

The end of another aircraft era was reached in the fall of 1958 when Northwest sold its last five DC3s, thus becoming the only major domestic airline to operate solely with four-engine equipment. With the sale of these twin engine planes, Northwest's fleet consisted of nine Stratocruisers, 14 DC7Cs, 20 DC6Bs, and 11 DC4s. Several of the latter were assigned strictly to cargo, with the other DC4s primarily serving cities whose airports were not yet able to handle larger equipment such as the DC6B.

Departure of the DC3s — much as they had contributed to the airline's career in their heyday — was cause for celebration, because it demonstrated Northwest had conquered the worst of its once seemingly insurmountable equipment problem, and was achieving the kind of financial results that promised still better days ahead.

Record revenues of $102 million in 1958 were 22% ahead of the previous year. More than a billion passenger miles had been flown domestically, with another 298 million revenue passenger miles on international routes, and the company-wide cost control program — which reduced expenses per available ton mile by 6¢, to a new low of 25.8¢ — was of key importance in setting a record net income of $5.6 million.

This continued good showing helped Northwest negotiate the financial arrangements critically needed to get ready for the hotly competitive jet age that was just around the corner, when an $83.5 million "package" was put together at the close of 1958.

Of this total, a $32.5 million credit was pledged by 15 on-line banks, $40 million was to be loaned by 12 insurance companies, and $11.5 million was obtained by selling 457,873 shares of preferred stock. Still another $10,231,000 was to be realized through trade-in of nine Stratocruisers and five DC7Cs when the new jet age equipment went into service.

The ability to negotiate a *predetermined* price on trade-ins to be made a year or more in the future was considered a real coup, because it made possible a precise completion of the airline's financing program, with no loose ends to be coped with later. (There's that word again — "precise.")

Part of the money raised in the new financing program was used to retire remaining debt on previously purchased DC6Bs and DC7Cs, while $67 million was committed to the purchase of five Douglas DC8 pure jets ($5,780,000 each) and an initial 10 turboprop Lockheed 188 Electras ($2,400,000 each), with the remaining $14,100,000 going for spare engines and parts.

By taking its time during a long and careful evaluation of new aircraft on the way, Northwest was able to order advanced-design, long range versions of the DC8 and L188 Electra, with superior performance over standard models of these two planes — a policy that became Nyrop's trademark over the years, contributing to safer, more efficient operation and better payloads.

This careful approach to the jet age made sense, because in the postwar period alone, the cost of an average plane *per passenger seat* had risen from $11,000 for the DC4 to $17,000 for the DC6, $24,000 for the DC7 and now approximately $45,000 for the DC8 jet.

The L188 Electra, often referred to as a "jet prop" because its propellers were driven by Allison gas turbine engines (rather than by reciprocating piston engines) was an efficient 400-mile-an-hour workhorse capable of carrying 77 passengers in the same kind of comfort offered by the slower Stratocruiser. Its standard fuel capacity of 5,360 gallons was increased by approximately 20% in the models ordered by Northwest, giving this plane easy transcontinental nonstop range.

The DC8s, ticketed for transocean nonstops to and from the Orient, carried up to 139 passengers, cruised at 550 miles per hour, and the custom-built fuel tanks holding 23,307 gallons gave Northwest's version of this aircraft nearly 25% more capacity than normal, with a full payload range of 4,385 miles. NWA also ordered the largest, most powerful jet engine then available, JT4A-9 (rather than the military J-75) which developed a 16,800-pound thrust for improved takeoff and load-carrying performance.

Electras were to begin arriving in mid-1959, with the first DC8 due by March, 1960, so a massive transitional job was begun at once to prepare for the task of carrying nearly twice as many passengers to their destinations in virtually half the time.

With completely new types of engines and air frames to service, many aspects of this preparatory work were like starting an airline from scratch. Approximately $11 million — over and above the cost of newly ordered planes and spare parts — was budgeted to get ready for the jet age.

The personnel training cost alone was estimated at $2,750,000, primarily involving flight crews, mechanics, engineers, equipment servicemen, meteorologists and flight dispatchers. Even the airline's regular instructors had to go to school before they could teach others. Another $4,830,000 went for tools and specially designed equipment needed to overhaul and maintain the new aircraft, with $2,100,000 invested in additional ramp servicing needs.

Because of its size, the DC8 required its own special passenger loading steps at every airport on its route ($10,000 apiece), not to mention mobile ground power units ($15,000 each) and jet engine starters at $18,000 per unit.

Both the DC8 and the L188 Electra operated on kerosene-type fuel rather than high octane gasoline — and at much higher rates of consumption than piston engine planes — so an entirely new fuel storage and distribution setup was added, including a number of underground tanks, trucks, and pipefield systems, at the cost of another $700,000.

So it went, as the entire airline buckled down to the job of maintaining present service while preparing for a whole new ballgame.

On January 1, 1959, the Civil Aeronautics Administration passed into history when its supervision of U.S. civil aviation was taken over by the newly created Federal Aviation Agency (F.A.A.) This was the same year Fidel Castro became dictator of Cuba, Charles DeGaulle took office as president of France, the St. Lawrence Seaway was opened (bringing seagoing traffic as far inland as Duluth, Minn.) and both Alaska and Hawaii achieved statehood.

Northwest's new L188 Electras began arriving by mid-summer that year, and in September — the first full month of passenger service — the initial three Electras, offering both first class and coach accommodations, racked up an astounding 82.67% load factor.

CAPTAIN PAUL SODERLIND, left, and Captain Ralph Render check out the cockpit of Northwest's first L-188 "Jet Prop" Electra in 1959. As Director of Flight Standards, Soderlind received the only gold medal citation for "extraordinary service to the airline industry" given by the F.A.A. to anyone outside its own ranks. (More about this award in Chapter 24.)

This heartening public acceptance was accomplished on highly competitive routes — New York-Seattle nonstops, New York-Twin Cities and Chicago-Twin Cities. Before year's end, all 10 L188 Electras were in service, and eight more were ordered, at an additional expenditure of $22,668,000, as the airline surged past the two-million mark in passengers for the first time in history, while a growing number of all-freighter schedules helped show a 42% increase in cargo revenues.

Despite the added expenses that always accompany introduction of new aircraft — long considered an almost inevitable harbinger of red ink — 1959s operation showed a record net profit of $5.7 million.

Nagoya, one of Japan's largest cities — population 2 million — was devastated by typhoon "Vera" in the fall of 1959. Torrential rains, tidal waves and 135-mile-an-hour winds left 5,000 dead, 15,000 injured and more than a million persons homeless. A Northwest Airlines DC6B loaded with tons of emergency supplies was the first relief plane to reach the stricken city, and NWA donated services of another plane to bring 5,000 pounds of clothing and medicines from the United States to Nagoya's storm victims, as a gesture of good will to the Japanese people.

Another Orient event also made headlines a few months later, in one of aviation's more remarkable demonstrations of the importance of well trained personnel.

A Northwest DC7C — en route from Okinawa to Manila with 51 passengers and seven crew members aboard — radioed that a runway propeller had started a magnesium fire which could not be brought under control. The captain — David G. Rall — reported he was forced to make a night-time ditching during a rainstorm and while flying under instrument conditions.

Thanks to the well-disciplined crew's directions in preparing everyone — including a group of retired school teachers — for the ditching, the water landing went off without a hitch and every person aboard was out of the aircraft within five minutes.

The plane's position — 67 miles from Manila — was radioed before the landing, and four hours after everyone had been collected in life rafts, the first of two rescue aircraft — a U.S. Coast Guard amphibian — arrived, followed by a naval rescue plane. One woman passenger did not survive the ordeal, but the others were so vociferous in their praise of the crew's courage and skill that flight attendant Yuriko Fuchigami of Tokyo was awarded the Imperial Order of the Sacred Crown, eighth class, by the Japanese government. She was the first living person to receive this rare medal.

"I only did what I was trained to do," said Yuriko in accepting the honor.

This final paragraph of the C.A.B.'s voluminous report on the ditching is of interest because it demonstrates a standard policy of Northwest in going beyond *required* precautions when it comes to ways of looking out for the welfare of passengers:

"It was noted that the illumination by a one-cell flashlight permanently attached to the life vests of survivors materially aided occupants of the life rafts in locating survivors in the sea during hours of darkness.

"Although Northwest Airlines had life vests with one-cell flashlights aboard this flight, the Board notes that such flashlight-equipped life vests are *not* a standard requirement for

overseas flight by U.S. air carriers."

Just as the nations' airlines were cranking up for the jet age with new and bigger aircraft, the U.S. economy began to stagnate at the end of the 1950s. Even the most conservative industry predictions of air travel growth collapsed when domestic traffic grew only 4% in 1960 and fell to 1% in 1961, the year John F. Kennedy was sworn in as president of the United States and Russia orbited the world's first man in space.

A variety of problems traveled hand in hand during 1960. First, Northwest's new DC8 jets were behind schedule. Next, after three different airlines — including Northwest — each lost an Electra, investigators determined that the engine mount of all Electras should be strengthened, and until this work could be completed, over a period of months, the government sharply restricted the plane's speed, thus temporarily removing one of its major advantages.

Optimism returned, however, when the DC8s arrived, and NWA launched the nation's fastest jet service to the Orient July 8, 1960, with two weekly flights to begin with and four per week as of July 31. The elapsed time from New York to Tokyo was faster than the nearest competitor by six hours and 31 minutes. In a 120-passenger configuration, the Orient flights offered 42 first class accommodations and 78 tourist seats.

The beginning of jet service coincided almost to the day with the first steps in a long and carefully planned move from St. Paul's Holman field to the giant new maintenance and overhaul base at Wold-Chamberlain, which was carried out with all the precision of a coordinated military engagement. Shop by shop, the various departments were moved over a period of more than three weeks, and of course much brand new equipment — ranging from overhead monorail and bridge crane units to a host of other specialized machinery and instruments — was already in place before the move began.

The last plane to be overhauled at Holman field was DC6B No. 578, which rolled out of the hangars on July 1.

Before the move to Wold-Chamberlain,

Donald Nyrop — noted in the industry for consolidating and centralizing many operations for greater efficiency — demonstrated a knowledge of decentralization, as well, when his evaluation of the Operations and Engineering Department (encompassing nearly 70% of the airline's employees) convinced him it had become too unwieldy during the airline's rapid growth since 1954. As a result, it was split into Maintenance and Station Operations plus a separate Flight Operations department.

Adding to the many problems of 1960 — the year America's U2 spy plane flown by Francis Gary Powers was shot down over Russia — Northwest, along with many other U.S. airlines, was caught up in a widespread jurisdictional struggle between pilots and flight engineers that came to a head as an outgrowth of the jet age. The pilots' union insisted the third seat in the cockpit of the DC8 — previously occupied by a flight engineer — be manned by a qualified pilot. Northwest offered to stand the cost of giving flight training to the engineers, but 31 of them assigned to the new jets went on strike October 11, and on January 9 expanded the strike to all aircraft.

A presidential fact finding board was convened late the following February, and flight schedules that had been sharply curtailed during the lengthy strike were resumed, with three instrument-rated pilots in the cockpit.

The airline had managed to maintain daily jet service across the Pacific, along with a greatly reduced schedule of domestic flights, but even with the resumption of normal service, crippling effects of the strike hung on because it took time to get customers back in the "Northwest habit." In the previous two Aprils, Northwest had enjoyed load factors of 65% and 71% between Seattle-Tacoma and New York using piston engine aircraft, while in the same month of 1961, the factor was only 25% on the DC8 jet.

Meanwhile, an enthusiastic crowd of 6,852 persons had turned out in the fall of 1960 to tour the new facilities when the airline unveiled its big new maintenance and overhaul base for the

FIRST PURE JET to be flown by Northwest was the DC8, five of which went into service in 1960.

160

general public of Minneapolis and St. Paul.

To encourage more tourist travel to and from the Orient, Northwest introduced a brand new fare — with C.A.B. approval — on December 1, 1960, cutting previous tourist class fares 14% by offering the public a new classification known as "economy fares."

Despite the year's vicissitudes, Northwest's careful cost control program managed to keep the airline in the black for the year, which also saw a final farewell to the much-loved — however expensive to operate — Stratocruisers.

As the airline continued to upgrade the quality of its fleet, the Stratocruisers were traded in according to plan as an aftermath of the Electra purchase.

Few of today's air travelers who enjoy a relaxing cocktail en route to their destinations are aware that in 1949 the Stratocruiser helped Northwest become the first U.S. air carrier to offer beverage service on flights within the continental limits of the United States.

In its own inimitable style, *The New Yorker* made this 1950 report on NWA's pioneering of the aerial cocktail:

"So far, the other domestic airlines have been sidestepping the manifold difficulties of inaugurating a bar service, content to let Northwest get some of the legal underbrush cleared out. National Airlines serves drinks on its flights between New York and Miami, but this is only an *apparent* exception to the rule; no liquor is broken out until the planes are over the ocean and well outside the three-mile limit.

"Northwest began serving drinks in October of last year, and thereby posed a number of nice legal questions, all of which have been settled amicably. At the outset, lawyers for the airline came forward with the argument that the air over the various states is free and therefore not subject to licensing restrictions, save by the federal government. Several states over which Northwest planes fly promptly protested that a plane, no matter how high up, is subject, by

IN ADDITION TO PIONEERING the idea of cocktail service on domestic flights in 1949, NWA next transformed each Stratocruiser's lower deck lounge into a touch of the Orient, with Japanese decor and a "Fujiyama tray" to complement mouth-watering menus featuring steaks and seafood.

virtue of the laws of common sense and gravity, to the jurisdiction of the state over which it happens to be flying. Northwest rather readily conceded this point out of court.

"Each state on the Northwest routes subsequently either granted an aerial liquor license, with whatever restrictions it saw fit to impose, or flatly refused to grant a license of any kind. There were two that took the latter action, New York and Illinois, both thoroughly wet at ground level.

"On Northwest flights from here to Seattle, the drinking situation is as follows. The stewards of the cocktail lounges ordinarily accept orders immediately after the takeoff, for the plane usually makes straight for New Jersey, which is wet in the air. By the time the stewards have prepared the drinks, with perhaps a modicum of time-killing, the middle of the Hudson River has been passed.

"If the stewards don't accept orders right after the takeoff, it is because the weather is bad over Jersey and the plane is going to proceed via upstate New York, in which case no drinks are served until after Buffalo. The Jersey aerial liquor license enjoins the planes to abide by local ordinances, so in theory they are supposed to shut down their bars while passing over dry towns, but this is such a difficult thing to keep track of, and towns are passed so quickly, that in practice Northwest gives itself the benefit of the doubt.

"After New Jersey comes Pennsylvania, which held out against aerial drinking until last March, and then announced that it would impose no restrictions beyond those in force on the ground. Next comes Ohio, which is wet, and then Michigan, which is wet, too, but says that a three-per-cent sales tax must be collected on all drinks served above it and makes an additional, rather fancy requirement: If a plane deviates from its course and a drink is sold over Canada, this deviation is to be regarded as an act of God and the tax is to be paid anyhow.

"As stated, Illinois is dry in the air. Wisconsin, Minnesota, South Dakota, North Dakota, Montana, and Idaho all are wet except on Sundays and Election Days. Over South Dakota, it is illegal to serve a spendthrift, but Northwest hasn't yet challenged a passenger under this statute. Washington, like Michigan, has a three-per-cent sales tax.

"In order that a lounge steward may know what state he is in, or over, and thus what laws are momentarily in effect, the pilot keeps in touch with him by means of the intercom. Because of severe restrictions as to space and weight — every bottle cuts into the pay load — Northwest serves a limited variety of drinks in its Stratocruisers. Martinis, Manhattans, Scotch, and bourbon are available, but not beer or champagne.

"For mixing purposes, you can have ginger ale, soda water, or, heaven forbid, Coca Cola. As drinks are apt to spill when the air gets bumpy, the stewards always shut down the bar at the first sign of turbulence. They also close it during all takeoffs and landings. During a descent, no one is allowed to hold a glass, lest he accidentally bite into or swallow it at touchdown. The steward takes all unfinished drinks and impounds them until the plane is aloft again."

It's only fair to the Stratocruiser's memory to point out that as time went by, its lounge offered a much wider variety of choice, including imported Japanese beer.

24

Fan Jets and Teamwork

UNLIKE MANY AIRLINES, Northwest bided its time at the start of the Sixties, refusing to rush the process of augmenting the original jets purchased in the need to remain competitive. There was good reason for this patience.

The much improved fan jet engine — with greater thrust, lower fuel consumption and quieter operation — was on the way, and NWA waited nearly a year before placing an order for the first six of an eventual 17 Boeing 720Bs in 1961, in order to assure itself of the pluses offered by fan jet equipment.

Another marked advantage of this approach to aircraft selection — which was to be noted on a number of future occasions — came when NWA eventually sold its 720Bs as part of a continuous program to upgrade the fleet. They were marketed readily at good prices, while owners of most non-fan jets could find no buyers, and were forced to junk them.

Commenting on Northwest's long range fleet improvement program and Donald Nyrop's deep personal involvement in these decisions, James H. Binger — a member of Northwest's Board of Directors for 33 years — pointed out at the time of the airline's golden anniversary: "We set up our debt structure as part of a major plan, rather than tackling it in drips and drabs. The

terms were not bad, either. The main reason was that lenders had great confidence in Don Nyrop.

"At various other airlines, we have noted much delegation of authority in areas highly important to success, such as the selection of aircraft. But not at Northwest. The chief executive officer doesn't and shouldn't delegate this because it concerns some of the most critical decisions he can ever make — especially at $35 million — and more — per airplane." (*Much* more, as time went by.)

The 720B — a 111-passenger jet capable of 600 miles per hour — was chosen to complement the airline's other modern aircraft in order to create this eventual pattern of operation: DC8s for the long transpacific routes; 720Bs handling nonstop transcontinentals, turnaround flights between the Pacific Northwest and Hawaii, Florida service and a variety of medium range domestic segments; newly modified Electra prop jets serving short haul and intermediate markets.

While the new 720Bs were on the way, Northwest moved ahead on several fronts to facilitate its transition to the jet age. The new General Office was completed in 1961, finally permitting the airline to begin reaping the benefits of centering its total operation under one roof; a new "continuous maintenance" concept was introduced, thus extending the productive hours of all aircraft; customer service was centralized in one department for unified and effective direction, combining the functions of communications, reservations (with a new computerized system), station operations, meals and in-flight cabin service.

The airline also moved into seven new terminal and hangar facilities across the system, with others under construction, including a $10 million terminal at New York's Idlewild (later, Kennedy) Airport, which Northwest built jointly with two other carriers.

With the entire airline industry struggling against a business slowdown in the early sixties, Capital Airlines — whose operational costs had risen from 24¢ per ton mile to a disastrous ton mile figure of 34¢ over a five year period — was on the verge of bankruptcy, and entered into an agreement to form the nation's largest airline by merging with United. Despite the documented objections of several carriers — including Northwest — which emphasized that the union would create a monopoly in 19 important markets, the C.A.B. approved the merger in 1961, and Capital was swallowed up, with United as the surviving corporation.

As an aftermath, Northwest and several other airlines filed briefs in what became the United Airlines Competitive Service Investigation. The major United monopolies under fire were New York-Cleveland, Cleveland-Chicago, Cleveland-Philadelphia and Philadelphia-Detroit. One of these segments — New York-Cleveland — involved more revenue passenger miles than the other three put together. Eventually, the C.A.B. awarded it to American Airlines, while Northwest was given authority to compete with United on the three lesser traveled routes — Chicago-Cleveland, Cleveland-Philadelphia and Detroit-Philadelphia.

Ironically, while American wound up with less competition after the merger, Northwest's situation was just the opposite. In some markets that had been served by Capital, American and United, the new lineup left only the latter two airlines. In others, where Northwest formerly had competed against Capital — such as on the Chicago-Twin Cities segment — it now had to take on the much tougher United.

Despite the difficulties of 1961, including increased interest charges of 4^1/_3$ million necessitated by borrowing for fleet expansion — plus the extra costs of integrating a new type of jet

720B AIRCRAFT LED THE WAY in Northwest's transition into an all fan jet airline.

164

aircraft into normal operations — NWA's rigid cost control policy helped show a profit gain, and Northwest entered 1962 with nearly 90% of its available seat miles in modern turbine powered equipment. One year earlier the percentage had been 30.

At a cost of $127 million in capital funds, the airline then was operating nine 720B fan jets, 16 Electra turbo props and five DC8s, in addition to its piston-operated DC6Bs and DC7Cs, several of which were converted into all-cargo freighters. New aircraft of all types purchased since 1955 then totaled 72, representing an expenditure of slightly more than $200 million.

The Twin Cities launched their own entry into the jet age by dedicating a brand new $10 million air terminal at Wold-Chamberlain late in January, 1962, shortly before Lt. Col. John Glenn of the U.S. Marines became the first American to orbit the earth on February 20.

In mid-year, Northwest finally said good-bye to Shemya Island for good, when its often foggy but always friendly air strip no longer was needed as a base for transpacific refueling, thanks to the advent of intercontinental jets.

The unlamented days when Northwest employes were forced to be apologetic about the scarcity and the age of the airline's flight equipment continued to recede into the background as the fleet grew. Winter schedules to Florida soon featured 10 720B jets daily between Chicago and Miami, not to mention eight jet flights from the Twin Cities, plus multiple connections with other on-line cities for sunshine-bound passengers.

Another improvement that year marked the start of a program to install enclosed "Top Flight loaders" at key cities, eliminating weather problems and stair climbing for passengers boarding or leaving NWA planes.

Late in 1962, the government canceled its 10% transportation tax on inter-city travel — a war-born levy that had hung on for 17 years after the end of World War II — and at the same time imposed a new 5% federal tax to cover the air carriers' share of operating U.S. airways.

Despite operational costs that rose 29½%, Northwest managed a 35½% increase in operating revenues, and reduced its breakeven passenger load factor to 45.5% in 1962, with a record net for the year of $7.23 million. One of the original five DC8 jets was sold and plans were made to sell the remaining four, because firm orders were placed for the first five in what became a long line of Boeing intercontinental 707-320s.

Their arrival in 1963 made Northwest the nation's first all fan jet operator.

These advanced Boeing jetliners were designed to Northwest's specifications, with a capacity of 112 passengers *plus* 10,000 pounds of cargo, which is just as much freight as the all-cargo DC7Cs could lift with no passengers aboard. An integral part of Northwest's design called for the only "big door" cargo loading facility in the industry (91 by 134 inches) to facilitate large shipments to and from the Orient. (Later versions of the 707-320 carried up to 165 passengers.)

Northwest's sales force rose to the challenge of larger and larger jets by intensifying cargo sales and devoting added emphasis to group travel, because surveys had made it clear that tour groups promised dramatic help in broadening the air travel market. Two examples: of 41 persons interviewed on one of Northwest's Hawaii tours, only eight had ever flown before, and just three of them had set foot in a jet plane previously. Another group of 35 had six former air travelers, none with jet experience.

Shortly after the airline had brought its total headquarters operation under one roof at Wold-Chamberlain field, new benefits of standardization were extended to Northwest's radio communications when NWA became one of the few U.S. trunk carriers to create its own centralized domestic radio system.

As the jet age approached, one of the decisions facing Northwest was whether to follow the lead of most other airlines by contracting with Aeronautical Radio, Inc. (a non-profit communications network in which all U.S. airlines own stock) to handle radio communications, or to rebuild its own obsolescent network.

After carefully analyzing and comparing the pluses and minuses of both possibilities, NWA engineers concluded in their written proposal to President Nyrop that a self-operated system would give faster, more reliable contact with all domestic flights, and save $132,000 a year in the bargain.

The execution of this recommendation was a textbook example of efficiency.

"We went from one extreme to the other," explained Robert Glischinski, former Vice President — Communications and Computer Services.

"Back in 1954, we had just about every kind of DC4 in existence — no two alike. And in communications, we weren't much better. We owned one of almost every ground radio device ever built. Even when we had two alike, they were wired differently. A lot of technical information was written down on the backs of envelopes, and that was just about par for the course among all the nation's airlines."

Under the new proposal, Northwest designed a completely modern radio station and central control point, then used the single blueprint of an ideal layout to create 37 identical "slave" stations at key points from coast to coast, at a total cost of only $100,000.

Every station, every unit, every wiring job was so alike and so carefully planned that to this day, only two men are required to service all 37 stations. Some of the 37 have been known to operate for a full year at a time with no maintenance call, and the two service specialists simply catch a red-tailed jet whenever their expertise is needed.

The central radio headquarters at Northwest's main base began with four separate networks, later enlarged to six. As a precautionary measure, some geographical areas are provided with identical radio stations in two different locations. For example, Miami and Fort Lauderdale backstop each other in case a hurricane should disable one of the transmitters.

As a further safety measure, double units are installed at several stations, so if one transmitter should develop trouble, a second one can be activated instantly. In addition, the 37 Northwest radio stations overlap each other in coverage, to assure immediate contact with the airline's planes.

By operating its own domestic radio networks, Northwest gains an advantage that might be compared to having a private telephone versus being on a party line.

When it comes to transmitting precautionary weather information, minutes really count, and NWA's private radio hookup gets this key data into the cockpit faster than any other system.

Mark Twain once said "everybody talks about the weather, but nobody does anything about it." He would be amazed at what Northwest's meteorology staff, working with flight opera-

DANIEL SOWA had a major hand in proving that Mark Twain was wrong.

tions specialists, has accomplished to belie his remark.

Over a period of years, Northwest Airlines has been honored by the F.A.A. and several other prestigious organizations for its industry leadership in developing a variety of important techniques that add to the comfort and safety of flying. Some of these advances involve weather research, others involve cockpit and operational procedures, and all of them were accomplished by teamwork.

Most of these developments had their origin in the middle fifties, and were made possible — in the words of Bill Hochbrunn, retired general manager of flight operations — by "management that believed in standardization, and realized safety could be enhanced if we spent the money needed to accomplish certain goals."

"Back in 1954," continued Hochbrunn, "our planes were a real hodgepodge — there were eight different types and configurations of the DC4 alone — different warning light systems, different switches, different locations for important controls, even different directions in which they were activated. And when you went from one plane to another — DC3s, DC4s, Stratocruisers and the first DC6s — the differences were far greater."

This, of course, not only undermined operating efficiency — it also involved the welfare and comfort of passengers.

A vast change that began right then is affectionately known to Northwest flight crews as "SOPA" — Standard Operating Procedures, Amplified.

SOPA is a two-way improvement over the past, because it involves both instrumentation and flight procedures.

A master cockpit arrangement plan was drawn up for *all* company planes, regardless of type or manufacturer, and management approved the necessary expenditures so Northwest aircraft — then and in the future — could be instrumented alike, to the airline's own specifications.

"This plan called for the same types of instruments in the same locations," explained Hochbrunn — "identical fuel panels, air conditioning panels, Automatic Direction Finder panels — your hand goes right to them without conscious effort, so you can devote your attention to the important business of flying. There's even standardization in the knobs on certain types of instruments — for example, square corners on some, while others are circular."

"Even if they were blindfolded," says retired Captain Vince Doyle, "our pilots could reach out and touch the flap indicator, the air speed indicator, the de-icing switch or any other instrument. No matter what NWA cockpit you're in, you feel at home."

At the same time, a complete evolution was effected in crew procedures.

"Pilots are great creatures of habit, and resist

NWA'S CAPTAIN PAUL SODERLIND, widely honored by the entire industry for his pioneering contributions to aircraft safety.

change," says retired Captain Joe Kimm, "but Paul Soderlind, then director of flight standards, hung in there and did a great job of selling us on the new system."

"Before SOPA," added Doyle, "every captain had his own pet way of doing things. Some of them wanted the first officer to tune the radio, others didn't want you to touch the radio. Same way with retracting flaps, or wheels, or whatever. You got hell for not doing things one way, and then another captain would give you hell for not doing it another. Now everybody does *everything* the same way."

"One of many reasons this is important," puts in another veteran — retired Captain Jack Deveny — "is that any one of our crews can work with anyone else, because we all know exactly what the other man is going to do, and how and when he is going to do it. SOPA brought discipline into the cockpit and became the foundation for valuable later procedures, one of which made Northwest the industry leader in noise abatement. Another made us the leader in fuel conservation."

At the same time SOPA was developed, four staff members teamed up to begin delving into the mysteries of air turbulence, winds, temperatures, and how to forecast unusual conditions in advance. These four were Dan Sowa (for many years chief meteorologist), Robert Trapp (then chief navigator, later director of flight dispatch), Soderlind and Roman Justiss (then chief pilot of the Western division.)

Aviation meteorology is directly related to — but far more complicated than — ground level forecasting, so "we learned our weather in the airplanes, working right along with the pilots," explains Sowa.

"We discovered that upstairs, things are different from what we had learned in text books," he adds. "And what helped us gather enough data to come up with some answers is that we use our flight crews as weather observers. As one example, when our planes call in on the radio every hour they're aloft, we get a temperature report, along with wind velocity and

direction. This is important because all weather is caused by changes in temperature, so flight reports help keep our air charts up to date.

"Over a period of time, we developed the ability to forecast clear air turbulence precisely. We learned what causes it, how to avoid dangerous turbulence, and when to advise the cockpit to put on the seat belt sign because moderate turbulence is ahead.

"We've been forecasting clear air turbulence since 1957, and developed a method of putting a precise turbulence plot into the cockpits of our planes in pictorial form in seven minutes."

(Said Joseph Ferrarese of the F.A.A.: "Northwest is the only airline that developed a turbulence plot. After this system had been in use for some time, to my knowledge Northwest was the nation's only major airline that had not one passenger injury caused by clear air turbulence.")

"When the jet plane came along," continues Sowa, "we speeded up our forecasts by spending considerable money to hook five teletype machines into the lines which carry coded messages from every Weather Bureau radar site in the United States to the Severe Storm Warning Center in Kansas City. We have a tap on it as it goes down to Kansas City, so there's no time lag whatever. We plot it instantly, and I expect our meteorologists to have the key data in usable form for our airborne crews in seven minutes.

"Other airlines have to wait and get the information on a facsimile machine, which delays things by an hour or so.

"We send the data to our planes by using a standardized format in all cases. Standardization has become a religion within the company. Our meteorologists follow precise techniques, and do not deviate from prescribed methods unless they can prove they have a better idea.

"A warble tone is used before transmitting turbulence information, to alert the cockpit that an important message is on the way. Four lines, no more and no less, are used for each transmission. *Line 1* gives a precise reading on the station or high altitude check point. *Line 2* gives the meat of the turbulence forecast. *Line 3* tells how long the forecast is valid, and *Line 4* indicates which previous message (if any) is canceled by the new information.

"This system makes it easy for the radio operator to send out, and it's easy to transcribe it into pictorial form in the cockpit, because they plot it on charts which are simply a reduction of our turbulence map at headquarters. Speed is the name of the game, because weather is a highly changeable commodity."

The Air Transport Association of America (A.T.A.) in an operations memorandum to all members October 4, 1973, reported:

"Recent correspondence from the F.A.A. pointed out that during 1972 there were 14 air carrier accidents directly attributed to turbulence that resulted in injuries to 51 passengers and 19 crew members. In 1973 to date, there have been eight air carrier incidents/accidents attributed to turbulence encounters which have resulted in injuries to 20 passengers and six crew members.

"F.A.A. also pointed out that, during this period and before, Northwest Airlines has not experienced one turbulence-related injury on domestic routes since its 'Turbulence Plot Program' was initiated . . . Northwest is presently planning to expand the 'Turbulence Plot Program' to cover its entire route structure.

"In view of the turbulence statistics referred to above, F.A.A. has recommended that A.T.A. member airlines implement a program for turbulence forecasting and avoidance so as to reduce injuries resulting from turbulence penetrations. To further discuss this subject, F.A.A. has requested a meeting of all A.T.A. member airlines.

"It is hoped that Northwest representatives will be present to brief the airlines on North-

PRETTY, BUT DANGEROUS, clear air turbulence was studied by Northwest scientists working along with pilot crews on hundreds of flights. Eventually they determined how to predict its path and warn NWA flights away from danger zones.

west's Turbulence Plot Program."

Northwest, of course, did as requested, because however competitive the airlines may be, they freely exchange much technical information for the good of the industry.

Oddly, a phenomenon which has been referred to as the "N.I.H. syndrome" (meaning "Not Invented Here") sometimes prevents the spread of useful new ideas, apparently because many feel "if we didn't think of it, then it can't be any good."

One example: back in the Fifties and early Sixties, studies conducted by Northwest meteorologists developed methods of predicting low level "wind shear" to help pilots avoid approach and climb-out problems caused by unexpected changes in wind direction and/or velocity.

"The other airlines thought we had gone ape when we told them we had started a low level wind shear forecast procedure in 1962," recalls Sowa.

"Many didn't feel it was important, and others didn't think it could be done," adds Paul Soderlind. "At an international air safety forum in England, one experienced meteorologist speaking to the group declared wind shear can't be predicted accurately, yet Northwest's procedures are super-accurate, and had been for 14 years at the time he made that statement."

The official records are full of examples such as this one: On March 4, 1971, at J.F. Kennedy Airport, New York, 22 airliners missed their first approach attempts because of sudden changes in head winds and tail winds at low level. Every Northwest flight into J.F.K. that day landed without incident, because the airline's wind shear forecast had prepared the crews for unusual conditions.

"Many airlines pay little or no attention to 'mountain wave' activity, which is a special kind of turbulence Northwest procedures have helped us avoid, or minimize, for years," adds Captain Jack Deveny. "Dan Sowa studied these mountain-induced air waves by getting out and riding in the airplanes. He eventually worked out a set of charts which show our crews deviation routes to follow for the most comfortable ride possible under mountain wave conditions."

Sowa's pioneering work over a period of many years in forecasting clear air turbulence and low level wind shear was given special recognition in 1976 when the Flight Safety Foundation presented him with the Admiral Luis de Flores safety award.

A whole new area of research and resultant flight procedures earned industry-wide fame for Northwest during the early Sixties, when a series of incidents — some major, others minor — afflicted many airlines in the first years of jet operation.

An NWA team, led by Soderlind and Sowa, conducted a detailed study of several unexplained mishaps that had been documented by the National Transportation Safety Board, and then carried out a series of risky personal experiments. They proved conclusively that jet aircraft required handling techniques in severe turbulence that were different from the old methods used with slower piston engine planes.

As the first hand evidence began to mount up — supported by readings from a battery of instruments when Northwest researchers risked their own necks and several million dollars worth of company aircraft by diving into dangerously turbulent weather — theory became a growing conviction.

Most automobile drivers are aware that when a car starts skidding, the quickest way of gaining control is to steer *into* the skid, rather than away from it, and then gradually turn in the desired direction. An adaptation of this strategy was part of Soderlind's theory, but by no means all of it. In piston engine planes, the policy had been to slow down in turbulent air to obtain better control. The jet experiments, however, proved very little — if any — speed reduction was desirable, and demonstrated the danger of overreacting at the controls.

Above all — because it was a team effort that involved meteorology know-how — the study established specific cockpit guidelines for *avoiding* severe turbulence altogether, as well as devising extrication measures.

The F.A.A. gave full cooperation to the Northwest experimental program, and Boeing participated in several of the flight tests. Recommended procedures thus developed were made mandatory for all airlines by the F.A.A., which "drafted" Paul Soderlind to give literally hundreds of pilot lectures, while the information was being disseminated to every carrier throughout the free world.

"The industry has not had a single 'upset' accident since that time," reported Joseph Ferrarese, former F.A.A. deputy chief of flight standards.

As a result of the "upset" research, Northwest Airlines received the Flight Safety Foundation safety award in 1964, and Soderlind — in addition to the Air Line Pilots Air Safety Award — was presented with the only gold medal citation for "extraordinary service to the airline industry" ever given by the F.A.A. to any individual outside its own ranks.

Among Northwest pilots — who presented Soderlind with the station wagon of his choice and a check for $2,700 in 1974 when he departed on a medical leave due to a balky heart valve — he probably will be remembered longest for his invention of the "bug" system.

The late Jerry Fredrickson, long time Director of Flying and — like Bill Hochbrunn — a contributor to Northwest's industry leadership in flight standards, once summed up the "bug" in these words: "It is so precise that it takes the guesswork out of flying, eliminating the mental gymnastics a man should not be bothered with when all his attention should be on flying the airplane."

The "bug" system, which has prescribed a *sequence* of landing and takeoff speeds for all Northwest planes ever since 1959, involves a metal template which fits around the air speed indicator, plus five movable "bugs" or pointers. The pilot sets these pointers before takeoff *or* landing, according to a scientifically devised system which takes into account such factors as weight of the plane, altitude, runway length, temperature and wind.

All mathematical data is pre-figured, so the pilot needs to look at only one side of a small card to get the proper settings.

Why five pointers? Simply because at each of five specific stages during takeoff, the plane should be moving at a precise speed, and the "bug" for each stage guides the pilot's throttle operation. For example, one of the "bugs" is set at the exact air speed that should be attained before flaps are retracted.

Similarly, there are four crucial speed stages during the *approach* to a runway, so only four of the pointers need to be pre-set before each landing.

"The beauty of the system," says retired Captain Jack Deveny, "is that there's no need to do any mental arithmetic while you're busy flying the plane. It's utterly fantastic how well it works."

Added the F.A.A.'s Joseph Ferrarese: "No other airline has effected this standardization of procedures. You never hear of an NWA plane landing short, and one of the big reasons is the bug system."

Dan Sowa and Paul Soderlind became part-time movie stars as a result of Northwest's pioneer work in meteorology and flight procedures. The F.A.A. used Paul as the key individual in a special turbulence-avoidance film prepared for distribution to all U.S. airlines, and also distributed 300 copies of another film he had produced for Northwest pilots demonstrating takeoff techniques with the Boeing 727 when this tri-jet was new to the industry. Sowa, in turn, starred with Danny Kaye (who often piloted his own jet) in an instruction film produced by Douglas Aircraft, and "his briefing of a flight crew on wind shear was the highlight of the film," said Ferrarese.

Back in 1960, Northwest pioneered an industry leadership in noise abatement that continues to this day.

"Management recognized the problem as

soon as jets began arriving," explained Jerry Fredrickson, "and Northwest began a series of research experiments aimed at minimizing the inevitable rise in decibels.

"The final result was an exact procedural system to be followed during all landings and takeoffs. It accomplished five beneficial results:

1. Reduced noise.
2. Reduced time of exposure to noise.
3. Reduced engine wear.
4. Greater operational safety margins.
5. Significant fuel savings.

"Northwest's solution helped minimize noise at the source, and increased its distance from the listener."

In layman's language, this is achieved on takeoff by a slightly steeper climb than normal (so a majority of decibels will be expended over the airport itself), after which flaps are retracted at 1,000 feet (to lessen drag and cut noise); next, engine thrust is reduced while the plane climbs 3,000 feet, after which climb power is reapplied when the aircraft is beyond congested residential areas. Essentially, a reverse of this process is followed on landings, with a one-notch reduction in flap settings as the prime key to less noise.

The reduction in thrust (Engine Pressure Ratio) is nicknamed "quiet eepers" (EPRs) by flight crews, and the total abatement procedure developed by Northwest saves money as well as eardrums.

In 1975 alone, NWA's noise abatement program saved 4,650,000 gallons of fuel on takeoffs and 3,940,740 gallons on landings. At an average then of 35¢ per gallon (the figure is much higher today, of course) this amounted to $3,004,755 in *one year.*

On top of this — as a financially successful airline — Northwest buys the newest planes, which have the quietest, most efficient engines, plus "SAM" (Sound Absorbent Material) in the engine nacelles. As Fredrickson summed up: "Our management puts its money where it counts — in top quality planes and equipment."

Impartial outsiders have saluted Northwest's noise abatement work several times. Twice the airline has been honored by awards from the National Organizaton to Insure a Sound-controlled Environment (NOISE) and in 1976 another award was presented by the Upper Midwest Chapter of the Acoustical Society of America.

Minnesota's Pollution Control Agency conducted a noise monitoring study in the summer of 1975 (350 families volunteered to participate) in which the agency specifically compared the Northwest Airlines takeoff method with that of other airlines following a system developed by the A.T.A. (Air Transport Association.)

A report issued by Alfonso E. Perez, chief of the agency's noise pollution control section, stated: "Summer measurements demonstrated lower peak noise levels and significantly shorter

PIONEER WEATHER RESEARCH by Northwest meteorologists has led to smoother, safer flying. Dan Sowa, above, for many years Chief Meteorologist and originator of the cockpit turbulence plot that is a Northwest exclusive, was honored by the Federal Aviation Administration for "distinguished service in the public interest on behalf of aviation."

duration for the NWA procedure than for the A.T.A. procedure presently used by other airlines."

Despite the "N.I.H. syndrome," word has been getting around. The president of one major airline, after learning about Northwest's money and eardrum savings in a conversation with Donald Nyrop, ordered his staff to adopt the same methods, lock stock and barrel.

The soaring price of jet fuel — which nearly tripled in cost from 1973 to 1976 — became one of the major problems faced by modern aviation. The savings that were made possible by noise abatement procedures have been carried one step further through still more operating refinements developed by NWA technicians, because to an airline using millions of gallons of fuel per year, even a small improvement pays big dividends.

The most spectacular additional fuel savings were developed by an unspectacular procedure under which all Northwest planes descending from cruise altitude merely cut their previous descent speed of 350 knots to 320 knots. In 1975 alone, this conserved 6,288,613 gallons then worth $2,201,000.

All of the industry-leading programs noted in this chapter — turbulence plots and avoidance techniques, "mountain wave" deviation routes, the "bug" system, SOPA, noise abatement, fuel conservation and low level "wind shear" forecasts — add a new dimension to Northwest's standardization policy that is known to comparatively few persons.

But in aviaton circles, these programs have attracted wide attention, "N.I.H. syndrome" or not.

In 1974, the F.A.A. hand-picked six outstanding retired pilots as members of its Special Air Safety Advisory Group (SASAG). These men spent weeks riding 600 different segments flown by all 27 U.S. scheduled carriers, to observe procedures and to make safety recommendations.

"We strongly recommended nationwide adoption of the Northwest Airlines turbulence plot system," summarized Captain Robert Buck of Moretown, Vt., a former T.W.A. pilot. "The technicians who developed it are giants of the industry, and the whole country needs the benefit of their work."

Despite accolades like this, the "N.I.H. syndrome" is still in evidence. To this day (1986) the cockpit turbulence plot remains a Northwest exclusive, and so does a still-more-sophisticated wind shear forecasting procedure developed by Dan Sowa and his associates over the years.

Sowa is a prophet with honor in many countries as well as his own. The ultimate honor came to him on his retirement in 1986. In addition to major safety awards received earlier from the Air Transport Association, the National Weather Service and the National Flight Safety Foundation, he received a citation from the Federal Aviation Administration for "distinguished service in the public interest on behalf of aviation."

F.A.A. administrator Donald Engen made a special trip to the Twin Cities to present Dan with this award. Engen found comfort in the fact that while Sowa is now retired, the benefits of his pioneer achievements in a 40-year meteorology career will fly on wherever the red-tailed fleet serves on three continents.

25

Momentum in the 60s

FOR NORTHWEST AIRLINES, the Fifties were a bootstrap operation, but the "domino effect" of standardization, centralization, cost control and careful money management began to pay off in a big way during the Sixties.

In 1963 — the year a Washington-to-Moscow "hot line" was opened, Cardinal Montini became Pope Paul VI and President John F. Kennedy was shot down in Dallas — Northwest continued to gather momentum, with record net earnings and passenger miles topping the two *billion* mark for the first time.

It also was the year Northwest ordered its first 11 tri-jets, the Boeing 727-100, which filled a need for an efficient medium and short range fan jet capable of carrying 93 passengers.

Many factors were involved in the airline's flight to the top of its industry, as Northwest became the darling of Wall Street in the Sixties, with rising dividends and three stock splits (one share became two, two became four and four became eight.) Before examining more of these factors, this table quickly summarizes NWA's remarkable growth in net earnings during the decade:

1960	$1.6 million
1961	$2.5 million
1962	$7.2 million

1963	$10.5 million
1964	$26.7 million
1965	$45.69 million
1966	$53.14 million
1967	$58.8 million
1968	$50.05 million
1969	$51.47 million

Even more remarkable than this growth is the fact that Northwest, although a distant seventh in size among major U.S. carriers, topped the entire industry in net profit both in 1968 and 1969, then did it again in 1970 and 1975 — a feat most businessmen considered as unlikely as for American Motors to outstrip General Motors and Ford.

When times were good in the Sixties, Northwest was the only major carrier to go into the equity market to build up its financing for larger jets that were on the way, and the airline's stock found eager buyers as dividends rose — before splits — to 5 times the quarterly rate of 1955.

Says Donald Hardesty: "Northwest does not believe in operating with too little equity. We raised money when the price of stock seemed right and when we weren't really hurting for capital, but knew we would be needing it in the near future. If you don't go into the equity market until lenders suggest doing so, word gets around, and the price of stock suffers."

Far-sighted money management helped Northwest retain the benefits of depreciation and investment tax credits by buying jets outright, while eight of the nation's major airlines wound up in financial straits that required them to lease many of their aircraft, thus losing these benefits.

As the conversion to fan jets was stepped up in 1963, a new marketing program keyed to "the fan jet airline" was developed, including a big effort aimed at the Florida market. Star attraction of this promotional campaign was another "different" advertising idea, featuring an upside-down map of the United States, with Florida seemingly at the northwestern corner of the nation. A heavy dotted line led to Florida, and the headlined message was: "Flying South to Florida? Go Northwest!"

The same approach was used on a huge lighted outdoor board in Chicago at the corner of Michigan and Randolph. The Chicago Daily News reported public reaction to the billboard was "fantastic!" Among other proofs that it got attention, a Bell Telephone Co. supervisor phoned Northwest's sales office and announced: "I think you ought to know the painters are putting your map upside-down."

With more and better Northwest planes serving Florida, the new sales effort added an extra 7,000 passengers to the airline's Chicago-Florida boardings in the 1963-64 winter season, and the successful "upside-down" map campaign was used in a variety of ways to help boost business for years.

Another important but little-known contributor to the airline's growing leadership position in the Sixties was marked by the creation of a Quality Control Division in the Maintenance and Engineering Department, employing many scientific discoveries and systematized procedures to augment the tender loving care NWA technicians give to aircraft engines and airframes.

UPSIDE DOWN U.S. MAP became the "surprise ingredient" in a long and effective advertising campaign that built public awareness of Northwest's routes to Florida. This big outdoor board in downtown Chicago was part of the print, broadcast and display promotion for several years.

At one time, it was necessary to rely on visual inspection for signs of wear and metal fatigue, and in many cases mechanics had to tear an engine down to see if its innards were in proper working condition. But not any more.

"We didn't have precise methods in the inspection division during the old days," recalls Eugene "Skelly" Skelton, retired head of the Quality Control Division, "but Mr. Nyrop and Frank Judd inspired a whole new approach to our operations in Maintenance and Engineering.

"In 1962, we put it all together. As a foundation for all other activity, we standardized on a system of written check lists, with signatures required for every item checked."

To replace the old tear-down method, a number of non-destructive testing procedures were adopted, including the use of isotope radiography, X ray, ultra-sonic, Eddy current and magnaflux procedures, all of which "see" through metal and spot potential trouble areas. Radio isotope photography required licensing by the Atomic Energy Commission, and Northwest personnel learned this new procedure by attending special courses in Cleveland prescribed by the A.E.C.

The net gain from these updated methods is twofold: first, preventive maintenance achieved big league status; second, more efficient utilization of aircraft followed automatically, as speedy and accurate testing replaced cumbersome ways of the past.

Computers joined the maintenance team in 1968, too. Engine performance is monitored in flight three times a day, and reports radioed in by the cockpit on power readings, fuel flow and a variety of other vital figures are fed into these electronic marvels for analysis as part of Northwest's preventive maintenance program.

By 1964 — the year New York staged a World's Fair, Tokyo hosted the summer Olympic Games and Northwest stockholders' equity nearly doubled (to $122.9 million) — NWA's jet fleet included eight 707-320s, with another five on order, 16 720Bs and the first three in a long line of tri-jet 727s, most of them the larger 727-200.

That same year, navigators became an endangered species when the F.A.A. approved the use of Doppler airborne radar and self-contained navigation systems, providing Northwest pilots with continuous position, ground speed and drift data, for greater safety and efficiency in all cockpit operations.

Northwest also added a new Univac Real-Time Computer system, with 10 times the speed of previous equipment, to handle reservations for constantly growing passenger traffic. The same system did double duty by taking over all automatic switching center functions of the teletype network — another example of the airline's efficient technology utilization.

In Alaska, 1964 was the year of the quake. Anchorage was hard hit by the strongest earthquake ever to hit North America, and the 131 casualties would have been far greater if the quake had not struck at 5:30 p.m. on a Good Friday — March 27 — when schools, theaters and most office buildings were virtually empty.

"We were used to tremors, but this thing hit without warning," reported Clayton Schule, who was Northwest's Anchorage station manager at the time. "It created tremendous damage in downtown Anchorage. On one four-block stretch along Fourth Avenue, the earth opened up and everything dropped about 20 feet.

"At the airport, the runways were O.K., but the terminal building was badly damaged, and when the control tower was knocked down, it fell directly on top of Northwest's food service kitchen. The man who had just taken over duty in the tower escaped with his life, but the operator he relieved was killed as he exited from the tower.

"Our kitchen at that time turned out 1,500 meals a day, because we serviced all international carriers using the airport, so I drove to Elmendorf field and managed to rent an old mess hall from the military base commander. Within 24 hours, when the airport was reopened to international traffic, we were supplying the usual 1,500 meals a day." (By 1975, the rebuilt

BOEING 727 has been a popular member of the fleet since 1964.

Anchorage flight kitchen was bringing in revenues of $2,941,871 annually from outside catering activities.)

As Northwest's net income zoomed to $45.7 million in 1965 — the year Medicare came in and the lights went out during a massive eight-state electrical blackout in northeastern U.S. — the airline added 16 new fan jets costing $93.5 million, and led all the nation's carriers in operating reliability despite the vicissitudes of cold weather operation, a winter-time problem Northwest lives with year in and year out.

Passenger miles flown topped the three *billion* mark for the first time, operating expenses per available ton mile were lowered to 16.4¢ and the number of employees increased nearly 1,000 — to 7,568 at year's end, including 178 newly trained pilots and another 498 flight attendants.

Once again, Northwest was tapped by Uncle Sam for military duty when President Lyndon B. Johnson announced U.S. ground forces in South Vietnam had been authorized to extend their support role by entering into actual combat against the Communist North Vietnamese. The airline was asked to increase passenger and

cargo charters already under way for the military to a variety of Far East destinations, and also operated a Pacific military supply mission based in Honolulu.

In 1966, Northwest's fleet had grown to 61 aircraft, with 20 more on order — a total of 81 fan jets acquired over a period of only 21 months — and at the same time Nyrop ordered his first 10 "jumbo jet" 747s for delivery in 1970.

A continuing series of coast-to-coast travel agent seminars boosted travel to Hawaii, Florida, Alaska and the Orient, while Northwest built its position with shippers by offering volume cargo service on the kind of priority scheduling normally associated with passenger operations. This was made possible by the addition of seven big door 727C freighters — convertible passenger-cargo versions of the standard 727 jet.

Although a 43-day machinists' strike against five airlines — Northwest, T.W.A., National, Eastern and United — put a crimp in summer operations, NWA managed a record $53.14 million net profit for 1966. The year also was notable for the fact that after 17 years of

1963 CORPORATE LOGO was inspired by the tail design of Northwest jets in the early Sixties.

persistent effort, Northwest finally was granted landing rights in the British crown colony of Hong Kong — one of the Orient's most exciting destinations — and daily through-plane service from New York City was launched October 1.

Osaka, Japan, and Hilo, Hawaii, were added as ports of call in 1967, the year all-cargo jet service was begun between New York and the Orient, and a few months later the airline retired its final piston airplane — a DC7C freighter.

The last of its breed was flown to Alexandria, Minn., where NWA presented it to a technical school operated by the Minnesota public school system, giving students an opportunity to learn maintenance and repair of aircraft instruments, radios and a variety of electronic components such as the navigation system, weather radar and automatic pilot.

Some of the plane's controls were dismantled to keep overly adventurous students from temptation, since the aircraft was in full operating condition when given to the school.

Over the years, Northwest has contributed much to the U.S. balance of trade through its international operations, and in the Sixties was singled out for a special honor — The Presidential "E" — for developing export markets and for its "Visit the U.S.A." promotion in the Orient.

About that same time, Northwest Orient Airlines completed one of the more remarkable financial "due bills" in aviation history. We noted earlier that Donald Nyrop — immediately after becoming president of NWA late in 1954 —insisted that Northwest become the first U.S. carrier to operate without government mail subsidy on transpacific and States-Alaska routes.

The joker in this deck is that Uncle Sam's minions finally decided to reduce Northwest's pre-Nyrop mail subsidies by $5,295,123, on the grounds that open rates for mail in the early Fifties had not been finalized. They submitted a bill for this amount.

In 1967, as a result, Nyrop became the first non-subsidized airline president in U.S. history who had paid a total of $5,295,123 in mail subsidies *to Uncle Sam.*

By 1968, inflation was sapping the vitals of U.S. business, and the entire airline industry was gripped in a cost-price squeeze that plummeted earnings. This marked the first time that many outside observers became fully aware of the benefits derived from Northwest's operating efficiencies, cost control policies and better utilization of personnel, because it was the year Northwest surprised larger competitors by leading the entire industry with a net income of $50.05 million.

"A flash in the pan," said some. But it was to happen again and again.

In addition to the onset of inflation, 1968 went down in history as a year of violence and unrest both at home and abroad. North Korea seized the U.S. Navy ship Pueblo, Dr. Martin Luther King, Jr., and Senator Robert F. Kennedy were assassinated, 3,000 demonstrators attempted to storm Democratic convention headquarters in Chicago during proceedings that nominated Hubert H. Humphrey to run against Richard

COMPUTERS GIVE INSTANT REPORT on the mechanical condition of every NWA plane. At a cost of $55 million, Northwest doubled its computer capability twice in recent years, largely due to changes that have occurred since the advent of airline deregulation.

M. Nixon for president, and Russia led four other Warsaw Pact nations in a bloodless invasion of Czechoslovakia.

Nevertheless, one bit of international goodwill was noted that summer when King Olav V of Norway renewed an old acquaintance while his party flew from Seattle to the Twin Cities on a Northwest Airlines jet captained by Norman Midthun, later to become manager of NWA's flight simulator operations.

A Minneapolis native of Norse descent, Midthun went to Canada at the age of 17 and joined the Norwegian Air Force after Hitler invaded Norway. He wound up as the king's personal pilot during an inspection trip to assess damage caused by the Nazi invaders of World War II.

After he had polished up his rusty Norwegian during a happy reunion with King Olav, Midthun made in-flight announcements on Northwest's special flight No. 2761 in Norwegian and in English. The king's party occupied the plane's first class section, served by an all-Scandinavian cast of NWA flight attendants: Terje Anderson, Siri Haugen and Eva Andresen.

Said His Majesty: "The most enjoyable flight in my experience."

Meanwhile, Northwest Airlines was in the midst of preparations for big things to come.

26

Big News and Big Aircraft

"MAN ON MOON" shouted a headline in the Japan *Times* when Neil Armstrong kicked up moon dust with his 9½B astronaut boots on July 20, 1969. Armstrong called it "a great leap for mankind," and after years of effort, Northwest Airlines made an important leap of its own that year — to California and on to Japan via Hawaii.

The long drawn out Transpacific Route Investigation, which had bounced back and forth like a badminton shuttlecock through the Eisenhower, Kennedy and Johnson administrations, finally came to a head, with a number of airlines receiving new routes.

In the domestic phase of the transpacific case, five new carriers were added to the mainland-Hawaii market, and competition from Seattle-Portland to Hawaii also was increased by the addition of a third airline; but NWA's long campaign to make the Twin Cities a major gateway to California and then to the Orient via the warm mid-Pacific was achieved through two of the awards made by the C.A.B. and President Nixon.

San Francisco-Hawaii-Tokyo service was launched by Northwest August 1, 1969, with transpacific flights from Los Angeles inaugurated the following January 6. Hawaii nonstops from Chicago began September 1, 1969, and nonstops from the Twin Cities to Los Angeles and San Francisco premiered shortly afterward on October 4.

The president's decision on international aspects of the transpacific case found no need for new Great Circle service to the Orient from California or the Pacific Northwest, but granted New York-Tokyo authority to Pan American via both Fairbanks and San Francisco, so Northwest's newly won routes were accompanied by more competition from the east coast as well as the west.

At the same time California-Hawaii-Orient service was being organized, the airline was engulfed in system-wide preparations for the advent of its first ten 369-passenger Boeing 747s.

No existing hangars were large enough to accommodate the giant 747 — each more than 2/3 of a city block in length — and with major overhaul operations centralized at the main Twin Cities base for greater efficiency, it was necessary to increase the physical plant at Wold-Chamberlain field by nearly 50% to get ready for the new generation of jets.

As an example of inflation's toll, this expansion cost more than the $17.5 million which had built the entire Wold-Chamberlain base a

GIANT BOEING 747s sporting the "new look" paint job were on the way in 1969, and preparations to handle these new 369-passenger jumbos kept Northwest busy all year. The 747 was to become No. 1 in the airline's international service picture.

few years earlier.

Approximately $18 million was required to fund a major expansion of shop facilities and build two king-size hangars; another $3 million went into a new Flight Services building, $8.9 million was invested in special ground support equipment for the new jets, and a $5 million expansion of Northwest's maintenance facilities at Seattle-Tacoma International Airport was necessary as well.

While all these projects were under way, instructor pilots were attending school at the Boeing factory in Seattle to prepare for transitional training of flight personnel; cabin attendants, mechanical personnel and ground crews also were being indoctrinated, and at the same time Northwest began absorbing its first 19 727-200s — a 128-passenger version of the basic 727 fan jet.

Once again, tangible benefits of standardization were evident, because the time and cost of preparing personnel for the operation of new equipment was reduced, and so was the cost of spare engines and parts. With an all-Boeing fleet containing four different types of aircraft to serve short, medium and long range destinations, only two *types* of Pratt & Whitney engines were required to operate all these planes.

In addition to serving new routes and carrying out preparations to handle the 747 at bases from Hong Kong to New York, Northwest in 1969 introduced a system-wide "new look" that changed the appearance of every aircraft, every ticket office, every installation, every piece of motorized equipment — in fact, everything from silverware and letterheads and napkins to ticket counters, service buildings, boarding passes or any other item that carried the Northwest name.

181

A new corporate symbol — a contemporary derivative of Northwest's long-established red tail device — was created by designer Clarence K.M. Lee, a Hawaiian of Chinese parentage, and a new lettering style was adopted for the "Northwest Orient" name. The familiar red, white and blue color scheme of the past was integrated into the new corporate look, and by year's end the updated "birth mark" was a familiar sight wherever the red tail fleet served, at home or half way 'round the world.

Four of the nation's trunk carriers found it necessary to omit one or more dividend payments in 1969, which was a troubled year for the entire industry, but Northwest increased quarterly dividends by 12½%, and for the second year in a row led all U.S. carriers in net earnings ($51.47 million).

Northeast Airlines — one of several which experienced difficulties in 1969 — agreed to a merger with Northwest shortly before the close of the year, giving Northwest the potential of several north-south routes along the U.S. east coast, plus a Miami-Los Angeles nonstop long considered a highly desired complement to Northwest's transcontinental service across the northern United States. However, while the C.A.B. approved the merger, it refused to permit inclusion of the Miami-Los Angeles route.

This left matters up in the air, because the negotiated price no longer included all of the properties which had been bargained for, so eventually the merger was abandoned. (Not long afterward, the C.A.B. permitted Delta to absorb Northeast.)

Shortly after the Northeast merger talks ended, Dudley Swim, chairman of the board of National Airlines — which came on hard times in 1970 with a loss of $6.2 million — proposed a merger with Northwest.

National's routes, while principally up and down the eastern seaboard and from the southeastern U.S. to California, also included flights between Miami and London. Combined with Northwest's national and international service to the Orient via both Alaska and Hawaii, the proposed merger would have created one of the nation's really great airlines, because the two route structures fit together like pieces of a jigsaw puzzle, promising many through-plane benefits to the traveling public.

In addition to the fact that the combination would not have disturbed effective competition (the only duplicate routes were short ones between Washington, Philadelphia and New York, plus the Miami-Tampa segment served by five other airlines), neither would it have created a giant, because six U.S. airlines still would have exceeded it in size.

Stockholders approved the merger, and next came more than a year of complicated hearings before the C.A.B. No decision was reached, and when Dudley Swim died, so did some of National's will to complete the merger. A time limitation had been part of the original agreement, and President L.B. "Bud" Maytag of the Miami-based airline notified Northwest that

SYSTEM-WIDE "NEW LOOK" introduced in 1969 featured this logo and a new aircraft paint design which — of course — retained Northwest's traditional red, white and blue.

National was exercising its option to withdraw.

Hollywood came to Wold-Chamberlain field in the winter of 1969, when Arthur Hailey's best-selling novel *Airport* — with a cast including Dean Martin, Burt Lancaster, Helen Hayes and many others — was made into a movie. A number of scenes were shot on location in the Twin Cities.

Among numerous Northwest employees who used their off duty hours to serve as extras in the film were four Northwest secretaries (Marianne Blomquist, Irene Sanders, T. Eileen Russell and Carol Larson), ticket agent Gordon Tibbs, mail room supervisor Harold Hageman, and a number of cabin attendants, equipment servicemen and baggage handlers.

Severe wintry weather was needed to carry out the film's plot, and the weather bureau obliged with a near-blizzard, which delighted Hollywood but did not thrill cold-toed Minnesotans at all.

Northwest closed out the Sixties with a financial record that was the envy of the industry. In one decade, stockholders' equity had risen from $52 million to $465 million, stock issued and outstanding went from 1,818,715 to 20,914,272 shares, and recomputed figures after three stock splits showed these gains over the 10-year period:

	Book Value Per Share	Dividends Per Share	Earnings Per Share
1960	$ 3.59	10¢	11¢
1969	$20.41	45¢	$2.55

Growth in overall efficiency showed a dramatic increase, reflected by the fact that over the same decade, expenses per available ton mile were reduced from 27.8¢ to 15.2¢, and expenses per revenue ton mile from 54.2¢ to 34.5¢. In 1960, it took 96.4% of operating revenues to cover expenses, while in 1969 this figure had been reduced to 82.4%. Employment, meanwhile, more than doubled — to 12,695 employees over the same period of time.

With inflation, recession and a world fuel crisis in the offing, Northwest was to need its financial strength and still greater efficiency in the years just ahead.

Northwest's eagerly awaited 747s began arriving in April, 1970, and first went on line June 22 between the Twin Cities and New York. The initial 10 jumbos — costing a total of $254 million — soon were serving destinations all the way to Hong Kong, although a five-month strike by the Brotherhood of Railway and Airline Clerks slowed down business during the normally heavily trafficked summer months.

The year also was marked by completion of a sparkling new $7 million satellite terminal at Washington National Airport. At the same time, NWA took on more competiton from the Twin Cities to New York and Seattle-Portland, and also between Milwaukee and New York, when the C.A.B. named additional carriers on these routes. Despite delays caused by the B.R.A.C. strike — including postponement of a

INITIAL 747 FLIGHT between the Twin Cities and New York was June 22, 1970. Donald Nyrop, left, and Frank Judd — Vice President-Maintenance and Engineering — congratulated each other on the inaugural.

newly awarded Twin Cities-Boston route until the following June 1 — NWA became the first airline to offer 747 service across the Pacific from the four major gateways of Seattle-Tacoma, San Francisco, Los Angeles and Honolulu.

Northwest completed its third straight year as the industry profit leader by ringing up a net of $44.4 million in 1970, but in addition to deep concern over the sagging U.S. economy, the nation's airlines suddenly faced a new and urgent kind of problem — skyjacking.

Effective airport security measures finally squelched the rash of U.S. hijackings which plagued carriers in the early 1970's, but some of these events were so bizarre that they went down in the record books as a permanent part of aviation history.

With many industry-leading "firsts" to its credit, Northwest Airlines was less than pleased to be involved in the world's first and only parachute skyjacking — engineered by a mystery man known as D.B. Cooper — although the smooth handling of this emergency speaks volumes for the thorough training and poised discipline of Northwest personnel.

It was Thanksgiving eve — November 24, 1971 — when Flight 305 took off for Seattle-Tacoma from Portland International Airport at 3:07 p.m. on the last leg of a flight that had started in Washington, D.C. The aircraft was one of the tri-jet Boeing 727s known as a "stubby" because it was the shorter of two 727 models in commercial use.

One nondescript passenger boarding in Portland bought a ticket under the name D.B. Cooper, and quietly took seat 18F in the coach section. As events were to prove, he was familiar enough with airplanes to know that only the "stubby" had a built-in exit and entrance ramp at the tail end — a ramp that could be opened in flight. (It cannot any more, thanks to changes sparked by Cooper's escapade.)

"The passengers had boarded through the aft door and Flo Schaffner checked tickets as they entered," relates cabin attendant Tina Mucklow

Larson. "Then we began our beverage service on the ground. Flo started at the back working toward the forward section, and I started at the front. Mr. Cooper in seat 18F had one bourbon and water. Later, the F.B.I. lifted his fingerprints from the glass.

"When Flo closed the galley, she went to the back jump seat while I proceeded to do the oxygen demonstration and to check seat backs. The captain ding-donged for take-off, and I hurried back to join Flo, who was sitting by the inter-phone connected to the cockpit. She had been given a piece of paper by this man Cooper, but until she read it, she thought it was just a mash note. The message said: 'Miss, I've got a bomb, come sit next to me — you're being hijacked.'

"Cooper had moved over to seat 18E, and Flo went to sit next to him while I read the note, then immediately called the cockpit via the inter-phone to tell them we were being hijacked. It was approximately one minute after lift-off, and they commented about it later, because we are taught you don't normally call the captain right after take-off — he has other things to do.

"Then the man dictated an additional message to Flo. He wanted $200,000 in $20 bills, and also four parachutes. I went up and kneeled beside her to ask if there was anything she wanted me to do. She told Cooper she was going to take his first note and the new one up to the cockpit, so I sat in her place in 18D, and over a period of time relayed dozens and dozens of messages back and forth over the inter-phone. Before it was all over I spent several hours talking with Cooper and on the phone.

"He had several afterthoughts, such as specifying the money should be used currency, and packed in a knapsack. He also insisted two of the parachutes be back packs, and two front packs, and that everything should be all ready on the ground before we landed in Seattle.

"He had no unusual characteristics — no accent — he was very plain and business-like, probably in his early forties, wore a dark suit, dark tie, white shirt and dark glasses which he kept on the whole time. He also had a black briefcase. He carefully explained how his weapon, or bomb, worked, and I'm sure this was his way of making sure I'd be more convincing while talking to the cockpit.

"He opened the briefcase and showed me the thing had a couple of red cylinders, and several wires. The only thing I could really be certain of is that there was a battery in there and that it was all wrapped with electrician's tape. My father is an electrician, and we always had that black, gummy tape at home.

"One of the terminals was hooked up and he kept the other wire in his hand — it had a little clip at one end, which he said would complete the circuit and detonate the charge if we didn't follow directions.

"While all this was going on, we circled for a couple of hours after the Captain (William Scott of Medicine Lake, Minn.) had radioed the ground with the man's demands." (Twin Cities headquarters and Seattle thus were alerted simultaneously over Northwest's private radio network.)

"The minute word reached our Twin Cities G.O.," adds Donald Hardesty, then the airline's financial vice president, "we informed Don Nyrop, and his decision was instantaneous: 'If the crew and passengers are endangered, pay the money.'

"George Harrison, our Seattle station manager, had contacted a local banker at his home, so I called this official and said we needed $200,000 out at the airport just as damn fast as they could get it there.

"The man was a stranger to me, so I explained to him we didn't have any money in his particular branch, but gave him the names of three men in the bank's main office who knew my voice and told him to have one of them call me back.

"This took only a few minutes, and the officer quickly left for the bank to supervise counting out $200,000."

"The money was easier to come by than the parachutes," according to Harrison. "We got two chutes at Boeing Field, and finally located two more at a flying service in nearby Issaquah, Washington. The weather was pretty bad — rain had caused several highway accidents — but the Washington State Patrol helped rush them to the airport."

Aboard Flight 305, the skyjacker was becoming irritable at the delay.

"At one point," continues Tina Larson, "a passenger came to the back of the plane looking for a magazine. Cooper muttered to me: 'If that's a sky marshal, I don't want any more of them.' So I called the cockpit and they announced over the P.A. system that there was a report of turbulence in the area and asked all passengers and crew members to remain seated with belts securely fastened.

"By using the ship's radio, they kept me informed on the inter-phone so I could tell Cooper about progress in getting the money and parachutes, including the difficulty in locating four chutes. He kept asking me what time it was,

TOKYO-HONOLULU-LOS ANGELES service began January 6, 1970, and aboard was a sack of first flight covers for stamp collectors.

and at five o'clock, Cooper got quite upset when we were still circling. That's the only point where he was kind of hostile.

"He kept repeating throughout the flight: 'I don't care what happens, but I'm not going to be taken alive.' He smoked a lot, and had me light a few of his cigarets.

"Cooper said the passengers were to stay on board until everything was completed, so before we finally landed, the captain made an announcement that no one was to leave his seat until orders were given to deplane.

"The aircraft was less than half full — 36 passengers plus Cooper on the Portland-Seattle leg — and while a few of them surely realized something unusual was going on, everything had been handled so calmly that there was no excitement whatever."

It was dark by the time the plane had come to a stop well away from the main Seattle terminal, and since Cooper insisted he wanted to be flown to Mexico, further negotiations by Captain Scott were necessary before Cooper would permit refueling trucks near the aircraft. Somewhat later, the money and parachutes were sent out to the plane in a private car. Captain Al Lee, who had happened by Harrison's office, volunteered to transport the 24½ pounds of $20 bills.

"Cooper asked me to go out and get the money and the chutes," adds Tina Larson, "and I asked him if I could get some help to carry the chutes. He said: 'No, you'll be able to manage OK.' He wanted the money first, so I went out, got the money and dragged it back into the cabin.

"Then I asked him: 'Why not let the passengers go, now? After all, you've still got the crew and the plane.' He thought about it a moment, then suddenly agreed, so I phoned the cockpit and they announced everyone should deplane.

"I remember wishing the passengers a happy Thanksgiving as they filed off. Everybody left quickly except for one man, who had forgotten his attache case. I got it for him as fast as possible, to keep Cooper from getting nervous again."

Asked if she had any thoughts of running, once she had left the plane to get the $200,000, Ms. Larson smiled: "You bet! But I felt I had to go through with it.

"Cooper sort of looked through the money, but didn't count it. After the passengers got off, the other two girls came back from the front of the plane — Flo Schaffner and Alice Hancock — and the hijacker offered us a small stack of twenties from the laundry bag, probably $200 or so.

"We told him we couldn't accept tips. Next he dug down in his pocket for the $19 in change he had received when he bought a drink with a $20 bill after coming on board, and offered us that. Again we said no. I told him Alice Hancock had been married quite recently and was planning to have dinner with her husband — a Northwest pilot who was coming in on another flight. Cooper then decided to let Alice and Flo get off the plane. He pointed at me and said: 'But you will have to stay.'

"He seemed to know quite a bit about aviation terminology and I got the impression he had

HONG KONG'S DOUBLE-DECKER TRAMS became traveling billboards in 1970 to promote Northwest's 747 transpacific flights.

been on Flight 305 before, or had flown between Portland and Seattle quite a bit. He knew the crew would be hungry by the time we got to Seattle, and one of his demands was that meals should be provided for us.

"Because he was planning on being taken to Mexico, he had even brought along a packet of Benzedrine for the flight crew in case they should get sleepy. I told him they wouldn't accept it, so he put the drugs back in his pocket.

"Shortly after the other girls left the plane, Cooper insisted all lights in the entire cabin be turned off except his reading light, the light over the aft jump seat and the aft stair light. All the shades had been pulled, on his order, and no one was to come back of the first class cabin curtain.

"When I asked if I could cook the crew meals in the galley, he said: 'No, I don't want anyone behind that curtain'."

Next Cooper haggled with the cockpit — Tina Larson serving as intermediary on the inter-phone — first demanding that the plane be flown to Mexico with the landing gear down, flaps down, and at an altitude of 10,000 feet. Captain Scott finally convinced him this was impractical, so Cooper agreed to Reno as a refueling stop, although it seemed obvious that somewhere en route he planned to parachute out the aft exit with $200,000.

"Shortly after takeoff from Seattle," resumes Ms. Larson, "Cooper asked me to show him how to activate the handle that would let the stairs down. Originally he wanted me to stay back and put them down for him, but I suppose he didn't want anyone to know when he left the plane, so it would be harder to pick up his trail.

"He stuck to his demand that we fly at 10,000 feet, so no pressurization would be needed. Finally Cooper told me to go to the front of the plane, pull the curtain between first class and coach, and not to come back. After that I stayed up in the cockpit, except that I used the forward lavatory once.

"At one point, Cooper used the inter-phone to tell the captain he couldn't get the stairs down. Then we knew he got them activated, because

the stair signal light in the cockpit flashed on a bit later.

"He cut some nylon cords from one of the extra parachutes to use in tying the money to his body, and apparently used two chutes for his leap because the other two were still in the plane after we landed at Reno.

"There are a lot of things I wish I had noticed at the time. Simple things, you know. Like afterwards, the FBI asked me if he wore a wedding ring, and I had to admit I didn't notice.

"When we got close to Reno, the men in the cockpit called back on the inter-phone and said: 'Put the stairs up now, because if we land with them down, we won't be able to take off again.' There was no answer. Then I made the same announcement over the loud speaker, but the signal light stayed on, so we landed anyway, with the stairs down. The captain called back: 'Are you still there?' No answer. So we went back through the curtains, and Cooper was gone. We looked through the plane, then Bill Rataczak (first officer) told me to get myself together and get off the aircraft."

Nyrop, Hardesty and a dozen other deeply concerned officials sweated out the ordeal in Northwest's offices into the wee hours of Thanksgiving Day, receiving frequent play-by-play reports over the phone from George Harrison as well as radio messages from the hijacked plane. Finally, well after 2 a.m., word came that the crew was safe on the ground in Reno, making the day truly one of thanksgiving.

A multi-state manhunt followed, involving helicopters, federal agents, sheriff's posses, police and volunteers, but the several hundred miles of rugged country over which the 727 had flown — plus the fact that the skyjacker's point of departure was unknown — gave up no clue to the parachuter's whereabouts, even though the hunt went on for years.

The preposterous aspect of the entire affair is that Cooper wasn't intelligent enough to realize no bank anywhere will package $200,000 in extortion money without recording the number of every bill, thus making that money as dangerous as the Lindbergh ransom that cost Bruno Richard Hauptmann his life. So in the unlikely event that he could survive his leap, he would have been shackled with a small fortune he did not dare to spend.

(It didn't reach the news media, but in the haste of counting out 10,000 $20 bills and listing their numbers, bank clerks accidentally bundled up only 9,998 of them — $40 short — a fact which came to light when numbers were checked at the time Northwest recovered the ransom from its insurance company.)

Did the money's extra 24½ pounds upset Cooper's parachuting calculations? Did he tie the laundry sack to his body so clumsily that it interfered with the opening of his chute? However he perished, most of his former hunters are convinced his remains lie at the bottom of a lake or hidden in the remote mountainous regions traversed on the way to Reno.

One thing is sure: Cooper's harebrained scheme adds up to what we all learned at mother's knee — crime does not pay.

27

The Big Engine that Could

NOT LONG AFTER the first ten 747s were introduced, five long range 747Bs — capable of 6,740 miles nonstop — were added in 1971. Next, Donald Nyrop startled the industry by announcing Northwest had ordered an initial 14 specially customized 236-passenger DC-10s, with 1,205 miles greater range than the standard model of this luxurious tri-jet.

Most of the eyebrow-raising was caused by the fact that his new version of the aircraft — designated as the DC10-40 — would be powered by the same basic Pratt & Whitney JT9D engine used in the 747, rather than by General Electric jets normally installed by the manufacturer.

This decision was not arrived at lightly. Nyrop's top engine specialist — Carl Magnuson, then Superintendent of Power Plant Engineering — had studied detailed technical drawings and evaluated the pros and cons of the engine substitution, not because Nyrop opposed the G.E. product, but because he knew the value of standardization.

Magnuson's research convinced him the rugged JT9D would do the job beautifully, and give Northwest DC10s greater range potential to boot.

Equally important, he and Nyrop reasoned that the inevitable "bugs" which must be eliminated from new mechanical equipment had been dealt with during more than a year of 747 operation, so adoption of the JT9D would mean relatively trouble-free integration of the DC10-40 into daily service.

It cost Northwest an extra half-million dollars per plane to make the engine substitutions — $11 million for an eventual 22 DC10-40s — but Nyrop laughed his way to the bank ever after because of the big savings that piled up.

"With the commonality of engines," he explained at the time, "we had a spare parts inventory of $116 million. That's only 9% of our fleet's cost at that time, largely due to standardization of engines and airframe parts, while the industry average is about 20%.

"At the industry average, we would have had $236 million tied up in spare parts, or an *extra* $120 million on which we'd have had to make a profit. Take 10% of that $120 million and that's $12 million more we'd have to earn per year —actually $24 million when you consider taxes."

So aircraft engine standardization saved Northwest a net $24 million every year?

"More than that. With interchangeable engines and parts, we make additional savings because fewer specialized tools are needed, as well as fewer employee training programs."

Savings like this take on a special meaning when one considers that in 1975, six of the nation's major airlines posted a loss, and only two of the others — led by Northwest's $43.4 million — earned a net profit that came even *close* to $24 million.

The observant air traveler will note that Northwest's DC10-40s have a third landing gear in the center of the plane (as opposed to only two on conventional models) which helps the NWA aircraft handle a larger total load — including extra fuel — enabling them to fly a greater distance than other DC10s.

Frequent reports published in *Aviation Week* and *Space Technology* have borne out the fact that Northwest DC10-40s exceed similar planes

CARL MAGNUSON, retired Superintendent of Power Plant Engineering, carried out the research that led to the decision that Northwest DC-10s could be powered by the same basic type of engine as the 747 — an unprecedented move that saved millions.

of all other domestic airlines in average ton capacity — as well as exceeding capacity figures of the competitive Lockheed 1011 — regardless of which engines are used by the competitors. Report after report also showed NWA's DC10 engine maintenance expense to be lowest in the industry in every respect — fewer problems, better engine durability, and less cost to overhaul.

As a sidelight to this success story, it's interesting to note another Nyrop trademark: whenever practical, he avoided committees. One of the nation's largest carriers sent a committee of 10 to observe Northwest's overhaul of a JT9D engine that had operated efficiently for an unheard-of 8,300 hours since its last previous disassembly. Chuckles engine expert Carl Magnuson:

"Northwest would have sent one good man."

To demonstrate the range of its new DC10-40, NWA made a nonstop demonstration flight from Los Angeles to Hong Kong — 7,677 miles — with F.A.A. officials and several representatives of McDonnell Douglas aboard, before introducing the plane in daily service. This record commercial airline flight took only 14 hours and 44 minutes, most of it against a prevailing head wind.

Among the more important components added to Northwest's fleet at that time were four wingless "aircraft" which cost $9,300,000, yet never lifted a paying passenger off the ground.

These computerized prodigies are flight simulators, which can duplicate any real life flying situation, and perform several other maneuvers that would be imprudent to carry out on purpose in an operational plane.

Internally, each simulator is identical with the completely instrumented cockpit of one basic type of jet in the fleet. Externally, the simulators resemble so many box-shaped moon probes, resting on skinny hydraulically-operated legs. For complete realism during four-hour training "flights," simulators are equipped with electronic visual systems, so the crew sees exactly what it would on an actual trip.

DRAMATIZING THE SIZE of this jet engine nacelle, three flight attendants climbed inside one to have this picture taken.

Flight instruction went big league when the airline bought its first digital simulator back in the Sixties, and since then Northwest has become noted in the industry for practical innovations that contribute to more effective pilot training.

This kind of leadership must be earned under the eagle eye of the F.A.A., which permits no carrier to modify approved training programs without first convincing this regulatory agency that a new idea will achieve better results.

From the not-so-good old days of the tiny Link trainer, right up to mid-1976, all airline instruction programs were geared to testing and improving the efficiency of *individuals*. Much as

this approach had accomplished, Northwest's flight operations men felt an important ingredient was missing.

"In the real world, a modern flight crew works as a team," explains Captain Tom Nunn, veteran director of flight training. "When a problem is encountered, all pilots in the cockpit must participate in a disciplined and coordinated plan to resolve the situation. So to begin with, our instructors worked out a series of training programs involving three flight officers, rather than the old one-man-at-a-time method of being tested by a check pilot."

These programs were refined after trying them out on 20 three-man teams of pilot volunteers, "and in only one month the terrific response from our crews made it clear we had a winner." Impressed by the program's complete success, the F.A.A. granted Northwest the nation's first exemption from past training methods in order to permit adoption of

FLIGHT ATTENDANTS acquired new uniforms about the same time the DC-10 began arriving in the latter part of 1972.

22 MCDONNELL DOUGLAS DC-10s with an original passenger configuration of 236 began arriving in November, 1972. They proved to have a range exceeding 7,500 miles.

"L.O.F.T." (Line Oriented Flight Training) as it is known today.

Soon afterward, the F.A.A. ordered *all* United States airlines to install L.O.F.T. — another in a long line of ways in which Northwest ingenuity has benefited the entire aviation industry.

When a flight crew reports for periodic proficiency tests (all captains are required to do so twice a year), everything is carried out exactly as if the men were assigned to fly between two NWA destinations. The captain files a flight plan, receives his usual briefing — including designation of an alternate airport — and studies all weather advices, including ground level and high altitude conditions.

Weather changes and other potential in-flight problems are activated by a check pilot, and the crew's handling of both routine and emergency situations is evaluated on a group basis.

"Modern flight simulators are so accurate and so realistic," comments Nunn, "that we'd use them even if they cost more than assigning line aircraft for pilot training. But expensive as they are, they save important money."

First of all, simulators make it unnecessary to take aircraft out of commercial use. Next, they conserve huge amounts of fuel. Just one four-hour check flight in a 747, for example, would consume 15,200 gallons of kerosene. Finally, simulators save on maintenance — and reduce air traffic, too.

Another important point about instructional philosophy: Northwest also pioneered the idea of rotating line pilots into instructorship positions, as opposed to those airlines which use a permanent instructor group.

"We believe in an operational approach," says Nunn, "and by rotating instructors on a carefully planned basis, we've found it helps them retain their proficiency and their touch with the real world of flying. We have no theoretical people making decisions — just down to earth practical guys in whom their fellow pilots believe."

FIRST DC-10 SERVICE TO THE ORIENT was celebrated by Tokyo personnel on June 2, 1973.

28

Problems — and a Golden Anniversary

A SEVERE ENERGY SHORTAGE and sharply escalating fuel prices hit the U.S. with a bang in the last quarter of 1973, when Arab nations established a total oil embargo against the United States and the Netherlands.

One of the few happy notes of that news-filled year was President Nixon's announcement on January 23 that an accord had been reached ending the long and wearying war in Viet Nam. In the months to follow, Senate hearings on the Watergate break-in filled the headlines, Henry Kissinger became Secretary of State, Vice-president Spiro T. Agnew resigned and was replaced by Gerald R. Ford, Pablo Picasso died, Marlon Brando refused an Oscar for his role in *The Godfather,* three U.S. astronauts spent 59 days in a space lab, and food prices also went into orbit.

Against this backdrop of national and international events, the government established an airline fuel allotment, granting carriers 95% of their 1972 usage.

This posed a temporary hardship for Northwest Airlines, since a 95-day pilot strike had restricted operations the previous year, but the entire fleet was kept in service, even though some flight schedules were abbreviated.

In Montana and North Dakota, where several communities are dependent on NWA for all or most of their air service, flights were continued on the same frequency as before. Where schedules had to be reduced, Northwest made these cuts solely on its own hook, avoiding any service reduction agreements with other airlines in competitive markets.

Efficient scheduling of aircraft — including a growing number of DC10-40s and 747s then on tap — helped Northwest end the year with a net of $51.85 million.

One of 1973's highlights was a temporary return to China, which Northwest still was authorized to serve at such time as the U.S. and Chinese governments chose to reactivate a mutual agreement. For the first time since NWA's forced evacuation of 1949, two red-tailed planes landed at the Peking airport under a special authorization to bring in supplies for the U.S. mission there, following success of the Nixon-Kissinger "ping pong diplomacy" which had helped warm up relations between the two countries.

A few months later, 14 Chinese government electronics experts visited Northwest's main base to observe computer operations which were regarded by many competitors as the industry's most efficient. One of many NWA sales tools that year was the first computer-generated airline ticketing procedure, introduced in January. In addition, Northwest used newly developed techniques to extend its "Insta-Res" system to Anchorage and — via Honolulu — to Tokyo, thus making NWA the first U.S. airline to provide reservations personnel with direct computer access to and from the Orient.

At the same time, new 24-hour-a-day reservations service was made available to all continental U.S. cities through telephone connections with a centralized reservations office in the Twin Cities. Another speed-up in passenger service was the addition of new X ray equipment for the security check of baggage at key airports.

Even the handling of U.S. mail — once the backbone of Northwest's business — was modernized when the airline introduced a new containerized mail system for the Postal Service, thus retiring the time-honored mail sack and enabling faster aircraft loading.

By the time 1974 rolled around, inflation had worsened and gasoline pump lines grew longer.

Maximum speed on U.S. highways was dropped to 55 miles per hour, and a full year of daylight-saving time was mandated to conserve fuel. Sharing headlines with the energy problem were the Patty Hearst kidnapping, Charles Lindbergh's death from cancer, Willy Brandt's resignation as Chancellor of West Germany and — for the first time ever — a U.S. President's resignation, when Richard Nixon stepped out and was succeeded by Vicepresident Gerald Ford.

The OPEC oil nations relaxed their embargo on oil shipments, but boosted prices to a point where Northwest's fuel costs more than doubled in one year, rising to $159.8 million in 1974, or 21% of total revenues. The C.A.B. granted offsetting fare increases to the industry, and during the year Northwest placed in service the final seven of its 22 DC10s, which helped achieve a new record in passenger and cargo miles plus a record net of $64.7 million. This was followed by another industry-leading performance in 1975.

To interviewers who pestered Donald Nyrop

GOLDEN ANNIVERSARY BOARD OF DIRECTORS in 1976 included, from the left, M. Joseph Lapensky, Donald G. McNeely, Lyman Wakefield, Jr., Raymond H. Herzog, Malcolm S. Mackay, Donald W. Nyrop, Melvin R. Laird, James H. Binger, Hadley Case and James N. Land, Jr.

with questions about what the airline was going to do when he turned 65 in April of 1977, he had a standard answer: "We've got a dozen well seasoned men around here who could run this airline just fine."

To prove his point, on the golden anniversary of Northwest's first mail flight — October 1, 1976 — Nyrop stepped out of the presidency and into chairmanship of the board, with M. Joseph Lapensky becoming the airline's first up-from-the-ranks president. Joe Lapensky — a summa cum laude graduate of St. Thomas College in St. Paul — came to Northwest as a junior account-ant in 1945, and worked his way up through a variety of important posts, eventually becoming vice president of finance and treasurer, as well as a member of the Board of Directors. At 57, he had 31 years of service behind him when he was named president.

The *Minneapolis Tribune* reported: "In New York, a leading Wall Street airline analyst seemed perfectly content with Lapensky's selec-tion, even though he knows very little about him. His reasoning was elementary: 'In building Northwest into the financially strongest airline in the industry,' he said, 'Nyrop's judgments have been impeccable. So why should I think he's suddenly screwed up in picking Lapensky? Besides, if Lapensky hadn't learned what it takes to run a profitable airline after 22 years with Nyrop, he wouldn't still be there'."

To celebrate Northwest's fiftieth year, the St. Paul Area Chamber of Commerce observed the birthday of its "godchild" in a novel way.

Since Colonel Lewis Brittin founded North-west while still an official of the St. Paul Association — predecessor of the Chamber —its membership decided to sponsor a salute to the airline at a huge civic luncheon in the Holman Field hangar where Northwest planes had been serviced in the early thirties. The cement-floored hangar was turned into a giant dining room for the occasion, and in addition to St. Paul's Mayor George Latimer and other dignitaries, the program included Robert F. Six, long-time president and by then chairman of Continental Airlines, as principal speaker.

"Northwest Airlines is a model for the rest of us in this business," said Six, then the nation's senior airline official in years of service.

"Northwest is first in profit as a percent of revenue in the airline industry . . . first in profit for four of the last eight years, first in retained earnings, first in shareholders' equity relative to airline size . . . and adds multi-millions per year to the Minnesota economy, a majority of it in payroll. These figures mark a triumph of ingenuity and application, of zeal and of judgment. They tell their own story of 11,500 men and women shaping their work lives to create a corporate unit which accomplished what free enterprise is all about.

"If it had not been for Don Nyrop, the Twin Cities today would be just another stop on the system of another airline. He gave direction, control, cadence and spirit to Northwest. He helped make air travel safe, swift, and efficient. This brilliant achievement in business enterprise has been accomplished with the aid of a highly professional staff and a magnificent fleet.

"You really got a winner in Don Nyrop. He made your airline fly higher than anyone ever thought it could."

Former stewardesses, some of whom served under Rosie Stein on the early DC3s in 1939, attended the golden anniversary luncheon garbed in their uniforms of years past, and two vintage aircraft — both dating back to the airline's fledgeling years — captured the atten-tion of luncheon guests just outside the old hangar.

These planes, a 1927 Waco biplane and a 1931 Stinson Junior monoplane, represent the hobby of a Northwest father-son pilot team — Captains Daniel F. Neuman and Dan Jr. — who located the old planes (one in Iowa and the other on a farm in North Dakota) and restored them to A-I flight condition.

Both aircraft carried the Northwest Airways emblem that was in use back in the Twenties and early Thirties, and made only one condescension to the present day — they were equipped with

ST. PAUL AREA CHAMBER OF COMMERCE saluted Northwest's fiftieth birthday at a special Holman Field celebration. A reconditioned 1927 Waco with original Northwest logo was the center of attention. Donald Nyrop is seated in the cockpit, and at the right is Robert Six, then chairman of Continental Airlines. Captains Dan F. Neuman and Dan, Jr., also shown.

totally modern radio equipment.

Even during the happy times of its golden anniversary, Northwest was acutely conscious of a problem affecting few other airlines.

That problem is what some observers call "the penalty of leadership".

A case in point was the launching of a new Seattle Gateway-Japan Service Investigation by the C.A.B. to look into possible need for another U.S. flag carrier from Seattle to Tokyo — a route on which Northwest had a bare breakeven load factor of 43%. Splitting that potential between *two* carriers would seem to promise both of them consistent losses, not to mention burning up an extra 25 million gallons of fuel per year unnecessarily.

Commented aviation writer Bill Henzey in

Airline Reports for February 16, 1976:

"It is no accident each year that either Northwest or Delta is the industry profit leader with the other not far behind. Both have achieved an efficiency of operation that is unique in American business, let alone the volatile field of air transportation.

"Last year, Northwest had the U.S. airlines' best profit performance with an estimated net of some $43.2 million. Second best — Delta, with $37.4 million. Yet, no matter how efficient or profitable, neither company is invulnerable and it is cause to wonder how much must be taken out of their hides before success stops being a burden and becomes a key to greater opportunity.

"We could recite a series of recent decisions in which both carriers made formidable cases for

197

new route opportunities but came up short in the decision-making process. The reasons varied in each case, sometimes with peculiar contradictions, but always there seemed to be the underlying belief that they were not in financial distress and therefore, could absorb the loss.

"Clearly, the problems facing C.A.B. in the carrier selection process are substantial, particularly with the largest carriers in the industry in financial distress. Also, the pure mathematics of the process dictate that for every new route winner there will be a half-dozen or so losers. It takes a lot of new route awards to spread things evenly and fairly.

"Such par-for-the-course reasoning, however, suffers when one tries to understand the contradictory logic of the new Seattle-Tokyo case. Little need, certainly none of the priority type, has been shown for adding new competition in a market well served by Northwest. No explanation has been given for shedding (in this market) the government's oft-stated concern with excess competition in the international field generally.

"The government's concern with Japan's

AT SPOKANE'S EXPO 74, Northwest used an authentic Chinese junk from Hong Kong as a floating "billboard."

feelings about a new U.S. carrier between Saipan and Japan apparently doesn't extend to that Nation's certain reaction to a new U.S. competitor on the long haul Seattle-Tokyo route. Ironically, JAL is almost certain to get Chicago if a new U.S. line is added between Seattle and Tokyo, but the U.S. incumbent on that route gets nothing save added competition all around.

"If success does not breed new opportunity, it should be apparent that it cannot long survive as a target for ill-conceived if not contrived efforts to take advantage of it. One more thing: the profit performances of Northwest and Delta were the industry's best last year — but, Northwest's was down $21.5 million from the previous year and Delta's was down $50 million. There is a limit."

Writer Henzey pointed out there have been numerous decisions where the stated intention of the C.A.B. was to give "route strengthening" to a carrier that was in the red, or close to it. The problem, however, is that in cases where the carrier's operating efficiency is not sufficient to turn a profit, new route awards become a burden instead of a boon.

One example he cited was the original Chicago-New Orleans Route Case. Northwest finances were in the black and Eastern was in the red, so Eastern's bid to compete with Delta's existing service was given the nod. Eastern, with a break-even load factor in the high 50s, began losing money on the route. According to their own figures, the highest load factor they achieved was 45% — so when the fuel crisis came along in 1973, Eastern asked for the right to suspend operation.

At that time, Northwest's breakeven load factor was slightly under 33%, so *for NWA*, 45% loads would have meant a profitable operation.

Eastern's departure left Delta operating the route as a monopoly. After long review of arguments in the Chicago-New Orleans case, the C.A.B. finally granted Northwest its first new route award in seven years when it voted approval of Chicago-New Orleans nonstops.

Three daily flights each way were begun June 8, 1977, thus restoring competition on this important north-south segment.

Twin Cities-New Orleans flights via St. Louis were added soon afterward.

At the time of Northwest's fiftieth birthday year, the contrast between its modern fleet and the aging aircraft in use at the time of the airline's darkest moments in 1954 stands out sharply in the following table:

1954 (all piston)

Aircraft	Capacity (each)
7 DC3	21 passengers
18 DC4	50 "
10 Stratocruisers	83 "
1 DC6	76 "
2 DC6 (rented)	76 "
38	

Total Passenger Capacity: 2,105

1976 (all jet)

Aircraft	Capacity (each)
17 Boeing 747	369 passengers
22 DC10-40	236 "
8 Boeing 707-320	165 "
32 Boeing 727-100	93 "
31 Boeing 727-200	128 "
3 Boeing 747F	105 tons cargo
113	

Total Passenger Capacity: 17,727

Fleet modernization expenditures by 1976 had reached $1.44 *billion* invested in 113 modern jets — including more roomy, wide-bodied aircraft for NWA's size than any other carrier. Another order for $134 million worth of planes was on the way, destined to make the NWA fleet — already leading the league in noise suppression — still quieter, because these aircraft

FLIGHT SIMULATORS cost millions but are important training aids. Computer-operated simulators shown here are for the DC-10, left and the 747.

INTERIOR OF A SIMULATOR is an exact replica of an actual plane's cockpit. Pilot crew "flies" the simulator while a check pilot activates its computerized trip through varying conditions and weather.

included the latest developments in decibel reduction.

But no discussion of Northwest's modern aircraft superiority would be complete without noting that an important factor in this leadership is the airline's success at selling used planes for top prices to make room for still more up-to-date models.

Like everything else that goes on at NWA, there's a reason. First, aircraft are depreciated on the books as fast as possible, which is why the airline commonly stands No. 1 in depreciation as a per cent of total revenue. Second, as Chester "Hanley" Holtan — a veteran Northwest pilot — once put it: "Northwest makes all the worth while engine and frame improvements suggested by the manufacturer to keep things up to snuff, so our planes are in demand."

This is a continuous process. For example, when the 747s were quite new, and significantly quieter than most other jets flown in the United States, Northwest spent $6 million to modify the engine nacelles in order to reduce noise still further, and extend Northwest's lead as the quietest airline in the nation.

In his 22 years as president, Donald Nyrop presided over the purchase of 223 aircraft and the sale of 141 — averaging out to more than 16 transactions per year. Clayton Brandt, vice president of purchasing and stores during much of that period, added up the sales one day and discovered they totaled up to $230 million, including several planes purchased by the late Aristotle Onassis.

The quality of Northwest planes is evident from this remarkable fact: all prices are firm, not subject to negotiation. The buyer makes a nonrefundable 25% down payment, and on delivery pays the remaining 75%.

Does this rigid policy work? In one six-year period, Northwest sold 50 jets for $177.9 million. This was $95.5 million *over* book value, so Northwest makes money while keeping its fleet up to date — just about the next best thing to discovering oil in the back yard.

200

29

The Home Town "Plus"

BEFORE MOVING ON from Northwest's golden anniversary year to another history-making era, this is an appropriate moment to pause for a brief look behind the scenes at more of the "grass roots" reasons for this airline's continuing success — reasons that aren't listed in financial reports.

They involve people — and a state of mind.

As a home town airline, Northwest — from top management on down — is peopled almost 100% with products of the towns, farms and cities of its area, and some of the most canny financial observers in the nation's largest money mecca — New York City — have noted what they consider a beneficial rural influence on the Northwest way of operating.

John S. Bliven, long-time first vicepresident of Bankers Trust Company and a student of airline industry economics for more than a quarter of a century, said on the occasion of Northwest's fiftieth birthday: "I saw a play about Lincoln recently, and whenever Abe had a difficult decision to make, he related it back to the farm and found a parallel — plus a solution. Northwest people seem to have the same knack. Maybe it's the advantage of headquartering in the Twin Cities, where there are no ivory towers."

Robert Ebert, retired personnel vice president, recalls the time many years ago when — in order to make a point during a discussion with several department heads — Donald Nyrop reminded them:

"When a farmer comes to a big rock while plowing his field, and merely detours around it, all succeeding rows will magnify the deviation. The only solution is to get off your plow and remove the rock."

Donald Hardesty, retired treasurer, financial vice president and director, made a practice of always carrying a red bandanna in his hip pocket, just to remind himself of his humble beginnings in the rural community of Watertown, Minn.

The first time Hardesty went along to a security analysts' meeting in New York, he remembers Nyrop told the group: "We're just a couple of country boys from the middle west trying to apply the basic philosophy of running a good farm to running an airline."

A few minutes later, as the room temperature kept rising on a warm spring day, Hardesty absently pulled out the bandanna and wiped his forehead. He couldn't have riveted the financial men's attention any better if he had clanged a bell, which was just fine because as things turned out, they were equally intrigued by the precise figures and background information presented by their visitors from Minnesota.

The precision of Northwest's financial information became a legend among the analysts. And over the years that Hardesty continued to take part in these presentations, they felt cheated if he didn't pull out his "farmer hanky" at least once per meeting.

Now that he's retired, Hardesty *still* carries a bandanna — even when he's spiffed up in a tux.

In keeping with the rural and near-rural origin of so many Northwest people, one of the airline's secret weapons might be described as "country boy ingenuity."

As a veteran maintenance specialist once expressed it: "When a farmer runs into trouble, he doesn't call up a service department to get the answers — he fixes the problem himself."

Consider

THE CASE OF THE DC10 LAVATORY.

It seems that on occasion, the rear-most lavatory door on all DC10s used to swing wide open when not latched properly after use. Because of close tolerances in the construction of airplanes, these open doors frequently were crushed by hydraulically-operated exit hatches when these hatches slid down into a closed position before DC10s left the ramp.

This created needless expense and — worse — each occurrence took a multimillion-dollar plane out of service until the door could be replaced. Along with other airlines, Northwest reported these occurrences to the manufacturer — McDonnell Douglas — which assigned some of its engineers to come up with a solution.

The result was Douglas Service Bulletin No. 25-230, complete with a series of detailed engineering drawings describing a complicated process whereby the offending lavatory doors could be made over into self-closing units.

Parts and labor called for in this service bulletin were priced out at $5,030 per airplane by the late Bill Huskins, then Northwest's maintenance and engineering vice president, totaling $110,660 to fix the lavatory doors on all 22

Northwest DC10s. Then Huskins, who used to work on a Minnesota farm as a youth, went shopping at his neighborhood hardware store. For 70¢ he bought a spring-loaded hinge of the type commonly used to keep a chicken coop door closed.

And for $4.49 he bought a much fancier version of the same spring-loaded hinge.

SELF-SUFFICIENT operation of Northwest's main base saves millions on jobs that some airlines "farm out." Here a massive 747 landing gear is being plated in NWA's own shops.

He shipped both purchases to Harold Bayer, a Douglas vicepresident, along with a letter which said, in part: "The engineering concept in your Service Bulletin 25-230 is merely a takeoff of the century-old chicken coop spring-loaded door hinge. In case some of your engineers don't believe the (enclosed) 70-cent hinge is esthetically a good choice, show them the improved easy-to-install substitute at $4.49.

"Your engineers and product support people must be directed toward simple, low cost, highly reliable answers to each design problem — not job-expanding, costly designs such as Service Bulletin 25-230. You may even have to remind some airlines, including Northwest, not to proliferate the complexity by asking that a design answer all whims and dreams of the user.

"McDonnell Douglas must become a leader in the fight to hold costs under control. The subject example is a poor display of that necessary leadership."

Huskins' letter sums up the philosophy under which *all* departments at Northwest operate, which goes a long way toward explaining why the airline has been so successful in its continuing battle to control costs.

A forthright reply to Huskins from Harold Bayer of McDonnell Douglas began: "What can I say? Your letter with regard to the lavatory device says it all . . . I have had several meetings with our Engineering and Pricing departments, reviewing this particular case in point, using your common hardware samples.

"As a matter of fact, (we) . . . intend to use this as a case study to re-emphasize to our engineers the fundamentals of a design-to-cost philosophy. Every once in a while we need a swift kick to put us back in the proper perspective, and your letter did just that."

So in addition to saving Northwest more than $100,000, the "chicken coop hinge caper" had carry-over benefits, as well.

Then there's
THE CASE OF THE CASTELLATED NUT.

Two of these nuts — notched on opposing sides to accommodate a cotter pin — are used in each engine that powers Northwest 747s and DC10s. Most spare parts for airplanes are so high priced that you might suspect they are made of precious metals, but when these ordinary-sized castellated nuts showed up on the supplier's parts list at $80 apiece, an NWA maintenance man asked: "What the hell kind of nut is worth 80 bucks?"

His investigation showed that the $80 item was simply thinner than a standard nut which can be bought in any hardware store for $1.50.

Net result: Northwest buys large quantities of the $1.50 version, machines them down to the proper thickness and runs them through the plating shop — at a total added cost of $2 per nut. In one year, this saving of $76.50 per nut totals up to $29,376 — not an earthshaking figure in itself but not exactly hay, especially when one remembers this type of ingenuity is displayed virtually every day at Northwest Airlines.

One key to these cost-cutting mechanical operations is the fact that NWA's main base operates like a self-sufficient factory, with special shops that can do everything from metal plating to the creation of highly expensive metal tubing and a host of other services that many other airlines farm out.

Often these operations do much more than save initial costs — they also speed things up and contribute to better aircraft utilization. Take THE CASE OF THE SONIC AIR FLOW BENCH.

When engines for 747s and DC10s undergo periodic reconditioning, it formerly was necessary to send metal blades from the JT9D turbines back to Pratt and Whitney for cleaning and testing, because this process must be carried out by creating jets of air that move at the speed of sound — a highly technical and difficult process that most carriers are willing to leave to the manufacturer.

"Why can't we do the job right here?" asked Northwest engineers. At the cost of $4,000 and a fistful of ingenuity, they fabricated a sonic air flow "bench" (an unlovely metal contrivance

ANOTHER EXAMPLE of self-sufficiency is the creation of costly metal tubing to order in Northwest's maintenance and overhaul shops.

about the size of a large office desk) which reconditions turbine blades on the spot.

During just its first year of operation, this innovation saved $651,840 in maintenance costs. It also speeded up the process of getting engines back in service, which is particularly important from an investment point of view, when one considers that each engine then cost $1,100,000 to begin with — the price of almost 100 Cadillacs at that time — not to mention expensive improvements added after purchase.

Even the routine job of painting aircraft lends itself to NWA ingenuity.

In 1975, an electrostatic painting process was installed, making use of the scientific principle that opposite charges attract each other. Each plane is given a positive charge, while the paint is charged negatively. This achieves two improvements. Paint thus applied goes on in a completely uniform thickness, and there is no overspray. This cuts paint cost 50%, and — in a switch from the past — allows maintenance men to carry out other tasks at the same time, because the air is not filled with solvents and paint.

Next,

THE CASE OF THE "HAY MOW DOORS."

When Northwest's 22 DC10-40s were on the way in 1971, their measurements were so large that the 58-foot-high tails of these luxurious new tri-jets posed a serious problem: the doors of four existing Main Base hangars in the Twin Cities are only 48 feet high.

The apparent solution was to build four new aircraft "barns" at an estimated cost of $9 million. Donald Nyrop asked his engineering department: "Why not cut auxiliary keyholes extending above the present doors, so the tails will slip through?"

"Impossible," was the answer. "This would weaken the trusses that hold up the roofs."

But Nyrop, who had a knack of challenging his cohorts to outdo themselves, insisted that the idea be pursued.

His engineers came up with a practical way to cut four new "hay mow doors," as they were known internally, without weakening the hangar structures. The total rehabilitation cost was $2,225,000, which saved $5,775,000 outright, to say nothing of the considerable expense that would have been involved in land acquisition and costly slowdowns in the assimilation of new aircraft.

And now,

THE CASE OF THE DOCTOR'S PROBE.

Back in the Stratocruiser days, a curious Northwest mechanic was struck by the fact that by use of an instrument known as a cystoscope, his doctor could examine the human bladder without the necessity of surgery.

"Why couldn't we make a similar probe that would check internally on the condition of valves, pistons and cylinders without spending the time and money to open everything up?" he asked. An enlarged version of the cystoscope was constructed, and it performed perfectly,

"HAY MOW DOOR" KEYHOLES allowed the high-tailed DC-10s to use existing hangars, and saved Northwest $5,775,000 in the process — another example of ingenuity at work.

when inserted through a spark plug hole.

Today, thanks to that mechanic's bump of curiosity, jet engines are made with special accesses for the new tool — known as a boroscope — and the condition of blades, vanes and other internal parts can be checked in a fraction of the time once required.

Northwest's unique ability to combine cost control with accompanying benefits has been noted earlier — such as pioneering noise suppression techniques that also save aircraft fuel. Another little-known example of this ability is the "fly-away acceptance" of new aircraft.

This was a maverick idea when NWA launched it in 1960, because it had been standard practice for all airlines to station one or more men for months — sometimes years — at

aircraft manufacturing plants where carriers had placed an order, in order to monitor construction work. But when its very first jets went on the assembly line, Northwest management concluded this traditional policy was a waste of manpower and an insult to the manufacturer.

That expression of trust not only saves manpower, but it also puts manufacturers on their mettle to deliver a topnotch product, with no one to share the blame if all specifications are not met.

Expert acceptance crews from the airline carefully check each plane out on the way to Minneapolis-St. Paul, and if they find any modifications are needed, Northwest makes necessary changes and bills the manufacturer. As a result, Northwest gets mint condition

AN INGENIOUS MEDICAL PROBE gave one Northwest mechanic the inspiration to create a tool known as the boroscope, which can check the "innards" of an aircraft engine.

aircraft, and both parties to the deal save money in the long run.

William Allen, who headed Boeing for many years, commented at the time of Northwest's fifitieth anniversary: "We have nothing but admiration for Northwest and its operating methods. They are tough but fair negotiators. You always know where they stand, and I like that."

As we've examined a variety of Northwest activities, it has been noted that the airline often invests millions in customized improvements of which the public is rarely aware — ranging from superior engines to state-of-the-art weather forecasting — and often saves millions through careful planning and ingenuity.

But a frequently overlooked point about the savings that accumulate is this: as the most consistently profitable operator in the industry, Northwest is commonly around the 50% income tax bracket (before investment tax credits.) So the "home town bunch" in Minneapolis-St. Paul, as students of practical economics, have updated an old saying: a million saved is *two* million earned.

They've also proved the secret of success begins with a dedication to doing the job right, even if it means "getting off the plow to remove a rock."

PART VII

Europe, Deregulation
and
the First Merger Ever
(1977-1986)

30

One More Ocean to Cross

WITH A SOLID LINEUP of domestic and transpacific routes, including Hawaii and Alaska, Northwest Airlines had eyed Europe for years as a means of adding still more balance to its revenue picture.

But for years international routes were difficult to come by. If acquired at all, the slow process was remindful of those sports trophies that must be won three times in a row before gaining permanent possession. First, there had to be a treaty or other inter-government agreement between the nations involved. Next, applicants competed for approval of an Administrative Law Judge and a majority of the Civil Aeronautics Board. Even then, the award is never final unless ratified by the White House — sometimes the toughest hurdle of all.

Nevertheless, in the middle Seventies Northwest saw an opportunity for an entering wedge into northern Europe. Pan American, as the 20-year holder of rights to serve Scandinavia and Scotland, had neglected these countries to a point where it carried only a skimpy 7% to 8% of all U.S.-Scandinavian traffic, offering flights between only one U.S. city and one in Scandinavia, with no service at all to Glasgow.

Pointing out that Pan Am's failure to gain anything even *close* to a 50% share of the U.S.-Scandinavian market was costing the U.S. more than $58 million a year in transportation revenues at a time when the unfavorable balance of trade had become critical, Northwest filed for the "orphaned" routes to Norway, Sweden, Denmark, Finland, Iceland and Scotland.

At a 1975 hearing before the C.A.B., Northwest proposed to replace Pan Am on these northern routes with a competitive schedule of fares and service with big 747 aircraft, and then underscored its argument with an effective presentation of the strong ethnic ties between Scandinavia and Minnesota, as well as several other nearby states served by NWA.

In the normal course of affairs, C.A.B. hearings are often grim and humorless, but this one was different. It ended up with the participants chuckling right along with Northwest Vice President J.W. "Bill" Campion — an Irishman — when he made a valiant effort to pronounce several words that would be duck soup for a Swede or a Norwegian, but not for a shamrock-wearing descendant of the "ould sod."

"I'm no expert at the Scandinavian languages," Bill told the Administrative Law Judge, "but if you want to see for yourself the community of interest between Minneapolis and northern Europe, I have two suggestions:

"Visit famous Minnehaha Park in the spring on *Svenskarnas Dag* and you'll be convinced that the entire city of Minneapolis is taking part in this giant celebration of Swedish Day, as it's called in English. Or in this same park you can see hundreds and hundreds of Norwegians in colorful costumes dancing up a storm on *Syttende Mai.*"

(Phonetically, these two Scandinavian holidays are pronounced "Svens-KAR-nahs Dahg" and SIT-ten-dee-MY," which is the Seventeenth of May — Norway's Independence Day.)

The C.A.B. was both entertained and impressed by Campion's presentation, and in July, 1976, approved Northwest's application. But then it languished on President Gerald Ford's desk until December, when he sent it back to the C.A.B. for review.

In the meantime, support for Northwest's bid continued to grow, and further arguments were placed before the Board in August, 1977. In C.A.B. parlance, the "Boston Parties" (Massachusetts Port Authority, Greater Boston Chamber of Commerce and the New England Council) summed up their case like this: "We support Northwest's position at Boston as a co-terminal to the North Country Route . . . we favor Presidential approval at the earliest opportunity . . . our support for Northwest is unequivocal."

Twin Cities and Minnesota officialdom chimed in: "In its first decision on this case, the Board decided that Northwest should operate the route . . . Nothing has since occurred that requires a different decision."

Detroit officials testified: "The Detroit Parties wholeheartedly endorse the certification of Northwest . . . a capable, aggressive and efficient carrier with extensive international experience."

Even the U.S. Department of Transportation shook its finger at the long delay: "There is no point in continuing the uncertainty about whether . . . Northwest's proposal should be accepted as a previous Board recommended."

By this time, the White House had a new occupant — Jimmy Carter — and after North-

west had sweated out another six months, the magic moment came on January 23, 1978, when Carter OK'd the C.A.B.'s final recommendation in favor of Northwest. Boston and the Twin Cities were named as co-terminals, and — happily — a previously recommended restriction that would have prevented Northwest from carrying local traffic between New York and Copenhagen was withdrawn.

There was little time to celebrate that an opening wedge into Europe had been achieved, because next came the demanding job of gearing up to handle these new routes — new personnel,

NORTHWEST SPEAKS MANY languages around the globe. This advertisement in Norway promotes executive class travel to the U.S. Similar ads also appear in Danish and Swedish.

new equipment, new offices, new airport "gates," new advertising, new everything in six more nations, five of them speaking new languages.

On top of everything else, a 109-day pilot strike in 1978 slowed things down, so even though Northwest managed an impressive $68.1 million profit for the year, a start on the northern route was deferred until early 1979.

All-cargo flights were scheduled first, while Northwest was getting used to the new routes, and the first passenger 747 across the Atlantic took off from the Twin Cities March 31 via Detroit and New York to Copenhagen and Stockholm. This was followed by Seattle-Twin Cities-Boston-Glasgow-Copenhagen passenger flights, with service to Oslo, Norway, beginning May 29, 1980.

At the same time the campaign to serve northern Europe was in full swing, Northwest set out to add another dimension to its transatlantic service by turning its attention to jolly old England.

London had been lurking in Northwest's hope chest ever since the "almost merger" with National Airlines, which owned a route to England's fabulous capital city. But now a brand new opportunity had arisen under an air rights treaty with the United Kingdom which provided that the U.S. could select one new gateway — and one airline serving that city — for nonstop London authority.

This news kicked off a wide open competition that became known as the "Wild Card Route Case," with 15 cities and several airlines locked in a free-for-all that somewhat paralleled professional football's "wild card" playdown to select an extra candidate for Super Bowl honors.

To Northwest, this was a battle for home town pride as well as for new revenues. Situated in mid America, Minneapolis-St. Paul — despite all the foreign cities already served by Northwest — still had not hit the "big time" as a nonstop international gateway to a foreign capital, but here was a chance to gain that distinction.

With 15 cities in the running, the odds were poor, but in its 60-year history, Northwest has shrugged off unfavorable odds on many occasions, and this was one of them.

Eventually, after all the competitors had filed lengthy briefs (one of the mysteries of life is that briefs never live up to their name) the rivalry narrowed down to a point where it seemed likely the winning gateway would be chosen from among Denver, Kansas City, Las Vegas, St. Louis, Pittsburgh, Tampa or the Twin Cities. Western and Northwest were running neck and neck to become the "Wild Card" airline if the Twin Cities should become the new gateway.

Then in 1979, good news and bad news walked in together.

The C.A.B's Bureau of International Aviation recommended selecting the Twin Cities and Northwest, but while the Board's Administrative Law Judge agreed on the Twin Cities, he endorsed Western as the carrier. This left Northwest with one last ditch chance — a final hearing before the full membership of the C.A.B.

A solid front of support for Northwest welled up in its home state before arguments were presented to the Board January 16, 1980. Enthusiastic endorsements of Northwest's selection came from Governor Albert Quie, the entire Minnesota congressional delegation, Mayors Donald Fraser of Minneapolis and George Latimer of St. Paul, T.E. Halloran, vice chairman of the Metropolitan Airports Commission, and numerous civic and labor groups. Many Northwest employees joined in by writing letters of their own.

The multiple supporting messages spotlighted five key reasons for choosing Northwest:

1. Its proposed fares and flight frequencies were the best submitted by any airline.

2. As a Twin Cities based carrier, NWA could best service the route.

3. Northwest already had the type and number of comfortable, widebodied aircraft needed to fulfill present and future schedules.

IN ENGLAND, Scotland and Ireland, travel prospects learn about Northwest's outstanding first class service via ads like this one.

4. As the most efficient U.S. carrier, Northwest could provide the best guarantee of superior service in both good times and bad.

5. Of Northwest's 12,000 system-wide employees at that time, half were Minnesotans earning $200.8 million annually, and the new route would increase local employment, further enhancing Northwest's already major impact on the Minnesota economy. (At that time, Northwest was paying $6.7 million in annual Minnesota taxes, plus another $9.1 million in airport use fees.)

The final result of this team effort was a smashing victory for Minneapolis-St. Paul and for Northwest. The C.A.B. made its formal recommendation on February 15, 1980, and after reviewing the findings, President Carter added his signature.

So another key date in Northwest's history went into the books when its new London "bridge" was inaugurated with a Boeing 747 on June 2, 1980.

Six weeks before the London flights began, Northwest generated considerable extra attention for the new service when President Joe Lapensky hosted an aerial press conference for 140 news reporters, government officials and tour operators aboard a brand new Boeing 747.

While this entourage was flown from the Twin Cities to Duluth and Minnesota's famous iron range, flight attendants served a champagne brunch and President Lapensky filled his guests in on details of Northwest's long-sought transatlantic routes. One of the out-of-town newsmen, knowing that Northwest then operated 29 747s in all, asked the cost of the plane in which the group was riding, and was amazed to discover that the going price for just one of the jumbos was virtually the same as the tab for Minneapolis' $50 million Hubert H. Humphrey domed stadium. (Six years later the price of a 747 had risen to the equivalent of *two* Humphrey stadiums.)

As the long fight for Twin Cities-London neared a climax, still another heated battle was under way for the right to become this nation's second carrier over the coveted Boston-London route. Four airlines — Northwest, Braniff, World and Capitol — set off in hot pursuit of this authority.

In order to introduce immediate competition on that route, the C.A.B. named World Airlines to provide service on a temporary basis pending an oral hearing attended by the competing carriers.

Undaunted, Northwest — already established as a major carrier with excellent facilities in the Boston market — set out to prove it should be

IN THE ORIENT, NWA advertising appears in Japanese, Chinese, Korean and English. This is a Japanese language ad promoting key U.S. destinations served by Northwest Airlines.

the No. 1 choice for permanent Boston-London authority.

After an evidentiary hearing, the Administrative Law Judge determined that in every significant measure of consumer benefit — primary market fares, behind-and-beyond-gateway fares, primary market service, additional single plane service and online support — Northwest led the field. The Bureau of International Aviation strongly supported these findings. In addition, Northwest proposed giving Boston its first service to Hamburg, Germany, via London under a new bilateral

agreement that had been filed with the Federal Republic of Germany.

When this welcome combination of benefits for the traveling public could not be equaled by the other competitors, Northwest won the right to launch Boston-London-Hamburg flights on April 26, 1981. The original two round trips per week were increased to five by early June, and later on, Frankfurt replaced Hamburg as the German terminus of this service.

While the "battle for Britain" was under way in late 1979, Northwest developed yet another opportunity to broaden its transatlantic market when TWA — as Pan Am had, somewhat earlier — filed notice of its desire to suspend service to Ireland, thus leaving that country with no U.S. flag carrier whatever.

TRANSATLANTIC travel, plus bargain sightseeing in the U.S., are featured in this German language advertisement.

NWA quickly leaped into the breach with an application for authority to add Shannon, Ireland, to its already going route serving Scotland and Scandinavia. Almost as quickly, the C.A.B. said "yes," and the Emerald Isle became a Northwest port of call for the first time on April 27, 1980. Later, Dublin became the second Irish market served by the red tail fleet.

The remarkable fact about Northwest's series of successes in transatlantic expansion is that it all had been accomplished in a comparatively short period of time, often with two or three projects overlapping each other.

So the net of these efforts was that by alertly going after several European markets that either had been neglected or abandoned, and by winning out in rugged head-to-head competition for additional routes that were highly sought after, Northwest ingenuity succeeded in putting together a highly viable "package" of service to the historic and eye-filling wonders of England, Scotland, Ireland, Germany, Norway, Sweden and Denmark.

What's more, despite heavy startup costs involved in serving still another continent, it took NWA only four years to put these new routes solidly in the black while bucking a severe recession that plagued the early '80s.

In the meantime, jubilation over these new routes across the Atlantic was tempered by the knowledge that a concurrent event was changing the airline business forever — an ongoing event known as deregulation.

31

The Deregulation Era — Boon or Boondoggle?

A WIDE RANGING debate over domestic airline deregulation came to a climax in the halls of Congress in 1978.

Proponents claimed deregulation would be a boon to everyone — better choice of service at competitive prices for the public, freedom for airlines to fly where they wished and set their own ticket prices — in other words, freedom to "get the government off their backs."

Opponents argued that sudden deregulation of one of the most henpecked industries anywhere would lead to serious imbalances of air service, ruinous price wars, financial failures, unemployment, overcrowded airports, and just about as much government red tape as ever.

After the Airline Deregulation Act became law in October, 1978, both sides wound up with plenty of opportunities to say "I told you so."

The new law created a wild free-for-all that spurred competition, as predicted, but its timing couldn't have been worse, because jet fuel prices more than doubled in 1979, just as the nation was sliding into a severe recession that was to hang on for three years. By then, 42¢ of every Northwest revenue dollar went to buy fuel.

It was in this climate of an already deepening squeeze on profits that upstart nonunion carriers — unburdened with multiple labor contracts — began to proliferate. Their prime weapon was — and is — that wages normally comprise the largest single cost of operating an airline, so the battle was joined, not only among long-time competitors but with many "Johnny-come-latelys" as well.

While the deregulation debate was heating up in 1978, Northwest noted two new "firsts" that year — one in Japan and one in the General Office. Primarily to house its own international passengers transiting Tokyo, NWA opened the brand new 212-room Narita International Hotel just a 15-minute ride from Narita airport — its first venture into the hotel business. Back in the G.O., a fast-rising young executive named Steven G. Rothmeier was named Vice President-Finance and Treasurer, at 32 the youngest chief financial officer among all the major U.S. airlines.

The puzzles of deregulation officially became President M. Joseph Lapensky's "baby" on January 1, 1979, when he took over the reins from Donald Nyrop as Chief Executive Officer. While it took a few months for the new law's full impact to be felt in the industry, some airlines behaved like a kitten after its first taste of catnip and gobbled up new routes so fast they had trouble absorbing them.

At the peak of the early rush, Braniff — later to go broke — entered 18 new cities in *one day*.

Northwest, however, carefully added only a few new destinations at a time. The first three were St. Louis, Las Vegas and Orlando, Florida, gateway to two Disney complexes as well as other popular tourist attractions. At that same time, NWA was busy expanding its transatlantic service and initiating 18 new nonstops between U.S. cities already served by the red-tailed fleet. Later that year, Phoenix and Fort Myers, Florida, also became new Northwest ports of call.

With three recession years still to come, the U.S. airlines had such tough going in the last half of 1979 that as a group their operating losses totaled $436 million. Northwest — despite the fact Uncle Sam had grounded all the nation's DC10s for a series of tests that took five weeks — ended 1979 with a net profit of $72.48 million, second highest in company history, but skinny times were ahead for all.

In addition to widespread financial woes, the nation's morale took a beating on the international scene that year when rabid followers of Iran's Ayotallah Khomeini took 63 Americans hostage in Teheran and sneered at the attempts of President Jimmy Carter's envoys to negotiate their release.

The following year — 1980 — brought U.S. airlines their worst year ever — worst up to then, that is — as a world wide recesion shrank air travel while jet fuel costs went ever higher, bringing the industry's operating losses to more than one billion dollars. Even though Northwest's operating expenses for the year exceeded operating revenues by $24 million, NWA came through with a $7 million net profit, thanks to sound financial planning that reaped millions in investment tax credits acquired by owning — rather than leasing — its planes, as many other carriers were reduced to doing. Only two other trunk carriers finished 1980 out of the red.

One happy note that year was Northwest's selection by the U.S. Department of Commerce to operate a 747F all-cargo charter to Peking, carrying displays for a United States Industrial Exhibition to be held in the People's Republic of China.

Next, NWA was asked to fly 200 officials and technicians to China for U.S. firms participating in the exhibition, and shortly afterward also carried 500 travel agents to this slowly reopening market. (It was to take four more years before Northwest received approval to reopen regular service to Shanghai.)

Another hands-across-the-sea project carried out in 1980 was Northwest's marketing abroad of "Visit U.S.A." passes, which provided extensive travel in the United States at a special fare, to help boost the recession-plagued tour business.

By the second year of deregulation, six regional airlines had gone bankrupt and 30 more — several of them commuter operations — closed their doors forever.

Then in 1981, with the recession deepening, Ronald Reagan — who had snowed Jimmy Carter under in the previous November election — was sworn in as President of the United States on January 20. That same day the American hostages held captive in Iran for 444 weary days were released and flown to freedom.

Scarcely seven weeks later, Reagan narrowly escaped with his life when he was shot during a bizarre assassination attempt by a troubled youth named John W. Hinckley. This also was the year the U.S. space shuttle *Columbia* became the world's first reusable spacecraft, and an illegal strike by federal air traffic controllers sharply curtailed the number of flights that could be handled throughout the U.S. An angered President Reagan ordered the controllers back to work. Those who refused were fired, with new controllers trained to replace them.

At the end of 1981, mounting operational losses sustained by the nation's carriers reached a frightful $1,485,000,000, with seven more regional lines bankrupt and another 13 out of business.

Layoffs and wage cuts had become common

NARITA INTERNATIONAL HOTEL, with 212 rooms, was opened by Northwest in 1978 near Tokyo's airport, primarily to house passengers transiting Japan.

in the industry by then, yet from the beginning of deregulation right up to this sixtieth anniversary year, Northwest has added employees continuously (more than 4,000 in all) and — instead of wage cuts — has granted increases to a point where the average increase in employee pay stands at 58%, but we're getting ahead of our story.

While managing a 1981 net of $10.46 million as one of only four carriers showing a profit, Northwest also initiated nonstops between Los Angeles and Tokyo, Tokyo and Guam (a favorite Japanese holiday destination) and between Taipei and Manila, while continuing to expand European service with Boston-London and Twin Cities-Oslo flights.

Also during this year still another example of Northwest ingenuity began contributing to the yearly black figures.

With the invention of a new type of airplane seat that was more comfortable yet less bulky than those previously in use, a fleet-wide program was launched in 1981 to increase the capacity — and the economic value — of NWA's existing 106 passenger aircraft by fitting them all out with these new seats, which increased a 727's capacity from 126 to 146 persons, a DC10's seating from 236 to 292 and a big 747's maximum from 367 to 394.

These modest-sounding increases per plane added up to a whopping total of 3,000 more places to put a paying customer — the equivalent of adding 15 new airplanes to the fleet, at a cost of only $33 million.

Fifteen new aircraft would have priced out at about $225 million. Thus the new seating project represented an initial saving of some $192 million, not to mention continuing benefits reaped by lowering the fleet's overall operating cost per seat mile.

Fare wars proliferated in 1982 as more nonunion carriers joined the competiton for passengers while the economy still limped along in low gear. When 12 more airlines went bankrupt, one of them hit the headlines everywhere because it was the first of the "big name"

lines to succumb. Braniff, after a series of disastrous losses, filed for protection under the bankruptcy laws and told its 9,500 employees: "Don't call us unless we call you."

While these events were going on, Northwest began serving eight new domestic airports — Denver, Dallas-Ft. Worth, Omaha, Kansas City, San Diego, West Palm Beach and Grand Rapids. NWA also negotiated an even dozen long term union contracts in an atmosphere of cooperation and understanding that saw the airline grant reasonable wage increases while the unions agreed to various productivity improvements that were essential to continue competing in the hectic world of deregulation.

The year also saw another step upward by the man destined to play an ever-growing role in Northwest's future when Steven G. Rothmeier — at the age of 36 — became Executive Vice President-Finance and Administration, and was elected to the Board of Directors.

Then on September 26, 1983 — eight days before his thirty-eighth birthday — Rothmeier was elected President and Chief Operating Officer, making him the youngest chief executive of a major U.S. airline. His election broke (by four years) the record set in 1954 when 42-year-old Donald Nyrop became the youngest Northwest president up to that time.

An outgoing individual with a deep feeling for people, Steve Rothmeier packed a variety of activity into his first thirty-eight years. A Minnesota native (Faribault, via Mankato) he earned a degree in business administration at the University of Notre Dame in addition to winning his varsity letter as an aggressive six-foot-two linebacker under football coach Ara Parseghian.

After college, Rothmeier joined the U.S. Army, earned a lieutenant's commission and served as a combat officer in Viet Nam, where he was decorated with several honors including the prestigious Bronze Star.

Back to civilian life, he entered the University of Chicago Graduate School and completed his Master's Degree in Business Administration in

M. JOSEPH LAPENSKY, former president, C.E.O. and Chairman of the Board, retired May 20, 1985, but still serves on the Board.

1972, before beginning his Northwest career as Corporate Financial Analyst.

M.J. Lapensky — who retained his position as Chief Executive Officer while stepping out of the presidency to make way for Rothmeier's newest promotion — had been named earlier that year by *The Wall Street Transcript* as 1982's "outstanding C.E.O. in the trunk airline industry" for his stewardship in helping keep Northwest profitable "through deregulation troubles, complicated by high fuel prices . . . and cutthroat competition."

Among several other major happenings during a news-filled 1983 was the welcome fact that the American economy began a dramatic recovery, even though the nation's airlines shuddered through still another billion-dollar operating loss while five more carriers went

bankrupt, including another of the majors — Continental — whose mounting debt exceeded a billion dollars.

Northwest, with its European routes already profitable, bucked the industry trend by boosting passenger traffic 13% in 1983 and raising its passenger load factor to 60% — the best since 1956 — while earning a net profit of $50 million.

That was the same year the OPEC countries cut oil prices for the first time in 23 years, Sally Ride became the first U.S. woman in space, American troops kicked Cuban forces out of Grenada and terrorists made two suicide bomb attacks on the multi-national peacekeeping forces in Lebanon, killing 241 Marines and sailors as well as 40 French paratroopers billeted just two miles away.

The 1983 demise of Continental Airlines — which had lost $471.9 million since January, 1979 — was followed by a unilateral cancellation of its labor contracts and across-the-board wage cuts, after which Continental resumed business as a nonunion carrier with about 30% of its former employees and a reduced network of only 25 cities, instead of 78. Its pilots saw $89,400 salaries slashed to $43,000, and only a third of 2,800 flight attendants were recalled, with former $29,000 salaries chopped to $14,000.

Even Delta, which frequently duels Northwest for profitability honors, recorded an $86.7 million loss for its fiscal year ending June 30, 1983, and promptly froze the wages of 32,000 nonunion employees while asking members of its only two unions — pilots and flight dispatchers — to defer pay raises or work longer hours.

As one means of self-preservation, all the leading carriers — including Northwest — found it necessary to work out a two-tier salary plan with their unions, under which current employees retained their pay scales, while those hired in the future would come in at lower levels.

Several airlines found that two-tiered salaries, plus paycuts and labor concessions, still were not sufficient to halt the financial bleeding, with further layoffs and wage reductions leading to months of labor strife.

At the time of Continental's bankruptcy, the Associated Press summarized the plight facing the nation's carriers:

"Desperately bleeding profits, major airlines are cutting costs to slow the hemorrhage, even as they are attacked from all quarters by new competitors that didn't grow up partners in one of the highest paid industries in the world . . .

"High labor costs have characterized the airlines for decades, but until deregulation opened the skies to new, low-cost competitors, the unions were in a position of strength, and the airlines generally passed the costs on to passengers through government-approved higher fares.

"And it wasn't just the glamour jobs with the high price tags. A report by the Civil Aeronautics Board says airline workers in general are paid higher than in the rest of the industry.

"For example, the C.A.B. said in 1980 key punch operators who worked for the airlines earned 31 per cent more than the average wage for all key punch operators. Typists at airlines were paid 41 per cent more; for computer operators the differential was 38 per cent.

"Among the major airlines, labor costs have almost tripled in the last decade, to $12.5 billion from $4.6 billion. According to the Air Transport Association, the average compensation in 1982 was $39,193, compared with $15,650 in 1972.

"Labor, as a percentage of airline costs, has declined to 35.3 per cent from 46.8 per cent, but only because fuel costs in the same period soared from $1.2 billion to $9.7 billion.

"The airlines have little control over fuel costs except to buy more efficient planes that they cannot afford. And since a jet runs on kerosene only, switching to some other form of fuel was not an available option.

"But labor is adjustable and most airlines have taken steps to bring costs down. Continental's petition to seek court protection from creditors while it reorganizes under the Federal Bankruptcy Act is the most radical, but some analysts say it may not be the last airline to file for bankruptcy protection to get out from under costly labor contracts."

The AP's review of airline troubles contrasted the situation of the old established carriers with one of the new breed of nonunion operators — People Express:

"Pilots for upstart People Express, which turned in a profit its first full year of existence, start at $36,000 and there is no shortage of applicants . . . and these pilots do more. In fact, virtually all of People's 2,000 employees are managers — flight managers (pilots), customer service managers (flight attendants) and maintenance managers. Each is a stockholder and each performs a variety of functions that their senior counterparts at other airlines are forbidden by their contracts from doing."

The AP forecast of more bankruptcies came true in a hurry, with 20 of them recorded in 1984, including Air Florida and Wien Air Alaska. Fourteen smaller carriers also closed up shop, even though U.S. airlines as a group finally posted more black figures than red.

This was the year Ronald Reagan was re-elected in a landslide, Indira Gandhi was assassinated by two of her own bodyguards, a violent Mexico City earthquake killed thousands, the summer Olympic Games were held in Los Angeles (with Russia sitting them out), Richard Burton died, the cruise ship *Achille Lauro* was hijacked in the Mediterranean and baseball's Pete Rose eclipsed Ty Cobb's "unbeatable" record of 4,192 career hits.

It also was the year that great planning, a strong marketing job and hard work made Northwest the No. 1 U.S. transpacific carrier — and by a wide margin over its old rival Pan Am. The return to Shanghai that spring — after a 35-year hiatus — was another welcome morale booster for the Orient Region.

Net earnings from operations totaling $86,964,000 in 1984 were reduced to a still highly respectable $55,964,000 by an extraordinary one time net charge of $30,903,000, when the U.S.

Supreme Court refused to review a lawsuit that had bounced around in the courts for 15 years.

The suit involved employment of male pursers as flight attendant supervisors in the Orient from 1967 to 1970. The attendants' union had ratified contracts covering this custom because at that time the Oriental culture did not accept women supervisors, but in 1970 a claim was filed on behalf of 3,354 female flight attendants under the Equal Rights and Equal Pay Acts. While the courts did not hold that Northwest intentionally discriminated against women, they ruled that the jobs of purser and flight attendant were not significantly different, and should receive equal pay.

Since the Sixties, female pursers have become

STEVEN G. ROTHMEIER became president of Northwest Airlines, Inc., September 26, 1983, eight days before his thirty-eighth birthday, and Chief Executive Officer on January 1, 1985.

accepted in the Orient, and Northwest equalized the pay differential between pursers and other attendants back in 1976.

At the annual shareholders' meeting in 1984, a new corporate identity was approved under which the airline began operating as a wholly owned subsidiary of NWA Inc., with one share in Northwest Airlines becoming one share in NWA Inc. The change was effected to facilitate future expansion and possible business diversification, both of which — as we will see shortly — were just around the corner.

By the close of 1984, Northwest had added 25 new U.S. cities under deregulaion, and on the first day of 1985 President Steven G. Rothmeier was elevated to Chief Executive Officer, placing him in full charge of the airline at the age of 39.

His 11-year-rise through eight different job categories had included — in addition to several key financial assignments — responsibility for personnel administration, industrial relations, communications and computer services, properties and, while he was Manager of Economic Analysis in the Regulatory Proceedings Division, Rothmeier represented the airline with great skill in Civil Aeronautics Board rate, route and fare proceedings.

An articulate communicator, on the day he was named C.E.O. Rothmeier made it clear that he believes in taking employees into his confidence and letting them know exactly where they stand in Northwest's game plan.

In Steve Rothmeier's view, they stand very high indeed, because "the airline cannot succeed without great customer service every step of the way."

"We want employees to know we have a plan, a direction, and they all have an important role in that plan," says Rothmeier. "Our individual standard of living and our corporate standard of living depend on winning the battle for market share. Each one of us is competing directly with his or her counterpart at all the other carriers — and the pie is not all that big, because there are 13 more jet operators today than when deregulation took effect."

In his first message to employees — which Rothmeier titled "Profit is Not a Four-letter Word" — he emphasized that profit, which he sees as a form of "shared winning," is the only source of job security for everyone at the airline.

He also pointed out that while Northwest has maintained an enviable (though sometimes slim) profitability throughout deregulation, profits were running $376 million behind actual requirements to keep updating Northwest's fleet.

NEW TECHNOLOGY 184-passenger 757s are the quietest and most fuel-efficient jets in the air. By the time Northwest's first 20 757s were in service, another ten had been ordered, plus 10 new generation 747-400s as part of a two billion-dollar purchase — the largest single aircraft expenditure in Northwest history. (That's Manhattan in the background, and Governors Island almost directly below.)

"Ten years ago," he explained, "a $50 million profit was equal to the price of seven 727 airplanes, while today a $50 million profit barely exceeds the cost of just *one* advanced technology 757." (And it now takes $100 million to buy one 747.)

At that time, Northwest had its first twenty 757s on the way, and then in 1985 signed a $2 *billion* purchase agreement for 10 more 757s, plus 10 new generation Boeing 747-400s and three long range 747-200s — the largest single aircraft order in the airline's history.

Among Rothmeier's many reasons for maintaining communications with employees on a continuing basis is this interesting fact: in the first six years of deregulation, Northwest employment increased by 4,000, and still another 4,000 were added to the payroll as replacements — chiefly for retirees — so with 8,000 relatively new members on his "team," the new C.E.O. sees employee indoctrination and training as vital to success.

"We're bringing in very bright, aggressive young people," he says, "and we're fortunate to have a world of experience in so many key areas that our people are melding into a solid group of winners. The opposition can't defense intelligence, speed, experience and superior service."

Nor is the opposition going to have an easy time defending Northwest's growing fleet superiority. The ultra-computerized new Boeing 747-400 will outperform any competing aircraft on Northwest's transpacific route, and the 184-seat 757 is the quietest, most fuel-efficient jetliner in existence, contributing important new gains in two areas of well-established Northwest leadership — noise reduction and cost-effectiveness of operation.

For example, on a nonstop segment from the Twin Cities to New York, the 757 consumes 31% less fuel than an advanced 727-200, and by carrying more passengers — 184 versus 146 — racks up a stupendous 46% fuel saving per available seat. Even compared to the larger DC-10, the 757 makes a 40% fuel saving per seat.

This kind of operating efficiency, of course —

added to many other kinds of cost control — enhances Northwest's ability to compete as a full service airline against the new breed of low overhead "bare bones" operators.

Also in the realm of efficiency, NWA has doubled its computer capability twice in recent years at a cost of nearly $55 million, and one of many new business necessities that brought this about is the whirlwind of change that now exists in the realm of air fares.

"In 1975," Rothmeier explains, "we had just three fares — first class, coach and Discover America. In the first 12 days of 1986, the industry had 989,000 fare changes. Even in a comparatively quiet week, there might easily be 100,000 fare changes nationally, 27,000 of them directly affecting Northwest. Since deregulation, the fare situation has become a totally different world."

Under Rothmeier, so has Northwest's management style.

Gone are the days when Donald Nyrop even made the decisions on what type of fabric — and what colors — would be used to cover the seats in company aircraft. Like Nyrop and Lapensky, Rothmeier keeps close tabs on what goes on throughout the airline, but he is realistic enough to know that with Northwest's tremendous growth, the time had arrived to decentralize a certain amount of authority and accountability by giving considerable decision-making power to trusted members of his management team.

To use a football analogy, Rothmeier — as head coach — establishes the play book, then it's up to his assistant coaches to execute the strategy and produce results.

One of Northwest's recent innovations is an annual report from management to flight attendants whose care and feeding of the traveling public leaves a lasting impression on the passengers' minds.

An article in *Twin City Business* on January 6, 1986, reported:

"At a recent meeting of 450 Northwest sales representatives, a vicepresident introduced the 12 'Flight Attendants of the Month' for 1985, with fanfare provided by the Richfield High School Band. After testimonials to the flight attendants' exceptional job performance and the company's appreciation of these efforts, the meeting ended with a standing ovation. Sales representatives lingered in the hall, reluctant to let go of this moment of employee-management unity."

Among those sales representatives were several men who specialize in one type of customer service that is little-known to the general public, yet now is approaching 20 per cent of all annual revenue.

It is no accident that by this sixtieth anniversary year, Northwest has become by far the largest freight carrier of all U.S. passenger airlines, and — even in competition with major cargo-only carriers — enjoys the fourth largest air cargo business in the *world*.

The commitment to go all out after air freight as an important adjunct of the passenger business — instead of treating it like a step-child, as some airlines do — began with Donald Nyrop and has been carried forward with great effectiveness under Joe Lapensky and Steve Rothmeier.

Every plane in the fleet contributes to the total, but the most dramatic gains have come since 1975, when Northwest became the first — and only — U.S. passenger carrier to buy three specially constructed Boeing 747 freighters (747F), with "big mouth" nose hatches to facilitate the loading and unloading of king-sized cargo.

Six weeks before the first 747F arrived, Nyrop called in three staff members — Rothmeier, then Manager of Economic Analysis; Allan Pray, at that time Director of Schedule Planning, and Reginald Jenkins, who was Vice President of the Orient Region — and assigned them the job of filling up the new freighters, with special emphasis on transpacific markets.

As part of their research, the trio learned from a Boeing analyst about a brand new source of commodity data at the U.S. Department of Commerce. They became the first to tap this valuable information while compiling an elaborate study that proved it was economically feasible to move a surprising number of items by air.

Their list of air-eligible commodities grew by the day, and ranged from asparagus, citrus fruit, lettuce, cherries and salmon to oil drilling pipes, cattle and automobiles.

Northwest's cargo sales people eagerly charged forward with this information in hand, and at the same time another $4 million was invested to install an extra loading hatch on the side of each jumbo freighter, large enough to accommodate a full-size American automobile.

The front nose hatch can, and does, swallow 190-foot long pipes used by oil drillers as far away as southeast Asia, as well as gulping down containers 11 feet wide by 10 feet high.

A year after the first three 747Fs had gone into service, Joseph F. Murphy, writing in *Air Transport World,* commented: "There were those in the airline business who thought Don Nyrop had made his first big bust last year when he took delivery of three giant 747Fs in about three months. Well, almost as if their presence had turned on a switch, the east-bound air freight business has been going like gangbusters ever since . . .

"And for those industry observers who thought Nyrop had flipped his lid by ordering three 747Fs, he has added an order for a fourth, to puzzle them still further."

It becomes somewhat easier to understand why it became economical to ship many perishable U.S.-grown foods across the Pacific by air when one considers these fairly common 1977 prices in a Tokyo market: oranges, up to 75¢ apiece; apples, $1 each; round steak, $16 up, per pound; hamburger, $5 or more per pound; fresh fish, $7 per pound.

When the first 747 freighters arrived, ground handling of containers at airports was speeded up by the addition of 10 huge custom-made cargo loaders ($177,000 apiece), each capable of hoisting 55,000 pounds with ease.

In addition to creating these physical shipping

LIKE A RAVENOUS SHARK, 747 freighter gulps down 105 tons of pay load. NWA is the largest freight carrier of all U.S. passenger airlines, and versus all-cargo carriers enjoys the fourth largest air freight business in the world.

aids, practical technical help was provided for shippers as well. One was a toll-free "Cargo Central" offering rate information and advice on how to load containers efficiently for the lowest shipping rate. The star attraction was a computerized cargo analysis service based on the Rothmeier-Pray-Jenkins research. For the first time, this made it possible to figure instant cost comparisons of air versus sea transportation, taking into account freight forwarding, packaging, surface handling, cost of capital, duties and a variety of other charges.

Eastbound cargo from the Orient also began to grow, when Orient shippers learned it was economical to send clothing and other textiles, cameras, tape recorders, hi-fi units, binoculars and many other products via Northwest, instead of by ship as in the past.

As business to and from the Orient continued to mount in volume, Northwest now has increased its fleet of 747 freighters to six, and among their more unusual cargoes have been entire plane loads of blooded cattle shipped to Korea for breeding purposes. With the addition of European destinations, of course, transatlantic freight has helped swell the company totals.

Domestic air freight has surged forward too. One of the reasons is that computer analysts have been able to show executives in several different fields that they can avoid the overhead of warehousing goods in a variety of different markets by the money-saving expedient of letting air freight deliver this material as needed, from a centralized manufacturing point.

"Air Freight is Cheaper Than a Warehouse" headlined the *Minneapolis Star* several years ago, while reporting that Munsingwear, Inc., had become the first U.S. clothing firm to save money by replacing a warehouse on the Pacific coast with Northwest air freight service.

The net of all this growth — accompanied by new and larger freight handling facilities in such key markets as Boston, Los Angeles and New York — is that Northwest cargo sales (including mail) have risen from $32.4 million back in 1972 to $408.53 million per year in 1985.

Another facet of Northwest's overall marketing strategy that received special attention in 1984 and 1985 was the development of an "Airlink" program, under which four regional carriers joined forces with Northwest to provide mutual feeder services, giving NWA connections to 38 additional cities and giving the regional lines convenient access to a wide variety of domestic, European and Orient destinations.

First to join in an Airlink marketing agreement was Mesaba Airlines, a Minnesota corporation serving cities in five states. The next three were Big Sky Airlines of Billings, Mont., America West, headquartered in Phoenix, and Fischer Brothers Aviation, serving destinations in Ohio and Michigan from a Detroit hub.

All Airlink cities appear in the Northwest time tables, and passengers receive one-ticket service to or from any NWA destination, plus check-through baggage service, pre-arranged connections and full Free Flight Plan mileage credit. All flights of the regional lines appear on the computerized Northwest reservations system.

Another significant 1985 business move was the first truly vertical integration for the new corporation known as NWA Inc., through the purchase of Mainline Travel, Inc. (MLT), a tour wholesaler with annual revenues of approximately $100 million. MLT markets travel

THE FIRST TWO ULTRA MODERN 757s added to Northwest's fleet were christened "The City of St. Paul" and "The City of Minneapolis" at a March 15, 1985, ceremony attended by 1,000 cheering bystanders and the mayors of both Twin Cities — Donald Fraser and George Latimer.

packages through 6,500 independent retail travel agencies, giving Northwest a sizeable presence in tour wholesaling for the first time in its long existence.

With Northwest now serving Europe as well as the Orient, Hawaii, Alaska and many scenic mainland regions from coast to coast, MLT becomes an important adjunct to NWA's continuing battle for market share.

Maintaining a remarkable record of having increased that market share every year since the start of deregulation — and having done so profitably — Northwest closed out 1985 with a net profit of $73,119,000.

Despite Northwest's showing, turmoil still rocked the airline industry. TWA, wallowing deeply in debt, was taken over by financier Carl Icahn, but in the first quarter of 1986 was reported still losing nearly a million dollars *a day*. Eastern — after three years of wage cuts, labor strife and layoffs — was staggering under a debt of 2½ *billion* and on the verge of bankruptcy when it was purchased for $676 million by cost-cutting Texas Air Corporation in early 1986, subject — as always — to government approval. And Pan American, which had been sinking deeper and deeper in debt since 1980, made a deal to sell its long-held Pacific routes to United for $750 million.

This, of course, poses a sharp challenge to Northwest's hard-won Pacific supremacy among U.S. carriers, because even before its new purchase, United already topped all this country's airlines in size.

But Northwest has played the role of giant-killer in the past, and with 40 years of know-how in the Pacific, is grimly determined to retain its laurels. One weapon in its arsenal of strategies was the decision to become the first airline to order the sophisticated new version of the Boeing 747 known as the 747-400. This new technology aircraft is expected to set the standard for passenger comfort and operating efficiency for the next decade and a half.

With a stretched upper deck and distinctive winglets that improve aerodynamic perform-

ance, the 747-400 (like Northwest's new 757) features a highly computerized instrumentation system that requires only a two-pilot crew. In addition, the new jumbos operate with a 22% fuel saving over the standard 747, while providing a passenger capacity of 450 and an 8,000-mile range that easily permits nonstops from New York to Tokyo or Shanghai.

The first seven years of deregulation produced a variety of side effects — some lesser known than others — in addition to the well publicized upsurge of new carriers, the rash of failures and outright bankruptcies with attendant unemployment, as well as fare wars, wage cuts, labor strife and mergers.

But much to the surprise of many, the big have gotten bigger. United and American Airlines between them accounted for 28.6% of the total operating revenues among 11 major U.S. airlines in 1980, but by 1984 their share had burgeoned to 31.9%. Obviously the architects of deregulation had no such eventuality in mind, but the facts speak for themselves.

Nor did the proponents of deregulation foresee the glut of arrivals and departures that has forced interminable delays on passengers at the busiest airports, even on ordinary travel days to say nothing of weekends and holiday periods.

For example, at the time deregulation became law, nine airlines served the Minneapolis-St. Paul International Airport, carrying approximately 11 million passengers in and out annually with 220,000 aircraft movements.

But in 1985, the number of passengers remained roughly the same, while 33 airlines — nearly *four times* as many as in 1978 — required 330,000 aircraft movements to handle them. The same pattern has been noted at many points throughout the nation, so it is no wonder aircraft noise complaints are at an all time high.

The Metropolitan Airports Commission of Minneapolis-St. Paul felt the problem had become so acute that in late 1985 its members adopted a resolution calling on the federal government to resume its old policy of regulating the number of flights allowed into the nation's airports from coast-to-coast.

While the general public is not aware of it, the government's hand still rests heavily on the shoulder of every airline when it comes to requirements for filing voluminous financial and statistical information — about 400 typewritten pages a year, in Northwest's case — and much of it is intimate traffic data which allows competitors to pick each others' brains.

Speaking before the International Civil Aviation Conference at The Hague, Netherlands, in a 1985 discussion of deregulation, former Northwest Chairman Joe Lapensky denounced the unfairness of such reports open to rivals:

"Segment load data, perhaps the best single key to a carrier's scheduling strategy and traffic plan, is laid bare for all to feed upon. Here the clear advantage goes to the mega carriers with huge computer systems capable of crunching sensitive competitive data into devastating market advantage."

With all deregulation's problems, few in the airline business would want to see a return to the old days of economic regulation, but virtually everyone is agreed that proprietary information about one's own business strategy deserves to be under house lock and key.

32

The First Merger Ever
— and a Birthday

NORTHWEST AIRLINES began its sixtieth year as the only major U.S. carrier to achieve that position without a merger.

But under deregulation, things were changing fast. The biggest operators were getting bigger, with merger and takeover rumors multiplying in financial circles — especially after it became known that despite objections by its own Justice Department, the government was going to approve United's purchase of the Pan American Pacific routes, making the largest U.S. airline a vastly more sizeable adversary.

Northwest, in good financial health, and Republic Airlines — rejuvenated after serious losses — figured in quite a few of the takeover rumors on Wall Street.

Steve Rothmeier and Stephen Wolf, his opposite number at the other Twin Cities-based carrier — Republic — "knew that their companies had to get substantially bigger — and quickly — or be gobbled up by others," as the *Minneapolis Star and Tribune* reported later.

One sunny day in June, 1985, Wolf phoned Rothmeier to suggest that the two get together to discuss deregulation problems and possible business alternatives that might lie ahead for the two airlines. This call led to a series of quiet meetings between the two at various Twin Cities hostelries. The meetings broke off in late July with an agreement to talk again before the end of the year.

Republic had been brought back from the brink of bankruptcy in 1983 when its unions agreed to a 15% pay cut as part of a deal under which employees were to receive 5½ million shares of stock.

Founded in Clintonville, Wis., as Wisconsin Central Airlines in 1946, the young carrier featured a mallard duck in flight as its emblem, but the insignia became affectionately known to the general public as "the blue goose."

Wisconsin Central changed its name to North Central in 1952 when company headquarters moved to Minneapolis-St. Paul, and by that time was serving 19 midwest communities on a route system that was largely the doing of energetic Hal Carr. Carr had become marketing vice president in 1947 and about the time of the Twin Cities move took over as president.

North Central grew and prospered, extending its route system as far as New York and Boston, in the east, and westward to Denver. With the advent of deregulation, North Central joined in a 1979 merger with Atlanta-based Southern Airways to create what then became Republic, thus acquiring much needed destinations in the lower half of the United States.

Republic followed this move by purchasing San Francisco-based Hughes Airwest, but acquisition costs that required heavy borrowing at a time of extremely high interest rates — plus the vicissitudes of deregulation — soon found Republic in the red. Losses mounted to $220 million between 1980 and 1983, but the airline gamely began a comeback that was accelerated by Stephen Wolf when he was appointed as president and C.E.O. in early 1984.

A hard working "graduate" of three other airlines — most recently as president of Continental — Wolf gained additional concessions from employees, restructured the route system, put together a successful marketing team, finished 1984 with a net of $29.9 million and 1985 with a whopping net of $177 million. (Republic's debt, however, stood at $674 million.)

On the day after Christmas, 1985, Wolf and Rothmeier resumed their meetings. But this time they were not discussions — they were *negotiations,* because both men were quite sure that the time for action had arrived.

New takeover and merger rumors abounded, although very few of the guessing games, oddly enough, involved a possible combination of Northwest and Republic.

In order to maintain tight security on all aspects of the bargaining, each C.E.O. involved only two associates in the negotiations. At Northwest, these men were James A. Abbott, Executive Vice President-Finance and Administration and General Counsel, and John Edwardson, Vice President-Finance and chief financial officer. Wolf's confidants included Al Maxson, Chief Financial Officer, and Ralph Strangis, Republic's Assistant Corporate Secretary.

Everyone on the two merger teams gulped when Minnesota Governor Rudy Perpich, fearful that thousands of Minnesota jobs might vanish if either Northwest or Republic — or both — should become a takeover target, publicly suggested that the two merge. They gulped again when Ray Glumack, Metropolitan Airports Commission Chairman, echoed the thought.

But no word of the Wolf-Rothmeier meetings seeped out, and confidential negotiations con-

ONE OF REPUBLIC'S 168 aircraft at the time the merger into Northwest was announced January 23, 1986, was this Convair 580, carrying the mallard duck symbol known to many as "the blue goose."

230

tinued right up to 3:30 a.m. the morning of January 23, 1986, when everything had been finalized except an exact price per share of stock.

Minutes before the Northwest Board of Directors was to meet on that date, Rothmeier telephoned Wolf with a final offer of $17 a share. Wolf accepted, and both airlines' boards of directors ratified the agreement, which called for Northwest to buy Republic in a cash-for-stock deal totaling $884 million.

Three years earlier, Republic's stock had sunk well under the $3 level, but its recent comeback — plus the impetus of takeover rumors — had brought the price up to $14 on the day the purchase was announced.

One Twin Cities official hailed the news as "a marriage blessed in heaven," not only because it would keep the Twin Cities on the map as a major air commerce center but because the "wedding" would avoid a mass migration of workers that would have followed if even one of the airlines had been absorbed by an out-of-town competitor.

Nearly half of Northwest's system-wide 17,000 employees live in the Twin City area, as do 5,500 of Republic's 13,400. The Northwest Minnesota payroll exceeds $336 million annually, with Republic's another $196.5 million, so it's no wonder Minnesota officialdom breathed a sigh of relief at news that the two airlines would combine at "home."

Out of the millions of Republic shares to be purchased for $17 each by Northwest, the 5½ million shares issued to Republic employees as part of their wage concession deal in 1983 were valued then at $6 apiece, so the gain of $11 per share for these holders totaled $60.5 million.

Republic's rapid expansion during deregulation had increased its network to 107 U.S. cities, with traffic hubs at Detroit, Memphis and the Twin Cities. Its 168 aircraft included 126 DC-9s, which are ideal for the large number of shorter haul markets on the route system.

Northwest — in most years the seventh largest U.S. carrier — logs approximately 22 *billion* revenue passenger miles per year, with Republic

— No. 9 — totaling 10.7 billion. Depending on year-end figures for 1986, the "new" Northwest is expected to become the third or fourth largest U.S. airline.

Stephen Wolf, who announced he would step out of the management picture once the merger was complete, commented: "It was the right deal for our shareholders and for the long term personal security of our employees."

The prodigious task of integrating the two airlines devolved on the strong shoulders of Steve Rothmeier, who called it "a unique opportunity to mesh the best of two cultures, to take the strongest aspects of two systems and combine them into one very large and competitive operation."

While the eventual approval of Republic's shareholders and the U.S. Department of Transportation was still to come, Rothmeier's merger task force began putting in 10 and 12-hour days to prepare for the moment when nearly 30,000 employees and 312 aircraft could begin operating under one banner.

Following government sanction of the purchase announced July 31, 1986, Northwest began preparations to eliminate the word "Orient" from its promotional vocabulary. Adopted unofficially in the late Forties to emphasize international stature, "Northwest Orient" does not reflect an airline that today spans two oceans and serves three continents. (While the term was used widely for years, the company's legal name has always remained Northwest Airlines, Inc.)

Well before merger talks moved onto the front burner, Northwest was in the process of constructing a handsome new glass and stone World Headquarters to replace the 25-year-old airport G.O. which the airline had outgrown.

This new General Office, six air miles due east of the airport in the suburban village of Eagan, was nearing completion at the time of the Republic acquisition. But one of the bittersweet problems of growth is that — even with 267,000 square feet of space — the new G.O. cannot accommodate all of Northwest's suddenly

NORTHWEST'S NEW WORLD HEADQUARTERS, an attractive glass and stone building in Eagan, six air line miles east of the Minneapolis-St. Paul International Airport, was nearing completion well in advance of the airline's sixtieth "birthday" October, 1986. Top view is from the northwest; lower view from the south shows all four levels of the new headquarters building.

232

enlarged "family" in Minneapolis-St. Paul.

As a result, existing Republic headquarters at the Twin Cities airport, plus a portion of the old Northwest General Office not required for current expansion of Main Base shops, will continue to house personnel whose activities require close proximity to the airport and NWA's maintenance base.

The history-making acquisition news all but eclipsed the fact that Northwest was about to celebrate its sixtieth anniversary in the fall of 1986 as the oldest U.S. airline with a continuous designation. (The closest rival for that title — Western — fails to qualify because for a time in the Thirties it was known as General Airlines.)

October 1 is observed as Northwest's "birthday," although incorporation papers were filed one month *before* actual Twin Cities-Chicago air mail flights began on that date in 1926 with Speed Holman at the controls.

While following our "people story" through the intervening 60 years, we have watched this one time Middle West puddle jumper earn its way into the elite of the United States aviation industry by establishing a standard of excellence that has made NWA the most consistently profitable airline among the majors.

This also makes Northwest an odds-on favorite to *continue* winning the battle of deregulation, because it is manifestly true that profit is not a four-letter word — it's an eight-letter word spelled s-u-r-v-i-v-a-l.

As we have seen, contributing importantly to the airline's strength is a healthy balance of income from domestic, European and Orient markets, with strong cargo revenues adding to

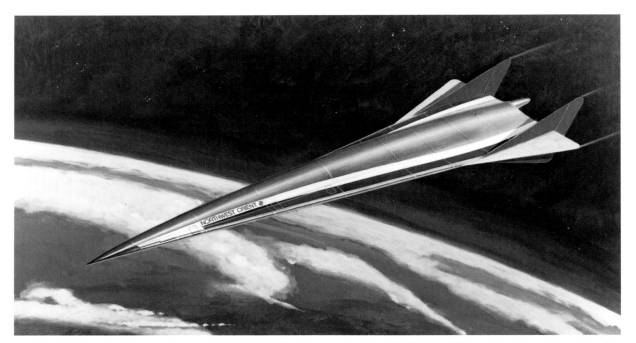

HYPERSONIC PLANE OF THE FUTURE, as conceived by McDonnell Douglas, is projected to fly at five to six times the speed of sound, making a New York-Tokyo flight a matter of about 3½ hours. Northwest President Steven G. Rothmeier has notified relevant government agencies of Northwest's desire to join in working toward realizing the goal of a "technically sound and economically feasible hypersonic aircraft."

the diversification in its "portfolio," along with NWA's recent entry into the wholesale tour business.

Today, Northwest jumps the two most famous "puddles" on the map — the Atlantic and the Pacific — as the only true two-ocean U.S. flag carrier. Quite a feather in the caps of the thousands of men and women who have contributed over the years to making this airline a world-wide industry leader.

How high can Northwest fly? Time — and people — will provide the answer.

But with confidence born of success and fired in the crucible of rugged competition, we may well see Northwest teamwork lead the way into a coming hypersonic era featured by fantastic airplane speeds that will eliminate jet lag and reduce once-awesome SSTs like the Concorde to the equivalent of an aerial skate board.

P.S. Things are happening so fast at Northwest Airlines these days that just as this book went to press — August 12, 1986 — Steven G. Rothmeier was named Chairman of the Board as well as C.E.O., with John F. Horn becoming President and Chief Operating Officer.

At 44 a Northwest veteran of nearly 20 years, John Horn had been serving as Executive Vice President — Corporate Planning and International. Immediately prior to that post he was Vice President of the Orient Region for more than four years during Northwest's surge into the lead as the No. 1 U.S. transpacific carrier.

At the same time, James A. Abbott, previously Executive Vice President — Finance and Administration and General Counsel, was moved up to Vice Chairman and General Counsel.

Appendix

NWA Operational Aircraft — 1926 to 1986

Dates listed indicate first year any plane of that type was acquired. Passenger capacity subject to different seating configurations. The "real world" cruising speeds shown — as opposed to manufacturers' claims — were arrived at after careful research by Carl Magnuson, Northwest's retired Superintendent of Power Plant Engineering.

In addition to operational aircraft pictured, in its early years Northwest also used several other planes, chiefly for company business or as "fill-ins," including the Stinson Reliant, Stinson "Junior," Fairchild F24, Cessna Bobcat, Fokker FIX and Stearman C3B.

THOMAS MORSE SCOUT, 1926. Rented to open mail service October 1.

CURTISS ORIOLE, 1926. Also rented to open mail service.

STINSON DETROITER, 1926. Four purchased; three-passengers. Cruising speed 85 M.P.H.

238

LAIRD BIPLANE, 1927. Two owned; used for mail only, cruised at 135 M.P.H. "Speed" Holman's personal plane was a Laird, which he flew in competition and in exhibitions.

WACO, 1928. Nine acquired, used mostly for mail. Waco Taper Wing cruised at 115 M.P.H.

HAMILTON METALPLANE, 1928. Nine purchased. Six passengers, cruised at 125.

FORD TRI-MOTOR, 1928. Five owned. Fourteen passengers, cruised at 125 M.P.H.

SIKORSKY S-38, 1931. Two purchased to serve Duluth harbor in absence of airport. Eight passengers, cruised at 110 M.P.H. The only amphibian ever owned by Northwest.

TRAVELAIR 6000, 1931. Four purchased; seven passengers, cruised at 118 M.P.H.

LOCKHEED ORION, 1933. Three of these wooden-framed planes with hand-retractable landing gear acquired. Five or six passengers. Cruised at 180, capable of 200 M.P.H.

LOCKHEED ELECTRA 10-A, 1934. Thirteen owned, plus one 10-B; 10 passengers, cruised at 140.

LOCKHEED ZEPHYR, 1937. Twelve acquired, carried 12 to 14 passengers, cruised at 160.

DOUGLAS DC3, 1939. Thirty-six purchased, 21 passengers, 140 M.P.H. cruise speed.

DOUGLAS DC4, 1945. Thirty-six owned, five leased; 50 passengers, cruised at 190 M.P.H.

243

MARTIN 202, 1947. Twenty-five owned; 36 passengers, cruised at 210 M.P.H.

BOEING STRATOCRUISER (B-377), 1948. Ten purchased; up to 83 passengers, cruised at 254.

LOCKHEED CONSTELLATION (L-1049), 1955. Four acquired; 74 passengers, cruised at 273.

DOUGLAS DC6, 1954. Twenty-four acquired, 17 the DC6B; 76 passengers, cruised at 259.

DOUGAS DC7C, 1957. Seventeen purchased; 82 passengers, cruised at 322 M.P.H.

LOCKHEED L-188 ELECTRA, 1959. Eighteen of these "jet props" purchased; 77 passengers, cruised at 400 M.P.H.

DOUGLAS DC8, 1960. Northwest's first pure jet, five purchased, 127 passengers, cruised at 550.

BOEING 720B, 1961. Seventeen acquired; 111 passengers, cruised at 550 M.P.H.

BOEING 707-320, 1963. Forty-one owned; 165 passengers, cruise speed 545 M.P.H.

BOEING 727, 1964. Sixty-five now in service, 56 of them the advanced Model 200 with original capacity of 128. Cruises at 550 M.P.H. Currently the Model 200 seats 146 passengers.

BOEING 747, 1970. Thirty-two passenger versions with original capacity of 369, plus six freighters capable of 105 tons each. Cruising speed 555 M.P.H. Ten new-technology 747-400s on order.

DOUGLAS DC-10, 1972. Twenty-two purchased, three later sold. Original capacity 236 passengers, cruise speed 555 M.P.H. Comfortable new seating now accommodates 292.

BOEING 757, 1985. Twenty purchased originally, 10 more on order. Passenger capacity 184, cruises at 535 M.P.H. Hailed as today's quietest, most fuel-efficient airliner.

The Officers of Northwest Airlines, Inc.
(April, 1986)

Steven G. Rothmeier*
President and Chief Executive Officer

James A. Abbott*
Executive Vice President—Finance and Administration and General Counsel

Benjamin G. Griggs, Jr.
Executive Vice President—Operations

John F. Horn
Executive Vice President—Corporate Planning and International

Thomas J. Koors
Executive Vice President—Marketing and Sales

Brent J. Baskfield
Vice President—In-flight Services

John W. Campion
Vice President—Regulatory Proceedings

John A. Edwardson*
Vice President—Finance and Chief Financial Officer

Terry M. Erskine
Vice President—Industrial Relations

Bruce H. Fillips*
Vice President—Comptroller

Phillip R. Gossard
Vice President—Ground Services

Roger D. Hauge
Vice President—Atlantic Region

Allen W. Johnson
Vice President—Orient Region

Benjamin H. Lightfoot
Vice President—Maintenance and Engineering

Robert A. Magnuson*
Vice President—Treasurer

Thomas E. McGinnity
Vice President—Purchasing and Stores

Bryan G. Moon
Vice President—Advertising

Walter H. Pemberton
Vice President—Communications and Computer Services

Allan K. Pray
Vice President—Assistant to the President

James F. Redeske
Vice President—Personnel Administration

R. James Thorne
Vice President—Properties

Steven D. Wheeler*
Corporate Secretary

William C. Wren
Vice President—Public Relations

*also officers of NWA Inc.

Board of Directors Members Through the Years

Since it is impossible to give individual recognition to the many directors who have contributed to the success of Northwest Airlines during its first 60 years, the following alphabetical roster is printed as a salute to their valued counsel and personal involvement in Northwest's growth.

Abbott, James A., Executive Vice President—Finance and Administration and General Counsel, Northwest Airlines, Inc., 1983 to the present.

Archer, Shreve M., President, Archer Daniels Midland Co., Minneapolis, 1931 through 1934 and 1939 through 1944.

Baird, Julian B., Secretary and treasurer, Northwest Airways, Inc., 1931 and 1932.

Binger, James H., Former Chairman of the Executive Committee, Honeywell, Inc., Minneapolis, 1953 to the present.

Black, Norman, Publisher, Fargo Forum, Fargo, N.D., 1931 and 1933.

Blair, Frank W., President, Union Trust Co., Detroit, 1926 through 1929.

Blanch, E.W., Jr., Chairman of the Board and C.E.O., E.W. Blanch Co., Minneapolis, 1980 to the present.

Brittin, Col. Lewis H., Vice President and General Manager, Northwest Airways, Inc., 1926 through 1929, also 1931 and 1932.

Butler, Francis D., Partner, Doherty, Rumble and Butler, St. Paul, 1939.

Case, Hadley, President, Case, Pomeroy & Co., Inc., New York City, 1957 through 1978.

Charpie, Robert A., President, Cabot Corporation, Boston, 1983 to the present.

Davis, Donald D., Vicepresident, General Mills, Inc., Minneapolis, 1930 through 1933.

Dayton, G. Nelson, Treasurer, The Dayton Co., Minneapolis, 1929 through 1933.

Donner, Robert, Vicepresident, Donner Steel Co., Buffalo, N.Y., 1933.

Emmons, Harold H., Attorney, founder of Emmons, Oren, Sleeper and Krise, Detroit, 1926 through 1929.

Evans, Edward S., President, Evans Auto Loading Co., Detroit, 1927 through 1929.

Ferguson, K.R., Vice President—Operations and Engineering, Northwest Airlines, Inc., 1943, 1944, 1949 and 1950.

Floan, A.E., Secretary, Northwest Airlines, Inc., 1944, 1945, 1965 through 1973.

*indicates current directors as of April, 1986

Fry, Morton H., Partner, Riter & Co., New York City, 1951 through 1970.

Gamble, Ted R., President, Mount Hood Radio and Television Broadcasting Corp., Portland, Ore., 1957 through 1959.

Gann, George K., Vicepresident, Tri State Telephone & Telegraph Co., St. Paul, 1929 through 1931.

Gardiner, William Tudor, Chairman, Incorporated Investors, Boston, 1945 through 1952.

Gardner, George E., Vice President—Operations, Northwest Airlines, Inc., 1939 through 1941.

Hannaford, Jr., J.M., Vicepresident, Gordon & Ferguson, Inc., St. Paul, 1927 through 1933.

Hardesty, Donald H., Vice President—Finance and Treasurer, Northwest Airlines, Inc., 1971 through 1974.

Hardy, R.M., President, Sunshine Mining Co., Yakima, Wash., 1940 through 1956.

Harris, Harold R., President, Northwest Airlines, Inc., 1952.

Heffelfinger, Frank T., President F.H. Peavey & Co., Minneapolis, 1929 through 1933.

Henderson, Col. Paul, Vicepresident, National Air Transport, Chicago, 1929 through 1931.

Herzog, Raymond H., Former Chairman of the Board, 3M Company, St. Paul, 1976 to the present.

Hunter, Croil, Chairman of the Board, Northwest Airlines, Inc., 1934 through 1969.

Irvine, H.H., President, Thompson Yards, Inc., St. Paul, 1931 through 1934.

Irvine, T.E., President, F.I. Products Co., St. Paul, 1938 through 1948.

Jacques, L.G., President, Motor Products Corp., Detroit, 1953.

Johnson, C.E., Vicepresident, Empire National Bank, St. Paul, 1927 through 1929.

Johnson, Joseph T., President, The Milwaukee Co., Milwaukee, 1939 through 1964.

Kalman, Paul J., President, Kalman Steel Co., St. Paul, 1929 through 1933.

Kellogg, Frank B., Partner, Kellogg, Morgan, Chase, Carter and Headley, St. Paul, 1929 through 1933.

Laird, Melvin R, Senior Counselor, Reader's Digest Association, Washington, D.C., 1974 to the present.

Land, James N., Jr., Financial Consultant, New York City, 1976 to the present.

*Lapensky, M. Joseph, former Chairman of the Board, Northwest Airlines, Inc., has served on the Board 1975 to the present.

Leffingwell, Lewis M., Vicepresident, Archer Daniels Midland Co., Minneapolis, 1935 through 1946.

Lewis, E.W., President, Industrial Morris Plan Bank, Detroit, 1927 through 1929.

Lilly, Richard C., President, First National Bank, St. Paul, 1929 through 1933, also 1939.

Mackay, Malcolm S., President, Foothills Co., Roscoe, Mt., 1947 through 1978.

Mayo, Dr. Charles, Mayo Clinic, Rochester, Mn., 1947 through 1951.

Mayo, William B., Chief Engineer, Ford Motor Co., Detroit, 1927 through 1933.

*McNeely, Donald G., Chairman of the Board, Space Center, Inc., St. Paul, 1968 to the present.

Morgan, Clyde B., President, Rayonier, Inc., New York City, 1957 through 1966.

Nyrop, Donald W., President and C.E.O., Northwest Airlines, Inc. 1954-1976; Chairman and C.E.O., 1976-1978; Director, 1979-1984.

Ordway, John G., Crane and Ordway, St. Paul, 1932 and 1933.

Pack, Robert F., Vicepresident and General Manager, Northern States Power Co., Minneapolis, 1929 through 1933.

Parker, John E., Special Partner, Auchincloss, Parker & Redpath, New York City, 1942.

Petteys, Alonzo, Vicepresident and Director, Farmers State Bank, Brush, Colo., 1945 through 1967.

Piper, H.C., Vicepresident, Lane, Piper and Jaffray, Minneapolis, 1929, 1931, 1932.

Rand, Rufus R., Capitalist, Minneapolis, 1929 through 1933.

Reavis, C. Frank, Partner, Hodges, Reavis, McGrath, Pantaleoni & Downey, New York City, 1951 through 1975.

Redpath, Albert G., Drexel, Burnham & Co., New York City, 1951 through 1975.

Reynolds, Earle H., President, Peoples Trust & Savings Bank, Chicago, 1929, 1930.

Rogers, A.R., President Rogers Lumber Co., Minneapolis, 1929 through 1931, also 1933.

*Rothmeier, Steven G., President and Chief Executive Officer, Northwest Airlines, Inc., 1982 to the present.

Shepard, Roger B., President, Finch, Van Slyck & McConville, St. Paul, 1927 through 1931.

Sheriff, Fred B., Manager, Sieben Livestock Co., Helena, Mt., 1933.

Shields, L.J., President, National Battery Co., St. Paul, 1929 through 1931, also 1933.

Stein, Camille L., Assistant Secretary, Northwest Airlines, Inc., 1934 through 1941.

Stern, William, President, Dakota National Bank, Fargo, N.D., 1938 through 1962.

Stout, William B., President, Stout Air Services, Inc., Detroit, 1926 through 1929.

Tegen, Albert F., President, General Public Utilities Corp., New York City, 1953 and 1954.

Wakefield, Sr., Lyman E., President, First National Bank, Minneapolis, 1931 and 1932.

Wakefield, Jr., Lyman E., Former Chairman of the Board, Resource Trust Co., Minneapolis, 1953 through 1981.

Weatherhead, Jr., Albert J., President, The Weatherhead Co., Cleveland Oh., 1953 through 1965.

Weesner, H.R., President, Wabash Screen Door Co., Minneapolis, 1929 through 1933.

White, Edwin, Chairman, Board of Directors, Kalman & Co., St. Paul, 1940 through 1950.

Whitney, Sr., Wheelock, Director and member of the Executive Committee, Truax-Traer Coal Co., Chicago, 1953 through 1956.

Whittemore, Fred, Vice President—Operations, Northwest Airlines, Inc., 1934 through 1938.

Whyatt, E.I., Executive Vice President, Northwest Airlines, Inc., 1934 through 1950.

*indicates current directors as of April, 1986

Growth Pattern of Northwest Airlines, Inc.

	Operating Revenues	Net Profit	Revenue Psgr. Miles	Cargo Ton-miles (incl. mail)
1927	$77,880	($1778) loss	unknown	unknown
1931	$1.15 million	$115,703	3.9 million	43,499
1936	$1.6 million	$312,289	unknown	unknown
1941	$4.67 million	$365,619	59.6 million	1.14 million
1946	$20.2 million	$157,300	378 million	unknown
1951	$49.11 million	$1.78 million	602 million	17.8 million
1956	$76.6 million	$3.23 million	1.09 billion	37.4 million
1961	$111 million	$3.66 million	1.02 billion	21.3 million
1966	$311.4 million	$53 million	3.7 billion	215.6 million
1971	$425.65 million	$21.4 million	3.6 billion	231.4 million
1975	$800.78 million	$43.4 million	9.9 billion	495.6 million
1980	$1.639 billion	$7.08 million	13.8 billion	667.3 million
1985	$2.655 billion	$73.2 million	22.34 billion	1.1 billion

Dates in NWA History

1926

September 1 — Northwest Airways organized as a Michigan Corporation. Base established at Speedway Field, later Wold-Chamberlain field, Minneapolis-St. Paul. Harold H. Emmons of Detroit, first president.

October 1 — First NWA air mail carried between Chicago and Minneapolis-St. Paul in two rented open cockpit biplanes.

November 2 — Northwest introduces nation's first closed cabin commercial plane — the 3-passenger Stinson Detroiter.

1927

July 5 — First ticketed passenger carried from Twin Cities to Chicago via La Crosse, Madison and Milwaukee; $40 one way.

Total 1927 passengers — 106.

1928

February 1 — Weekly Twin Cities-Winnipeg flights via Fargo began.

April 2 — First scheduled air express carried into Twin Cities.

September 1 — First coordinated air-rail mail service, Twin Cities-Chicago.

September 15 — Route added to Green Bay via Fond Du Lac, Oshkosh, Neenah-Menasha and Appleton, Wis.

1929

May 1 — Passenger service begun to Rochester, Minn. (Mail contract not awarded until following year.)

August 1 — First night air mail, Twin Cities-Chicago.

Government adopts Northwest "U.S. Air Mail" emblem for *all* carriers.

Twin Cities businessmen buy control of Northwest Airways, and elect Richard C. Lilly of St. Paul as president.

1930

March — Service added to Rockford and Elgin, Ill., and Janesville, Wis.

May — Weekly flights, Twin Cities to Sioux City, Iowa and Omaha, Neb., later suspended.

July 1 — Operations base moved to St. Paul downtown airport.

First NWA ground radio installation purchased.

1931

February 2 — Daily service to Winnipeg via Fargo and Grand Forks. (Transfer to Canadian air line required at Pembina, N.D.)

May 31 — Duluth service added with two amphibian planes.

June 2 — Bismarck extension with stops at Valley City and Jamestown.

Arthur R. Rogers of Minneapolis elected president.

1933

March 2 — Billings, Mont. added via Glendive and Miles City.

October 23 — Route extended to Spokane via Helena, Butte and Missoula.

October 31 — Stop added at Dickinson, N.D.

Government mail pay reduction canceled service to Madison, Green Bay and Duluth.

December 3 — Northwest achieves "Northern Transcontinental" to Seattle.

December 4 — Tacoma service added.

1934

April 16 — Re-incorporation under Minnesota law as Northwest Airlines, Inc., with Shreve M. Archer of Minneapolis as president.

Col. Lewis H. Brittin, founder of Northwest Airways, resigns.

Roosevelt cancels all air mail contracts. In re-shuffle, Northwest loses route from Chicago to Fargo, then buys contract back from Hanford Airlines at year's end.

1935

October 10 — Through service to Winnipeg approved, eliminating transfer at Pembina.

Lewis M. Leffingwell of Minneapolis elected president.

1937

Croil Hunter named president — first operating officer to hold this title.

1938

May 14 — Portland-Yakima service begun.

July 27 — Northwest pioneers first practical aviation oxygen mask.

1939

March 6 — Service resumed to Madison, Wis.

First stewardesses employed on the new DC3.

1941

Annual passenger revenue exceeded mail revenue for the first time.

February 14 — NWA common stock went public.

1942-1944

Northwest carried out 11 major government wartime assignments including lifeline to Alaska, bomber modification center and variety of special projects; employment leaped from 881 to 10,439 during war.

(Service to several smaller cities suspended when government commandeers half of Northwest's fleet.)

Northwest receives Army-Navy "E" for operation of bomber modification center, credited with big assist in eventual Allied victory.

1945

June 1 — Northwest becomes the fourth transcontinental air carrier, Seattle to New York, via Twin Cities, Milwaukee and Detroit.

256

1946

March —   First operations into Newark.

September 1 —   Service begun from Seattle to Anchorage, Alaska.

1947

January 2 —   "Inside" route to Anchorage launched from Twin Cities.

April 27 —   Jamestown and Aberdeen service begins.

June 21 —   Bozeman added.

July 15 —   Orient service began from Twin Cities via Anchorage and Shemya to Tokyo, Seoul, Shanghai and Manila.

September 25 — First service to Okinawa.

November 12 — Permanent certificate awarded for service to Great Falls.

1948

February —   Red tail paint job adopted for all Northwest aircraft.

March 15 —   Washington, D.C., service inaugurated via Cleveland and Pittsburgh.

December 2 —   Hawaii service launched between Honolulu, Portland and Seattle-Tacoma.

1949

March 24 —   Northwest begins nation's first transcontinental all-coach flights.

May 15 —   Civil war in China forces suspension of Shanghai service.

August 1 —   Northwest becomes first carrier to offer beverage service within the U.S., (on the Boeing Stratocruiser.)

1950

April 30 —   Edmonton approved for passenger service. (Formerly only a fuel stop.)

June 3 —   Taipei added to Orient route.

July 25 —   Korean War forces temporary halt of service to Seoul. (Northwest named by government as prime contractor for Korean air lift.)

1951

March 19 —   Service to Hong Kong is begun via connecting service with Hong Kong Airways.

1953

September 27 — Seattle-Portland flights begin.

Harold R. Harris serves briefly as president.

1954

September 27 — Donald W. Nyrop named president.

December 10 — Interchange flights to Miami arranged with Eastern Airlines.

1955

January 1 —   Northwest voluntarily becomes first airline to operate without government subsidy on transpacific and States-Alaska routes.

October 30 —   Chicago-Detroit-New York service opened.

1956

January 1 — Northwest leases Shemya from the government, becoming first carrier to operate its own airport. Also makes decision to centralize operations at new $17.5 million base, Wold-Chamberlain field.

1957

"Imperial Service" introduced on first class flights.

Clear air turbulence forecasts pioneered by NWA.

1958

December 6 — Florida service launched. (Chicago-Miami route approved nonstop or via Atlanta and Tampa. Nonstops later added from Twin Cities and Milwaukee.)

1959

June 1 — New York-Anchorage-Tokyo polar service inaugurated.

September 27 — Atlanta service begun on Florida route.

1960

January 1 — Fort Lauderdale flights added.

July 8 — Fastest U.S. jet service to the Orient is launched (DC8s).

July — Northwest occupies new maintenance and overhaul base at Wold-Chamberlain.

August 31 — Chicago-Anchorage-Tokyo service begun.

Northwest pioneers jet noise abatement procedures.

1961

New General Office occupied, bringing entire main base under one roof.

1962

Northwest originates wind shear forecasts, to warn of sudden changes in head winds and tail winds.

1963

Northwest becomes nation's first all-fan-jet operator.

1964

October 5 — Cleveland-Chicago flights begun.

Northwest receives Flight Safety Foundation safety award for turbulence research.

Presidential "E" presented to NWA for development of export markets and "Visit the U.S.A." promotion in the Orient.

1965

April 1 — Cleveland-Philadelphia and Detroit-Philadelphia service inaugurated.

1966

July 17 — Through-plane service begun to the Orient from Philadelphia, Detroit and Twin Cities via Seattle-Tacoma.

October 1 — After 17-year wait, Northwest certificated to serve Hong Kong.

1967

April 1 —   Osaka becomes newest Orient stop.

December 17 —   Hilo added as destination in Hawaii.

1968

Northwest leads entire industry in net profit for the first time.

1969

August 1 —   San Francisco-Honolulu-Orient flights begun.

Northwest again industry profit leader for the year.

October 4 —   Twin Cities-Los Angeles and Twin Cities-San Francisco flights launched.

Northwest adopts new corporate symbol and "new look".

1970

January 6 —   First service connecting Los Angeles and Tokyo via Honolulu.

September 1 —   Hawaii nonstops from Chicago begun.

For third year in row, NWA leads industry in profits.

Northwest first to offer 747 transpacific service from the four major gateways of Seattle-Tacoma, San Francisco, Los Angeles and Honolulu.

1971

September 1 —   Boston-Twin Cities service inaugurated. Also Twin Cities-San Francisco.

Northwest honored for noise abatement leadership by National Organization to Insure a Sound-Controlled Environment.

1973

January —   First computer-generated airline ticketing procedure.

First direct computer reservations service to and from the Orient.

1974

June 7 —   Service resumed to Edmonton, Alta., after 12-year suspension.

1975

Industry profit leader for fourth time.

1976

July 1 —   First airline to install co-ordinated flight crew training, now known as L.O.F.T., which has become an industry standard mandated by the F.A.A.

October 1 —   M.J. Lapensky named president, Donald W. Nyrop becomes Chairman of the Board.

October 15 —   Northwest's golden anniversary feted by St. Paul Area Chamber of Commerce.

1977

June 8 —   Nonstop service added between Chicago and New Orleans; also between Chicago and Tokyo.

1978

October 12 —   Seattle-Fairbanks nonstops launched.

1979

January 1 — President M. Joseph Lapensky named Chief Executive Officer.

January 20 — Nonstops began in the following markets: Philadelphia-Orlando; Orlando-Fort Lauderdale; Boston-Fort Lauderdale; Boston-Orlando; Boston-Cleveland; Minneapolis/St. Paul-St. Louis and New Orleans-Tampa.

February 1 — Nonstops added in these markets: Philadelphia-Fort Lauderdale; Boston-Tampa; Boston-Philadelphia; Boston-Detroit; Boston-Washington, D.C. (Dulles); Newark-Pittsburgh; New Orleans-Miami; Chicago-St. Louis; Portland-San Francisco; and San Francisco-Las Vegas.

February 9 — New York-Boston-Glasgow all-cargo service launched.

March 2 — All-cargo service added to Copenhagen.

March 31 — Transatlantic passenger service to Copenhagen and Stockholm began from the Twin Cities, Detroit and New York.

April 29 — Transatlantic passenger service to Glasgow and Copenhagen added from Seattle, Twin Cities and Boston.

Nonstops inaugurated between San Francisco and Seattle.

June 8 — Los Angeles-Seattle nonstops launched.

July 1 — Nonstops inaugurated between Seattle and Seoul and between Honolulu and Osaka, Japan.

September 12 — All-cargo flights added Amsterdam-Manchester-New York, and New York-Boston-Prestwick-Amsterdam.

November 15 — Phoenix-Twin Cities nonstops originated.

December 18 — Fort Myers, Florida, service began.

1980

April 27 — Began service from Boston to Shannon, Ireland, and New York to Shannon; also flights from New York to Oslo, Norway, and on to Stockholm.

June 2 — London service launched from Minneapolis-St. Paul, continuing on to Hamburg, Germany.

1981

January 7 — Taipei-Manila service began.

April 26 — Boston-London nonstops inaugurated.

April 30 — Tokyo-Guam nonstops and direct flights from Guam to Seoul, Korea, added.

June 10 — Twin Cities-Oslo nonstops began.

September 8 — Nonstops launched between Los Angeles and Tokyo. International 747F cargo service added at Houston and Los Angeles.

December 17 — Nonstops between Twin Cities and Orlando, Florida, began.

1982

April 25 — Nonstops added between Boston and Chicago O'Hare, plus 747F all-cargo service to San Francisco.

May 19 — Omaha, Kansas City, Wichita and Dallas-Fort Worth came on line.

July 1 — Denver-Twin Cities flights began.

July 25 — San Diego became newest California destination.

August 1 — Grand Rapids, Michigan, service added.

October 1 — International cargo service added at Atlanta, plus weekly 747F cargo flights from the United States to Oslo.

December 16 — West Palm Beach, Florida, came on line.

1983

September 26 — Steven G. Rothmeier elected President and Chief Operating Officer.

December 15 — Tucson, Az., service added, as well as direct service between Tokyo and San Francisco, NWA's sixth gateway to the Orient.

1984

March 15 — M. Joseph Lapensky, C.E.O., elected Chairman of the Board.

April 30 — Direct flights began from Minneapolis-St. Paul via Boston to Frankfurt, West Germany.

May 2 — Shanghai, China, now served direct from Seattle and Tokyo.

May 21 — Northwest shareholders approve adoption of a holding company corporate structure — NWA Inc. — a Delaware corporation.

June 8 — Nonstop passenger service from the Twin Cities to Frankfurt was launched.

Direct flights from Phoenix to San Francisco and Seattle begun, linking the Arizona city to Orient destinations.

June 9 — Direct service from Boston to Dublin, Ireland, made Northwest the only U.S. airline to serve the Irish capital.

September 5 — All-cargo 747 freighter service was launched from the United States to Singapore.

December 1 — Northwest and Mesaba Airlines announce major marketing agreement called "Northwest Airlink" — the first of several mutual feeder arrangements to be established.

1985

January 1 — Steven G. Rothmeier, NWA President and Chief Operating Officer, named Chief Executive Officer.

"Flight Attendant of the Month" program, and Annual Report to Flight Attendants are inaugurated.

March 2 — Northwest became the only U.S. airline to offer direct service from Dallas/Ft. Worth to Tokyo and Hong Kong.

March 15 — Kuala Lumpur, Malaysia, came on line.

May 21 — Northwest and America West Airlines sign another Airlink marketing alliance.

May 28 — NWA Inc. announces purchase of Mainline Travel, Inc. (MLT) of Minnetonka, Minn. — a tour operator — including its principal affiliate Sun Country Airlines, Inc.

June 6 — Nonstop Los Angeles-Seoul flights began.

July — Another Airlink marketing agreement reached with Big Sky Airlines of Montana.

December — Largest aircraft order in Northwest's history announced — $2 billion for ten 747-400s, 10 more 757s and three more 747-200s.

December 23 — Fourth Airlink contract signed with Fischer Brothers Aviation of Detroit.

December 31 — 1985 net profit, $73,119,000.

1986

January 23 — Northwest announced purchase of Republic Airlines for $884 million.

August 12 — Steven G. Rothmeier elevated to Chairman of the Board and C.E.O.; John F. Horn named President and Chief Operating Officer, James A. Abbott became Vice Chairman and General Counsel.

October 1 — Northwest's sixtieth birthday.

Bibliography

Books and Other Publications

"Airways" by Henry Ladd Smith.
"North to the Orient" by Anne Morrow Lindbergh.
"Airlines of the United States Since 1914," by R.E.G. Davies.
Office of War Information reports.
Gopher Air Mail Society news bulletins.
Annual reports, all major U.S. airlines.
RENPA bulletins.

The Congressional Record
Time Magazine
Newsweek
The New Yorker
Corporate Report
Air Transport World
Minnesota Gopher
Aero Digest
Fortune
F.A.A. and C.A.B. reports
Air Transportation
American Aviation Daily
Airline Reports
Aviation Week & Space Technology
Air Transport Association reports
DC Flight Approach
Sponsor
Advertising Age
Wisconsin State Journal
Chicago Sun-Times
U.S.A. Today

New York Times
St. Paul Pioneer Press
St. Paul Dispatch
Minneapolis Morning Tribune
Minneapolis Journal
Minneapolis Daily Times
St. Paul Daily News
Chicago Tribune
Japan Times
Detroit Free Press
Detroit News
Cleveland Plain Dealer
Omaha World Herald
Seattle Post Intelligencer
New York Herald Tribune
Seattle Times
Washington Post
AP, UPI and INS dispatches
Anchorage Daily Times
Manila Chronicle
Sarasota Herald-Tribune

Additional Sources

Personal interviews with more than 100 men and women who have figured in Northwest's past and present; minutes of the airline's Board of Directors; files of the Minnesota Historical Society and Michigan Historical Society; public libraries of Minneapolis, St. Paul, Chicago, Detroit, Billings, Washington, D.C., and Venice, Fl.; Campbell-Mithun Library; Milwaukee Airport Log; "Passages" and all previous NWA employee publications dating back to 1939; numerous historical documents and personal letters gleaned from Northwest Airlines files, which were generously opened up to me on a "no holds barred" basis.

And finally, I am indebted to dozens of individuals who dug through old pictures and scrap books to provide background material that helped bring Northwest's 60-year history to life, with special thanks due to Captains James Borden, Vince Doyle and the late Walter Bullock.

k.d.r.

Index

(Note: NWA aircraft are catalogued in the appendix. Nearly 200 city destinations are shown in the route map at the front and back of the book. Research sources, including numerous publications, are listed in the bibliography.)

Kenneth D. Ruble

About the Author

Ken Ruble's path has intermingled with that of Northwest Airlines off and on during all three of his business careers — as newspaperman, advertising executive and author. In fact, he is the proud wearer of an NWA service pin because he once took time out from his writing projects to originate the post of Orient Region Advertising Director.

More than a dozen lively nonfiction books have been turned out by Ken's versatile typewriter on subjects ranging from travel to midwest history, plus numerous magazine articles, a humorous "whodunit" and the lyrics to a song that made the "Hit Parade."

He sold his first book manuscript at 17, and as a star reporter and humor columnist ("Under Your Hat") for the Minneapolis newspapers, covered some of the dramatic events chronicled in this book.

While a captain in the U.S. Marine Air Corps during World War II, Ken and his squadron won a Presidential Citation for their record in the climactic battle for Okinawa, eventually a Northwest port of call which Ken was to visit many times on business for the airline. As vicepresident of the largest advertising agency in the western half of the United States, he was the first account executive to manage Northwest's advertising campaigns when Donald Nyrop moved the account to Minneapolis from New York.

Later, Ken gained an opportunity to study the airline from within when he put aside his typewriter for a year and joined Northwest's ranks to help restructure the Orient Region's advertising program during the busy times of 1969 when California routes and a system-wide "new look" were introduced.

A native of Willmar, Minn., Ken lived in the Twin Cities area for many years, but as a free lance writer now makes his home in Florida. A widower, he has two sons in Minneapolis, three grandchildren and is an alumnus of the University of Minnesota.

Among his books are narrative histories of several other nationally known firms headquartered in the midwest, including Land O'Lakes, Peavey Company, Andersen (Windowalls) Corporation and Rayovac.

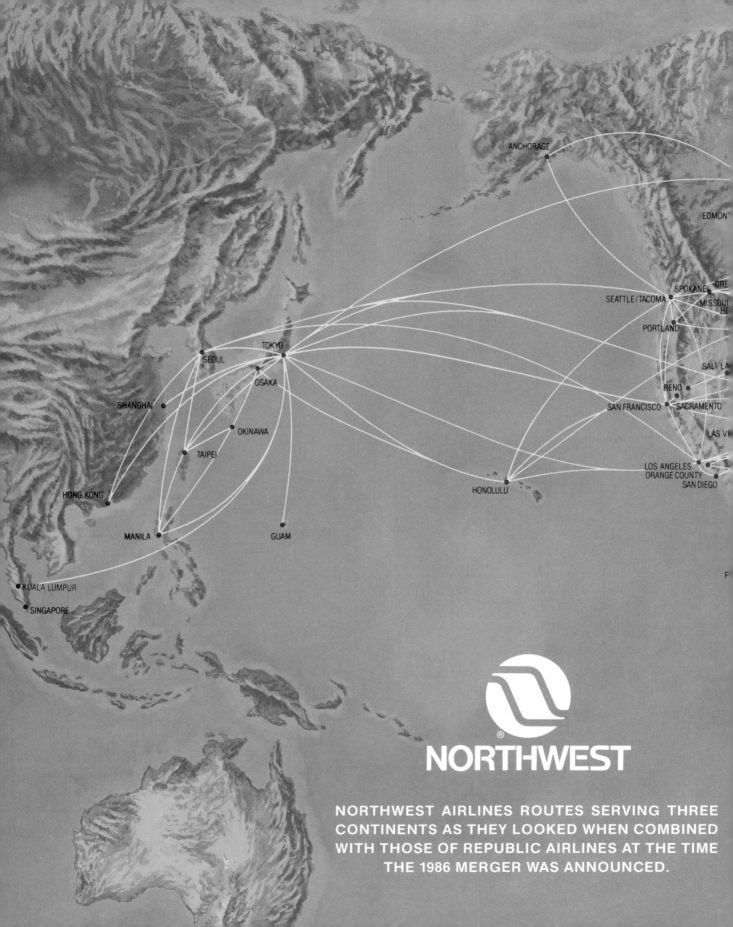

**NORTHWEST AIRLINES ROUTES SERVING THREE
CONTINENTS AS THEY LOOKED WHEN COMBINED
WITH THOSE OF REPUBLIC AIRLINES AT THE TIME
THE 1986 MERGER WAS ANNOUNCED.**